MW00424697

THE THEOLOGICAL AND THE POLITICAL

THE THEOLOGICAL
AND THE POLITICAL

ON THE WEIGHT OF THE WORLD

MARK LEWIS TAYLOR

Fortress Press
Minneapolis

Cover image: "La Protesta," David Alfaro Siqueiros (1896–1974). Oil on masonite. Copyright © 2010 Artists Rights Society (ARS), New York / SOMAAP, Mexico City.
Cover design: Joe Vaughan
Book design: PerfecType, Nashville, TN

Library of Congress Cataloging-in-Publication Data
Taylor, Mark L. (Mark Lewis), 1951-
  The theological and the political : on the weight of the world / Mark Lewis Taylor.
      p. cm.
  ISBN 978-0-8006-9789-1 (alk. paper)
  1. Political theology. I. Title.
  BT83.59.T36 2010
  261.7--dc22

                          2010044670

The paper used in this publication meets the minimum requirements of American National Standard for Information Sciences—Permanence of Paper for Printed Library Materials, ANSI Z329.48-1984.

Manufactured in the U.S.A.

15 14 13 12 11 1 2 3 4 5 6 7 8 9 10

For Wonhee Anne Joh

I see growing on the ripples of the water
The revivifying specter
Of a barbarous freedom drunk on its tears.

Victor Serge
"Stenka Razin,"
Resistance: Poems by Victor Serge

CONTENTS

PREFACE

> . . . the entire parapenal institution, which is created
> in order not to be a prison, culminates in the cell, on the
> walls of which are written in black letters: "God sees you."
> —Michel Foucault, Discipline and Punish[1]

Allow me to introduce the theological. It is not to be confused with Theology, which I render here in capital letters to mark its status as guild discipline, a credentialed profession in especially the Christian West that typically reflects on doctrines of a religious tradition and fosters an ethos of transcendence. The theological is a specter haunting Theology, is already unsettling it, perhaps dissolving it, disseminating it anew among other languages and other disciplinary discourses—on the way to revealing something much more significant than Theology's doctrinally structured ethos of transcendence. The theological strikes a "neither/nor" approach to the binary of transcendence/immanence, but recasts both of these in a milieu of what Jean-Luc Nancy terms "transimmanence," a haunting and ghostly realm of seething

---

1. Michel Foucault, Discipline and Punish: The Birth of the Prison (New York: Pantheon, 1977), 294.

presences.[2] It is a milieu within which we must reckon with a new belonging of the theological and the political to one another.

This book, *The Theological and the Political: On the Weight of the
World,* argues that the theological is this transimmanence as a dimension
of agonistic political thought and practice. This theological comes to its
fullest expression in the prodigious force of artful signs deployed in spectral practice, and it is born of the struggle of those bearing, resisting, and
finding life under "the weight of the world," particularly that weight as
shifted, or concentrated, in structures of imposed social suffering. Unlike
the dominant ethos of Theology, the major concern of the theological is
not transcendence, and its primary language is not doctrine. Nevertheless,
it is a discourse that is alive with force to rival stultifying and repressive
sovereignties, what I will treat as the onerous and concentrated weight of
the world. The theological is a discourse that is disciplined, not so much
by doctrinal formation, but by reflection taking place at multiple sites of
the academies and other public thinking. The theological not only identifies and sharpens political differences in the agonism that marks political
being, but it also facilitates human organizing to redress the social exclusion and repression that keep imposed social suffering ever bearing heavily upon those in its agony. Notions of "agony" and "agonistic" derive from
the concept of *agōn,* meaning struggle, and for political theory have been
reworked by nineteenth-century German and, increasingly, U.S. political
thought.[3] Agonism, and agonistic politics, are terms used in this book
for struggle that entails human pain and suffering (agony), and includes,
though cannot be reduced to, the antagonisms and contradictions in social
being that often generate such struggle and agony. The theological will be
a distinctive discourse, issuing from this agonistic dimension of political
and social life.

The theological can be introduced further with the aid of the epigraph above from Foucault. The passage is from his *Discipline and Punish,* a segment in which he writes of imprisonment.[4] In an analysis that is
vintage Foucault, the prison is analyzed within a larger political matrix,

---

2. On this notion of "seething presence," see Avery F. Gordon, *Ghostly Matters: Haunting and the Sociological Imagination* (Berkeley: University of California Press, 1997), 17,
21, 195.

3. Andrew Schaap, ed., *Law and Agonistic Politics* (London: Ashgate, 2009), 1.

4. Foucault, *Discipline and Punish,* 294.

an "entire parapenal institution." This political matrix is an intricate assemblage of power. The matrix has an entirety, a larger parapenal and institutional setting, that reaches into the extensive and complex workings of many social processes. All this even includes a pervasive intention *not* to be a prison. And yet, what is envisioned here is not just a politics of complexity, an ever proliferating, polymorphic matrix. The "entirety" culminates in the cell, a place of agony, a site where someone's flesh is constrained, bounded by wall and bar, by all the apparatuses of force that create the prison cell. This may be taken not just as reference to the cruelties of incarceration in the France of Foucault's time,[5] or to the astounding increase in mass incarceration in recent U.S. history.[6] It can refer as well to the confinement and imposed weight borne by those constructed and subordinated as sexual or gendered others, as racialized and colonized others, and also, simultaneously, exploited as the impoverished others of the global South.

What this book foregrounds as "the theological," then, emerges within and from such agonistic sites of imposed suffering. Such sites are often marked by Theology with some backing of the transcendent. Foucault thus inscribes on the cell wall the words, "God sees you." The theological is not this phrase; it is the seething discourse and practice that is alternative to that marking and making of the cell's agony. It envisions a liberatory and different way through the weight of the world. It is the way those who endure imposed social suffering "weigh-in" with an alternative to the world that is often weighted against them and buttressed by the discourses of transcendence. As we will see, these sufferers usually do this by wielding the force of the artful image from their liminally intense sites of suffering.

For all the agony within the places we would demarcate as a cell, a realm of confinement, it is also an agony that is woven into the wider public world, its fabric of social and institutional life. It is, after all, a "culmination," as Foucault puts it, of an "entire parapenal institution." As I will show below, even the acute agony of the torture cell is woven into the fabric of everyday living, as a subtext of horror at work in the political

---

5. David Macey, *Lives of Michel Foucault* (New York: Random House, 1998), 283ff.
6. Bruce Western, *Punishment and Inequality in America* (New York: Russell Sage, 2007).

in which twenty-first-century U.S. citizenry and "civility" are enmeshed. The weight borne by the tortured in that cell is inscribed in the burden that is the weight of the world, as borne in various ways, too, by the many "outside" the cell.

"God sees you," here, appears as a sinister symbolic inscription of the divine within a most material and political site. The agony of the confined, suspended in a matrix of power, an entire political configuration, is here overseen by God. It is a case of what Stefanos Geroulanos calls "theoscopy"[7]—being seen, transparent to, and thus surveilled by an omnipotent God, locked into place at a site of agony, in part, by the gaze that is projected as coming from an all-seeing figure. The theological of this book, born of the agonistic political, contests this transcendent discourse of theoscopy, without positing a simple obverse. There is a more liberatory way.

This book's argument for the theological is not so much a political theology, as it is a political theorization of the theological. This latter is already ongoing, especially in political philosophy, where scholars like Gayatri Chakravorty Spivak,[8] Slavoj Žižek,[9] Enrique Dussel,[10] Alain

---

7. Stefanos Geroulanos, "Theoscopy: Transparency, Omnipotence and Modernity," in Hent de Vries and Lawrence E. Sullivan, eds., *Political Theologies: Public Religions in a Post-Secular World* (New York: Fordham University Press, 2006), 633–51.

8. Gayatri Chakravorty Spivak admits deep into her *Critique of Postcolonial Reason* to having "dreamed of animist liberation theologies" for "an ecologically just world, inspired, in part, by Christian liberation theologies." In a long footnote she writes in the same text, she more formally muses, when analyzing Kant through the writings about the "Kierkegaard-Levinas-Derrida" line, that "the name of God . . . may be seen as *a* name of the radical alterity that the self is programmed to imagine in an ethics of responsibility." *A Critique of Postcolonial Reason: Toward a History of the Vanishing Present* (Cambridge: Harvard University Press, 1999), 355 n.59, 382.

9. Slavoj Žižek drops references in his political theory to the "mystery of the incarnation," to Che Guevara's "weird Christological aura," to atonement theory, and to G. K. Chesterton's *Orthodoxy*, even as he inspires complex monographs in ontology and on transcendental materialist subjectivity that hardly mention a word about these theological components. See Slavoj Žižek, *In Defense of Lost Causes* (New York: Verso, 2008), 433. See also Adrian Johnston, *Žižek's Ontology: A Transcendental Materialist Theory of Subjectivity* (Evanston, Ill.: Northwestern University Press, 2008).

10. Enrique Dussel, *Ethics and the Theology of Liberation*, trans. Bernard F. McWilliams (Maryknoll, N.Y.: Orbis, 1978).

Badiou,[11] Giorgio Agamben,[12] Jacques Rancière,[13] and others find themselves marching upon the theological. These thinkers will enter this book's
writing at various points, as will others, such as Abdul R. JanMohamed,
Avery Gordon, Judith Butler, Jacques Derrida, Chantal Mouffe, Theodore
Schatzki, Pierre Bourdieu, and especially Jean-Luc Nancy. It remains to
anticipate the itinerary of the book along which such thinkers find their
place.

The introduction, "The Theological in a Post-Theological World," places
my critical presentation of the theological within the context of contemporary discussions of the post-theological and the postsecular. These "post-"
markers are signs of crisis and transition in the understanding of Theology
and of religious expression in contemporary, especially Western, societies. The distinctive route my examination of the theological takes will be
delineated against the backdrop of other routes being forged in this post-
theological moment.

Chapter 1, "Thinking the Theological: A Haunting," has three major
functions. First, it identifies the creative interplay of Michel Foucault's
theory of power with select critical theories of spectrality in order to set
the conceptual background for thinking the theological. Second, I follow the interplay of power and specter into a particularly significant part
of philosopher Jean-Luc Nancy's work—that is, his reflections on world
and weight—in order to clarify the book's meaning of "the weight of the
world." Third, I show how this approach to thinking "the theological"

---

11. The prolific philosopher Alain Badiou, author of *Being and Event* and *Logics of
Worlds*, "cares nothing" for Paul's gospel, and says so, but issues a book-length analysis of
Paul's militant subjectivity and about the apostle's respect for "the Event." Alain Badiou,
Saint Paul: The Foundation of Universalism, trans. Ray Brassier (Stanford: Stanford Univer-
sity Press, 2003). For further examination of the many treatments of Paul by philosophers,
see *Paul, Philosophy, and the Theopolitical Vision: Critical Engagements with Agamben,
Badiou, Žižek, and Others*, ed. Douglas Harink (Eugene, Ore.: Cascade, 2010).

12. Italian political philosopher Giorgio Agamben also has written his own philosophical commentary on Paul, *The Time That Remains: A Commentary on the Letter to the
Romans*, trans. Patricia Dailey (Stanford: Stanford University Press, 2005). In another text,
Agamben also proposes a "theological genealogy of economy" to understand Foucault's
notion of political apparatus. Giorgio Agamben, *What Is an Apparatus? And Other Essays*,
trans. David Kishik and Steefan Pedatella (Stanford: Stanford University Press, 2009 [Italian
2006]), 8–12.

13. Jacques Rancière treats in his political theory certain "theologies of the novel."
Jacques Rancière, *The Flesh of Words: The Politics of Writing*, trans. Charlotte Mandell (Stanford: Stanford University Press, 2004).

involves a wandering labor through the "body of sense" that is the world, an approach that haunts with liberatory effect the imperio-colonial sense of Theology as a guild discipline. The theological in relation to Theology exists as a kind of teeming multiple, a Hydra figure through whose many new voices and discourses there is a thinking that haunts Theology's interpretive procedures.

Chapter 2, "The Agonistic Political," delineates the kind of being that is carried by practices of the political, from which the theological emerges. This delineation is a political ontology, but less the kind that searches for "fundamental structures" of an "onto-theology," and more an "historical ontology," an "ontology of ourselves" articulated by Foucault, and by others after him.[14] The chapter depends heavily on the social-site ontology of Theodore Schatzki and the social theory of Pierre Bourdieu's theory of socialized bodies, of *habitus* and symbolic capital. The aim of the chapter is to show how the conjunctures of being with practice, and then of power with symbol, constitute the agonistic political. Again, it is from this agonistic political that the theological rises.

Chapter 3, "Transimmanence," treats the hallmark trait of the theological, the terrain of transimmanence that opens up within and as provoked by agonistic politics. Transimmanence is shown to be a distinctive way through and beyond the transcendence/immanence binary. Crucial here are the cues I take from artists working from the deep places of human agonistic travail, such as Richard Wright's poetry written from a lynching site, the poets caged at Guantánamo, and one, Catarina, from a zone of social abandonment. The centerpiece of this chapter is an extended meditation on one passage in Jean-Luc Nancy's work, which clarifies this notion of transimmanence. The theological as transimmanence emerges in this chapter with a "sacred" power of prodigious images, a force that both sharpens differences in a "singular plural world" (Nancy), but also dramatically engages, to quote Nancy again, the "brutal collision" of creative world-making, on the one hand, with homogenizing globalization projects of the West, on the other. The theological emerges as the emancipatory sign-force that weighs-in from under, but against, the weight of the world.

---

14. See, for example, Ian Hacking, *Historical Ontology* (Cambridge: Cambridge University Press, 1998).

Chapter 4, "The Weight of Transimmanence," deepens the book's reflection on the powers of those bearing the world's weight, their presence, and their sign-force for weighing-in with alternatives amid the agonistic political. The theological thus comes still more fully into view. Crucial here is the notion of practice, of movements, that give prodigious art forms a spectral power in history, the weight of transimmanence. Those whom Judith Butler discusses as "spectral humans" wield poetic and other artful images, the force of which can pose through networking practices a challenge to the transcendentalizing sovereignties—of state, religion, and Theology—against vulnerable flesh. Special attention is given here to the practice of torture, where the sovereignty of the torture cell instantiates and serves the aesthetic regime and sovereignty of the state. The practice of spectral imaging, then, engages and marshals new, artful practice against the sovereignty of the torture state. While the symbolic force of spectral practice, and reflection upon it, is not usually the primary concern of guild Theology, it can be a concern for many thinkers who, from whatever disciplinary or public site, trace "the theological" as an emancipatory way of spectral humanity.

Chapter 5, "Transimmanence and Radical Practices," focuses more concretely the ways "spectral humans" challenge sovereign power and discourse. In a critical and close reading of Sister Dianna Ortiz's account of torture survival, *The Blindfold's Eyes: My Journey from Torture to Truth*, I trace not only her singular practice of survival and spectral imaging, but also distill four key modes of spectral practice amid the agonistic political: somatic performance of the wounded body, anamnestic solidarity, revivifying naturalism, and a grotesque transcendentalism. For all the debates about torture in current U.S. culture, there is a disturbing failure to acknowledge and analyze what survivors of torture have to teach, in the ways their wounds might congeal as practices that enable some survival, and then haunt, with both threat and promise, the states that would wield torture. This final chapter seeks to learn from that survival and haunting, and so limn for our futures a set of radical practices—discursive practices of the theological—to undertake works of liberation amid the weight of the world.

Introduction

THE THEOLOGICAL IN A POST-THEOLOGICAL WORLD

What is the fate of theology in a post-theological moment?—
Corey D. B. Walker[1]

Corey Walker's query in the epigraph provokes a number of other questions. We need to ask, for example, what is this "post-theological moment" in which the fate of Theology might be considered? What is meant by the often controversial notions of "Theology" and "the theological"? These questions are central for understanding this book's overall purpose, which is to foreground "the theological." It is the purpose of this introduction to clarify the notion of a "post-theological moment," and then to provide a preliminary sketch of what this book will explore as "the political," and then as "the theological."

A Post-Theological Moment

Take first the question of a "post-theological moment." Maybe a groan and a sigh greet the emergence here of yet another "post-" word, to join

---

1. Corey D. B. Walker, "Theology and Democratic Futures," *Political Theology* 10, no. 2 (April 2009): 199–208, at 200.

1

poststructural, postmodern, postcolonial, perhaps also post-Christian and postdemocratic, among others. How long before we are debating the meaning of the hyphen in this new term, *post-theological?* All these terms can be wielded in ways that show a deficit of careful thinking, marking instead the next academic project's "cutting edge." Moreover, the "post-" designation often functions largely in a chronological sense, suggesting that some new era—the one we are in, of course—is now underway, in a time that is supposedly "after" that of the structural, the modern, the colonial, the Christian. Whatever these older formulations may have meant, we can lay them to rest, so it might be thought, to move into some new period, in which we have "come of age." (And always we need to ask: Who is this *we?*) Sometimes, particularly with the terms *post-Christian* or *post-theological*, the intent seems to be not to exult in the coming of age, but more to lament the passing of an era, to mark a degeneration of one's epoch from some better past.[2]

As slippery and obfuscating as these "post-" terms can be, there are lessons to be learned from their coining. What all of them share is not primarily a claim that the present moment constitutes a new epoch in a chronological narrative, but that there is a crisis in understanding underway, as well as, perhaps, an opportunity for fresh thinking. This is especially so with the post-theological. Some may use it to lament the passage of an era when theology, as in fourteenth-century Europe, could be touted as the reigning "queen of the disciplines because of an alleged supernatural origin of its principles,"[3] or in various other times when it was thought possible to formulate and celebrate theology's beliefs and practices within some Christian haven, thinking them protected from the challenges of secular thought, of other religions, or of the plurality of other Christian cultural readings.

The notion of the post-theological is an important one to engage because it marks a certain crisis in which Theology is interrogated anew. Moreover, it usually connotes also an ethical query, which asks about

---

2. Walker, of course, is not the first to use the term *post-theological*. Philosopher John T. Lysaker uses it to discuss Ralph Waldo Emerson's challenges to Christian theology, referring to it as "post-theological," in *Emerson and Self-Culture* (Bloomington: Indiana University Press, 2008), 137–39. Another author, writing mainly to evangelical audiences, uses the term to lament a problem that evangelical theology might rectify. See Stanley J. Grenz, *Renewing the Center: Evangelical Theology in a Post-Theological Age,* 2d ed. (Grand Rapids: Baker, 2006).

3. Edward Farley, *Theologia: The Fragmentation and Unity of Theological Education* (Philadelphia: Fortress Press, 1983), 38.

the value and the good of these discourses we call "Theology." What I find particularly important about the post-theological is that the notion emerges especially as reflection on the relation of the theological to the political. This moment has often been discussed as the resurgence of a particular kind of "theologico-political," viewing Theology, with its diverse beliefs and practices of its faith as rife with political meanings and consequences for wide sectors of secular and public life, even for purportedly nontheological and nonreligious sectors. This "theologico-political" is often today linked to discussions of Spinoza's 1670 *Tractatus Theologico-Politicus*, and ushering in a new take on "political theology."[4]

Again, I stress that I am not offering here a political theology—that is, say, a Christian theology that unfolds its meanings for political life, advocating political forms or treatment of political processes from the viewpoints of, for example, a belief in God, a Christology, some view of the church, and so on. Instead, the book is a political theorization of the theological. It is an analysis of the politicality of Theology, which persists as "the theological." Although this is not a political theology, the conjunction of the political *with* Theology in this post-theological moment is crucial to understanding what the theological is. Corey Walker's discussion explores the political and theological conjuncture as "the problem of multiple theologies animating various forms of religious fundamentalisms,"[5] not only the much-referenced Islamic fundamentalisms, but also those of the West. The laudable goal of a "separation of church and state" has not meant a successful quarantine of religion from politics and state power, or of theology from statecraft. George W. Bush's citing of prayer and scripture as playing key roles in his calculus for the U.S. invasion and occupation of Iraq in 2003 is almost too facile an example of a resurgent theologico-political that can be destructive of the international community.[6] To think the post-theological, then, is not to endorse a political theology, nor is it to think we can simply be done

---

4. Hent de Vries and Lawrence E. Sullivan, eds., *Political Theologies: Public Religions in a Post-Secular World* (New York: Fordham University Press, 2006), 25–31.

5. Walker, "Theology and Democratic Futures," 200.

6. To assess the destructive impact on the international community, one excellent starting place is Ahmed Rashid, *Descent into Chaos: The United States and the Failure of Nation Building in Pakistan, Afghanistan, and Central Asia* (New York: Viking, 2008), esp. 265–316.

with Theology. It is to realize that Theology is freighted with powers in our present that have potent political import. They are not easily set aside. Although often declared dead and spent of strength, the powers of Theology roar back upon us with a vengeance, romping through our time with their political claws.

Interestingly, this discussion of the post-theological overlaps with yet another "post-" term of our period, "postsecular." The two terms may seem like simple opposites—the first *theologically* concerned, the second more *secular*—but their discourses set us on the same ground, if from somewhat different starting places, namely, on the terrain of the theologico-political. In the extensive collection *Political Theologies: Public Religions in a Post-Secular World*, editors Hent de Vries and Lawrence Sullivan cite a host of literatures that chastise secular confidence in its modern or postmodern criticisms of religion and theology. Those criticisms presume they can lay aside, or move beyond, theology and religion as determinative phenomena in public life. Such confident criticisms are described as "utterly misplaced" or "to have missed the point." They conclude that "the wall between religion and government is now so porous as to be an unreliable guide to attitudes and actions."[7] The notion of the postsecular, writes de Vries instructively in his own introduction to the volume, refers not to a return to religion, a repenting of secular critiques, but to a "changed attitude by the secular state or in the public domain with respect to the continued existence of religious communities and the impulses that emerge from them."[8]

Again, as with the post-theological, so with the postsecular. The center of concern becomes the nature of the theologico-political, that is, the political as variously charged, animated, driven, and maybe dominated by theological beliefs (in God, sacred scriptures' inviolability, future promises that theologians derive from religious beliefs, and so on). The present "moment" is felt as especially charged by the resurgence of theological fundamentalisms—a "clash of fundamentalisms"—whether an Islamic fundamentalism assumed to be at work in the September 11, 2001, attacks in the United States, or a Christian fundamentalism of the "Christian

---

7. De Vries and Sullivan, *Political Theologies*, x.
8. Hent de Vries, "Introduction: Before, Around, and Beyond the Theologico-Political," in ibid., 3.

Right."[9] Whether as post-theological or postsecular, our moment is one of renewed contemplation on the theologico-political.[10]

The Political

This book does not and cannot survey all the ways Theology—or notions of the theological—animate and interact with the political. Because the book's main argument, however, is that the theological is a dimension of the political—in particular, of the agonistic political—it is necessary to offer here a first introduction to the notion of the political as it bears on the emergence of the theological. I do this by discussing, first, the scope of the political, and then what makes it distinctive.

As to its scope, the political is much more than what is usually referred to as politics. It refers to a certain mode of organizing the human practices that structure social interaction and the dynamics of collective action in history, but also, by extension, the interests, beliefs, and ideologies of individual actors. The social practices of the political are not to be identified with governmental policies or state and party functions, typical understandings of "politics," but more importantly with our very ontological condition in all spheres of human living. Chantal Mouffe puts it well when she emphasizes that "the political cannot be restricted to a certain type of institution, or envisioned as constituting a specific sphere or level of society. It must be conceived as a dimension that is inherent to every human society and that determines our very ontological condition."[11]

This scope of the political is so broad, one may wonder, next, what makes it distinctive? What I term its distinctiveness not only further clarifies what the political is, but also partly accounts for its ontological scope already mentioned. I suggest that the social practices that distinguish the political are those pervaded by agonistic tension and strife. This agonism extends from the ways social orders are fragilely dependent upon and in

---

9. For more studies and a problematization of the very term "Christian Right," see Mark Lewis Taylor, *Religion, Politics, and the Christian Right: Post-9/11 Powers and American Empire* (Minneapolis: Fortress Press, 2005), 61–62, 71–95.

10. De Vries and Sullivan are well aware that they are writing about political theologies now reconnected to a discourse of the "theologico-political" that characterized Spinoza's 1670 *Theologico-Political Treatise*. For the treatise itself, see Spinoza, *Theological-Political Treatise*, ed. Jonathan I. Israel (Cambridge: Cambridge University Press, 2007).

11. Chantal Mouffe, *The Return of the Political* (New York: Verso, 2005), 3.

tension with orders of nature, to the ways different social groups interact (cooperate, contest, compete) with one another. My claim is not that every element of nature and human being is agonistic. After all, as Abdul JanMo-hamed suggests when reflecting on the agonistic friction of Hegel's master/slave dialectic, there is an ethnographic record that suggests, in contrast, that "in practice, human sociality is grounded in the immediate and abun-dant offering of recognition."[12] There may be a problem, he admits, that the West, especially following Hegel, has been too quick to assume a primary agonism in all social life. Nevertheless, this book will follow Jan-Mohamed and others who decide that a certain primacy of the agonistic mode cannot be avoided. Even the more pacific and generous options in "the ethnographic record"[13] have those options amid their awareness and anxiety concerning the costs of social agonism. This awareness and anxiety point to a certain inevitability of the agonistic. For this and other reasons, this book's notion of the political remains agonistic, tapping into a tradition of political theory as explicated by Andrew Schapp in his *Law and Agonistic Politics*.[14] This distinctively agonistic character of the politi-cal opens up that critical space in the political, the body politic, where large segments of the population—"the part that has no part," as politi-cal philosopher Jacques Rancière describes them[15]—are often rendered absent or subjugated to structured and systemic violence.

The political, in sum, is rendered in this book as a mode of being affected by our socially and historically mediated ontological constitution. This is the broad scope of the political. The agonism of the political, what is distinctive of the political for this book, means that the world's being—which is always socially and historically mediated being—is weighted with agonistic tension. What Johannes Fabian in *Time and the Other* describes as the "scandal of domination and exploitation of one part of

---

12. Abdul R. JanMohamed, *The Death-Bound Subject: Richard Wright's Archaeology of Death* (Durham: Duke University Press, 2005), 267.

13. Mohamed doesn't cite "the ethnographic record," but of many possible, see histo-rian Donald Fixico, *The American Indian Mind in a Linear World: American Indian Stud-ies and Traditional Knowledge* (New York: Routledge, 2003), esp. 142–79.

14. Andrew Schaap, *Law and Agonistic Politics* (London: Ashgate, 2009). I am grateful for Princeton Seminary doctoral candidate Elías Ortega-Aponte for calling my attention to this work amid his own groundbreaking research and writing on U.S. Latino/a ethics and theology.

15. Jacques Rancière, *Disagreement: Politics and Philosophy* (Minneapolis: University of Minnesota Press, 1998), 7–14.

mankind by another"[16] is an affliction that weighs heavily upon, even as it is culminant of, an "entirety" of systems and structures, to recall Foucault again. The sufferers' acute pain and struggle is a culmination of a struggle borne by the whole, even if agents of domination have their singularities and responsibility. All this is the weight of the world, and it is the distinctive feature of the political, the agonistic political.

The agonistic political emerges in a number of contemporary theorists' discourses, and in different ways. Groups weighted by imposed social suffering, in modes both blatant and subtle, both covert and overt, are enmeshed within and constituted by what Achille Mbembe terms a "necropolitics." This is a set of political practices effective toward death, marked by what Mbembe terms "a generalized instrumentalization of human existence and by the material destruction of human bodies and populations."[17] The world is heavy, then, with social practices that generate and organize death and dying. Though this necropolitics consigns more and more people to "zones of abandonment,"[18] relegating increasingly larger numbers to the status of surplus populations or disposable peoples, those subordinated to the necropolitics nevertheless rework the agonism, insist on being human, "weigh-in" with counterpractices that are not only agonistic in their own right but also are often motivated by nonagonistic visions and practices. Nevertheless, as nonagonistic as they may be in their visionary origins, they do not escape having to be fought for in an agonistic world of being and practice.

The weightedness that marks the agonistic political is also operative in the patterns of exclusion that are revealingly traced in its more subtle mode, in what Gayatri Spivak has termed "foreclosure." This is a dynamic that is evident, for just one example, in Immanuel Kant's clear decision in his *Critique of Judgment* to dismiss "New Hollanders" and "inhabitants of Tierra del Fuego" as subjects who shed any light on "why it is necessary that men should exist."[19] Their exclusion occurs with little fanfare in

---

16. Johannes Fabian, *Time and the Other: How Anthropology Makes Its Object* (New York: Columbia University Press, 1983), 31.

17. Achille Mbembe, "Necropolitics," trans. Libby Meintjes, in *Public Culture* 15, no. 1 (2003): 11–40, at 14.

18. See João Biehl, *Vita: Life in a Zone of Social Abandonment* (Berkeley: University of California Press, 2005).

19. Gayatri Chakravorty Spivak, *A Critique of Postcolonial Reason: Toward a History of the Vanishing Present* (Cambridge: Harvard University Press, 1999), 26–29. For the passage in Kant that Spivak addresses, see Immanuel Kant, *Critique of Judgment,* trans.

Kant's book, but it discloses a significant part of a foreclosure that Spivak interprets as part of an "axiomatics of imperialism."[20] There seem to be no operative norms compelling Kant and his readers to see these peoples as "recognizable," to adapt Judith Butler's language; certainly there seem to be few schemas in Kant's thought to make their subjectivity intelligible or valuable.[21] With a few penned phrases he can assume readers will not object if he waves them aside as he moves on through his argument. A reader might not advert to the foreclosure at all. Kant simply apprehends his sensible world through what Rancière points to as an "aesthetics" at the core of politics, one that subtly determines "what is seen and what can be said, organizing, in fact, determinations of who has the ability to see and the talent to speak, around the properties of spaces and the possibilities of time."[22] The sensible world is subject to divisions, the most notable one for the political being the dividing off of those social groups who are a part of society but without rights to participate equally, "the part that has no part."[23] Kant's subtle but emphatic distinction among worthy and unworthy lives—those undeserving and deserving of grief, as Judith Butler addresses this problematic[24]—is judged quickly in passing. This, too, is all part of the agonism of the political that structures human being in society.

The foreclosures Spivak discusses, and the framing of affect (Butler) or the divisions of the sensible world (Rancière), are all important for seeing how relations transpire in the powerful worlds of colonizing and largely European-American settings. It should not be forgotten, however,

---

J. H. Bernard (New York: Heffner, 1968 [1790]), 225. Kant's foreclosure of these peoples, not treating them as "subjects" in his analysis, but instead dismissing them as beings not at all helpful for reflecting on human existence's purpose, is exemplary of the moderate mainstream Enlightenment, which, unlike an earlier, more "radical Enlightenment," accommodated itself to a racial hierarchy of inequalities. See Jonathan Israel, *The Enlightenment Contested: Philosophy, Modernity, and the Emancipation of Man 1670–1752* (New York: Oxford University Press, 2006), 40, 49, and 590–614. On Kant and racial hierarchy, see Robert Bernasconi, "Kant as an Unfamiliar Source of Racism," in *Philosophers on Race: Critical Essays,* ed. Julie K. Ward and Tommy L. Lott (New York: Blackwell, 2002), 145–66.

20. Spivak, *A Critique of Postcolonial Reason,* 330. Compare with pp. 19, 34, 26, 48, 120–21, 340, 409.

21. Judith Butler, *Frames of War: When Is Life Grievable?* (New York: Verso, 2009), 9.

22. Jacques Rancière, *The Politics of Aesthetics: The Distribution of the Sensible,* trans. Gabriel Rockhill (New York: Continuum, 2004 [French 2000]), 13.

23. Rancière, *Disagreement,* 10–12.

24. Butler, 22–31.

that the likes of Kant and Hegel could also be far less subtle, more bla-
tantly antagonistic to foreclosed peoples, with Kant advocating outright
eradication of these "others" and Hegel deciding that "Africa has no history," no spirit, and so on.[25]

The agonistic political is not carried simply in thinkers' manifestations
of an antagonistic viewpoint toward subordinated and colonizable others;
or, conversely, in those thinkers who decry their subordination and colonization. To be sure, those stances are ways to participate in the agonistic
political. But the agonism of the political is first and foremost that which
is at work in the more general dissemination of practices and powers that
mark our very ontological condition. It is this agonistic political that will
figure prominently in this book, and from which the theological emerges
with its haunting power.

The Theological

The political, understood as this ontologically constituting, agonistic
dimension of human thought and practice, then, sets the stage for understanding "the theological." The theological is a discourse that discerns
and critically reflects upon the motions of power in this agonistic dimension. More particularly, it traces and theorizes the ways that persons and
groups rendered subordinate and vulnerable by agonistic politics and its
systemic imposed social suffering nevertheless haunt, unsettle, and perhaps dissolve the structures of those systems. The theological traces and
theorizes the way this haunting congeals into specters and forces both
threatening and promising alternative patterns and lifeways. Again, the
theological as a discourse should not be confused with Theology, the
guild discipline long established in the theological institutions, seminar-
ies, divinity schools, and, more controversially, in some Western university religion departments.[26]

---

25. These attitudes of Enlightenment philosophers were traced early on by such
works as Cornel West's *Prophesy Deliverance!* (Philadelphia: Westminster, 1988), and more
recently by J. Kameron Carter, *Race: A Theological Account* (New York: Oxford University
Press, 2009), 79–95.

26. By "the West," I refer to those cultures and regions where Eurocentric views of
modernity predominate, both politically and ideologically. Crucial to the notion is that
the West sees its European heritage as leading to, and then descended from, a period of
"modernity," the latter held to be a good and originative with European peoples, then

Some may query, given the difference between Theology and what I propose as "the theological," why keep the adjectival form at all? My response here is threefold, even though each point will become clearer only against the backdrop of the book's entirety. First, *the theological* names the kind of discourse deployed by nontheologians, especially political theorists, when they delve into sources and meanings of Theology without sanctioning its traditional concerns as guild discipline. This hardly makes them "anonymous theologians." That is not my claim. The theorists often express their ambivalence about these deployments from Theology. Recall Alain Badiou's claim "to care nothing" for Paul's gospel, while yet writing a full-length text on Paul's militant subjectivity as exemplary. We could cite also Spivak's dreaming of an "animist liberation theology" that might express her "impossible vision of an ecologically just world." She then adds, however, and this is telling, "Indeed, the name theology is alien to this thinking." Moreover, not only does she not embrace Theology, especially "individual transcendence theology," she also announces her conviction that none of the major religions should be invoked to facilitate our reach for "that impossible, undivided world of which one must dream," which is the internationality of ecological justice.[27] Note that both Badiou's and Spivak's retrieval of, or desire for some part of, Theology's discourse is occasioned by reflection on the agonistic political. Thus, Paul's "militant subjectivity" is attractive to Badiou in spite of his gospel, and Spivak mentions liberation theologies because, especially if worked out in an "animist" mode, they enable contestation with a financialized and unjust international order. Because their sense of agonistic politics drives them to consider and deploy notions from Theology, I refer to discourse like theirs as "theological." But because of their severe ambivalence about their own moves, rooted in a critical rejection of Theology and the religions, its discourse cannot properly be said to belong to Theology. It is, instead, a discourse of the theological, occasioned and provoked by the agonistic political.

A second reason for preserving the term *the theological* is that there is no antitheological anti-space that might be counterpoised to the cultural history that has been shaped and stamped by Theology and its practices

---

diffused outward to other peoples and continents. In the ideology of "the West," the colonial roots of modernity are usually unacknowledged and unstudied. On Eurocentrism and the West, see J. M. Blaut, *The Colonizer's View of the World: Geographical Diffusionism and Eurocentric History* (New York: Guilford, 1993).

27. Spivak, *A Critique of Postcolonial Reason*, 382–83.

in the West. This reason may offer the cultural historical condition for the first reason given above. If the likes of Badiou and Spivak find it necessary to engage, however tangentially and ambivalently, the offerings of Theology, this is because even those who reject it must work in the ruins of its failure. Later in this book I will discuss Ernesto Laclau's notion of "failed transcendence." Even for those who argue that there can be no return to transcendence, there is still a necessity to work in its ruins. Especially in the contexts of agonistic politics, where contestation will often necessitate working in, and reworking, the ruins of transcendence and of Theology—precisely there is it appropriate to speak of this puzzling notion of the theological.

My third reason for preserving the term *the theological* is not the most significant, but does warrant comment. Etymologically, it is not necessary for theologically interested discourse to make reference to a transcendent or to "a God," even less to require belief and reverence for such. Many may assume this and, indeed, the standard etymology for "theology" (*logos*, "discourse," about *theos*, "God") would seem to confirm this. But further digging into the etymology of the Greek, *theos*, opens out more possibilities. Among them is the possibility that its meaning is bound up not so much with a singular divine figure, a god, but with a multiplicity of "gods," and, perhaps more elusively, with a revered presence.[28] Then, too, there are the playful etymological musings that Plato has Socrates offering up in his *Cratylus* (397d), well known for its speculative punning on word origins. Recall Socrates's musing on why the planets in motion were called "*Theoi.*"

> *Socrates*: My notion would be something of this sort: I suspect that the sun, moon, earth, stars, and heaven, which are still the god of many barbarians, were the only gods known to the aboriginal Hellenes. Seeing that they were always moving and running, from their running nature (θεῖν) they were called Gods (θεούς) or runners (θέοντας); and when men became acquainted with the other Gods, they proceeded to apply the same name to them all. Do you think that likely?
>
> *Hermogenes*: I think it very likely indeed.[29]

---

28. "God," *Oxford English Dictionary*, eds. J. A. Simpson and E.S. C. Weiner, volume VI (Oxford: Clarendon, 1989), 639.

29. "Cratylus," in Edith Hamilton, ed., *The Collected Dialogues of Plato: Including the Letters* (Princeton: Princeton University Press, 2005), 435.

Again, Plato's thoughts in the musing of Socrates does not in itself con-stitute an argument for what the theological is or should now be taken to be. This passage, however, from the mythology and reflection of the past, does indicate that the theological need not be so closely attached in its first meanings to a notion of god or gods, but instead may attach to something more inchoate, indeed, perhaps unfocusable, too—here, the "moving and running," the "running nature" of the world and its bodies. If the theological of this book is a tracing of, and critical reflection upon, the motions at work in an agonistic politics, upon the diverse modes of motion in the weight of the world, we are—granted, in a most general way—in keeping with this early musing on the theological as related to running and moving, not just to a god or gods.

More particularly, however, how will the theological differ from The-ology? To be sure, Theology is not completely incapable of harboring the theological as I will unfold it in this book, but usually its discourses depart from the theological in two senses. First, the primary discursive language of guild Theology, especially in Christian theological institutions of the West, tends to focus on doctrinal loci, traditional topics of God, creation, sin, Christology, Holy Spirit, church, eschatology, and so on, all of which provide an ordering function, its parts drawn from established church formulae, creeds, and the biblical narrative's view of history.[30] Strictly observed, arrangements of these loci structure a sense of "ortho-doxy," and in some quarters are enforced over and against other notions of "heresy." More loosely held in modern and contemporary theology, the loci still limn a "web of symbols" that the guild looks to in order to distinguish their work, even if they often accept the task of reworking them in imaginative and often radical ways.[31] The concerns of the theolog-ical may intersect with some discourses of the traditional loci, but doing so is not the distinctive focus of the theological.

Instead, the primary discursive language of the theological is the art-ful image, with symbolic force to convey the promise and threat of the spectral, the haunting by peoples and groups who are often rendered disposable, excluded, and oppressed. Their imagery, their art forms—in

---

30. Alister E. McGrath, *Christian Theology: An Introduction*, 4th ed. (New York: Wiley-Blackwell, 2006).

31. Rebecca Chopp and Mark Lewis Taylor, eds., *Reconstructing Theology* (Minneapo-lis: Fortress Press, 1994), 14–15.

song, poetry, story,[32] literature, painting, graffiti, the sewn designs of the *arpillera* quilts of culturally traumatized peoples of Chile and Peru,[33] for example—all these and more constitute the primary discourse of the theological, insofar as they convey and constitute the haunting power of peoples bearing the weight of the world, but weighing-in spectrally with resistance and flourishing. As a foretaste of the powers of this language, which I will discuss in detail across later chapters, I offer these haunting stanzas from Richard Wright's poem "Between the World and Me,"[34] in which, as Abdul JanMohamed observes, Wright both gives persona to a man being lynched and burned in the Jim Crow era and also works readers' identification with his horror:

> And my skin clung to the bubbling hot tar, falling from me in limp patches.
> And the down and quills of the white feathers sank into my raw flesh, and I moaned in my agony.
> Then my blood was cooled mercifully, cooled by a baptism of gasoline.
> And in a blaze of red I leaped to the sky as pain rose like water, boiling my limbs.
> Panting, begging I clutched childlike, clutched to the hot sides of death.
> Now I am dry bones and my face a stony skull staring in yellow surprise at the sun . . .[35]

In this language there is not simply a recounting of a brutal event. Wright does not merely traffic in horror. His poem, to the contrary, is

---

32. The role of the story—written, but especially oral—has been frequently remarked upon in this regard, especially in indigenous nations' traditions. It is dramatically exemplified in Leslie Marmon Silko, *Ceremony,* 30th anniversary ed. (New York: Penguin, 2007 [1988]), 2–3.

33. "Threads of Hope: The Story of the Chilean Arpillera," *International Center for Ethics, Justice and Public Life,* Brandeis University, http://www.brandeis.edu/ethics/events/past/tellingthestory/agosin.html, accessed September 13, 2010.

34. I discussed this poem previously in my essay "Today's State of Exception: Notes on Abu-Jamal, Agamben and JanMohamed," in *Political Theology,* special issue on "Theology and Democratic Futures," ed. Corey D. B. Walker, 10, no. 2 (April 2009): 305–24.

35. This segment from Abdul R. JanMohamed, *The Death-Bound Subject: Richard Wright's Archaeology of Death* (Durham: Duke University Press, 2005), 29. For the full poem, see "Between the World and Me," in *The Richard Wright Reader,* ed. Ellen Wright and Michel Fabre (New York: Harper & Row, 1978), 246–47. Used by permission of the Estate of Richard Wright.

poignantly and startlingly about a "face," yes, a "stony skull," but one "staring," engaging the present, indicting its perpetrators and indeed all "humanity." Wright's art—here and in his other writings, in his and others' creativity—works a most severe mercy, exorcising the social death lived by such sufferers, but releasing them toward a radical engagement with liberating possibilities that he and others might mobilize in the present. Thus, what Avery Gordon would term a "seething presence" is created, as bodies live in spite of death through such symbolic force in artful form. Gordon's notion of seething presence is used also by her for the power of Argentine women writing about absented/forcibly disappeared friends and family.[36] As "seething" they make striking impressions. Their artful language "makes everything we do see just as it is, charged with the occluded and forgotten past," but with an eye to an "emergent solution," a material practice of "something to be done."[37] The force of this kind of language constitutes the theological that this book will explore. In terms of liberatory and transformative potential, Theology's doctrinal language is no rival to the symbolic language of such an art-force.

Second, guild Theology, as I refer to it, departs from the theological in that the former is usually marked by some discourse of transcendence, that is, a thinking across (*trans-*), which involves a going above, a climbing (*scandere*), beyond the finite, somehow to another dimension above world and history. The kind of transcendence involved may be complexly structured, with discourses about a "this-worldly transcendence," or of "the immanence of the transcendent," but still the opposition of the transcendent and the immanent remains,[38] with guild Theology's distinctive concern focused largely on a valuation of the transcendent that can "go immanent." Even in some radical embraces of "pure immanence," the transcendent retains its controlling power by being the obverse that must be countered.

By contrast, this book does not seek to replicate the binary—transcendence *or* immanence—by simply shifting to embrace or celebrate

---

36. Avery F. Gordon, *Ghostly Matters: Haunting and the Sociological Imagination* (Berkeley: University of California Press, 1997), 195.

37. Ibid., 195, 202.

38. William Temple, *Nature, Man and God,* the Gifford Lectures at the University of Glasgow, 1932–1933, 1933–1934 (London: Kessinger, 2003). This text is still a key example, with its two parts being "The Immanence of the Transcendent," and "The Transcendence of the Immanent."

an immanence over and against transcendence. It surely is not marked by proposing a new version of transcendence, however attractive some recent attempts to do so may be.[39] Rather, the theological of this book discerns, within the agonistic political, a distinctive realm of human being and social practice, what I will explore, with the aid of Jean-Luc Nancy's thought, the "transimmanental." I hasten to add that in this turn to Nancy for interpreting the theological, I do not seek to "theologize" Nancy, reintroducing some notion of the divine or of transcendence into his project. I thus welcome B. C. Hutchens's telling critique of theologians who would use Nancy to somehow rescue a notion of God, or to guide some ability to trace divinity in human experience. Nancy's discourse of transimmanence does not offer Theology a way to cling, in some new fashion, to its desperate faiths in god; rather, as Hutchens writes, Nancy "enables the secularist to wrest poetry's transcendent value from the theologians."[40] Even this secularist avowal by Hutchens, however, makes too much of the transcendent, here mainly transporting its function to the poetic. The transimmanental is sufficient, it seems to me, for pointing to the power of the poetic and of the theological without bringing in either transcendence or immanence.

So what is transimmanence? As a first statement, I present it as a practice or reflection that steps *into* and moves *within* the political. It is the liberating opening and closing, and continual opening and reopening, of existence to itself, to and through its many singularities and pluralities. Transimmanence is existence thus refusing to be locked in place, "locked down" in systems that resist continual opening and reopening. It is a kind of passing, a traversing of manifolds and relations of immanence, which can be discerned especially along the boundaries marking agonistic strife between the powers that seek to dispose of weaker peoples and those peoples who resist being so disposed.[41] Transimmanence is disclosed especially in that realm of life and struggle where the prodigious

---

39. Regina Schwartz, *Transcendence: Philosophy, Literature, and Theology Approach the Beyond* (New York: Routledge, 2004); and John D. Caputo and Michael J. Scanlon, *Transcendence and Beyond: A Postmodern Inquiry* (Bloomington: Indiana University Press, 2007).

40. B. C. Hutchens, *Jean-Luc Nancy and the Future of Philosophy* (Montreal: McGill/Queens University Press, 2005), 95.

41. Vijay Prashad, "Thinking in the Wound," unpublished presentation, Columbia University/Barnard College conference, "Live from Death Row—Mumia at the Crossroads in the Age of Obama," April 3, 2010.

art form—as in Wright's poem "Between the World and Me"—wields the figural form of the oppressed to show that their powers and presence have not been erased.

Transimmanence, then, while pervading the entire human condition, abides in and flashes forth along the agonistic boundaries of being, especially as agonistic tension shifts from a fruitful balance of power into a more concentrated and onerous exercise of power over others. The theological addresses this concentration, grates against it, engages and deflects it. Ultimately, tracing the transimmanental will offer us a way to discern the powers that sustain and liberate world, through the at-times strange conspiring of human flesh, heart, will, and mind, all of which are at work in the specters of the dying and lost, particularly of the excluded and oppressed, in ever creative ways. These whom Judith Butler renders as "spectral humans" amid the agonistic political, then, take on a surprising power to haunt, and at times also to dismantle and erode, the forces that freeze and subjugate. In more poetic language, we may recall the words of Victor Serge, activist for the dead and dying of many contexts, who suffered imprisonment in both Western capitalist as well as Soviet revolutionary societies:

> in time flesh will wear out chains
> in time the mind will make chains snap[42]

What kind of power of the flesh is this? What sort of flesh might "wear out chains?" What manner of flesh with what mode of mind can step into the world, be steeped in it, and so inhabit time and space to have such a wearing power? Whatever it is, Serge saw it as a power *in* the world to open another future one:

> I see growing on the ripples of the water
> The revivifying specter
> Of a barbarous freedom drunk on its tears.[43]

Discerning and reflecting on the possibility of such a future, heavy with the dead upon the living, but transimmanentally weighing-in with the

---

42. Victor Serge, "Be Hard" (fragment), in Victor Serge, *Resistance: Poems*, trans. James Brook (San Francisco: CityLights Books, 1972), 33. Used by permission.

43. Victor Serge, "Stenka Razin," in ibid., 21. Used by permission.

specter of revivifying practices, gives us a foretaste of the critical space of the theological.

The Theological and Post-Theological Alternatives

It is against the backdrop of three theological tendencies, in present post-theological discourses, that we can clarify still further the theological that this work focuses as transimmanence of the agonistic political. Walker has given his own expression to these three, and though I recast them somewhat in my own terms, I depend on the options he identifies for situating my sense of "the theological." As will become apparent, the theological of this book is closer to the third tendency, but with some important differentiations.

A first tendency is viewable in the works of John Milbank and other theologians working in support of projects in Radical Orthodoxy. This group seeks to engage the political order, making extensive use of secular theories of modernity and rationality, aiming to forge a radical politics (the "radical" part), but then also moves deeply into the biblical and ecclesial traditions (here's the "orthodoxy" part) in ways that shift theology from the margins to the center of public intellectual discourse. The result, as Walker notes, is not only a retrieval of writings by theologians and orthodox theologians, both mined for their politically transformative meanings, but also a "bulwarking" of Christian claims and doctrines that are given a "*sui generis* gloss," one that sets theological discourse over and against critical and secular theoretical discourses.[44] The result of these maneuvers is often more orthodox than radical, as in Daniel M. Bell Jr.'s critique of liberation theology, which faults Latin American liberation theology because its leading themes of oppression and justice lead, allegedly, to a vengeful reactive spirit. Instead, Bell proposes for liberation theologies a new discovery of the Christian message of forgiveness, expressed by victims toward their oppressing agents.[45] Bell's book evidences a trait of this post-theological tendency, especially as Walker formulates it: "Such projects are indebted to and predicated on historic and traditional flows of conceptual certainty, epistemic privilege

---

44. Walker, "Theology and Democratic Futures," 202.

45. Daniel M. Bell Jr., *Liberation Theology after the End of History: The Refusal to Cease Suffering* (New York: Routledge, 2001), 189–95.

and theoretical imperialism that mask the exploits and consolidations of political and intellectual power."[46] As a part of this problem noted by Walker, there is also the tendency of Radical Orthodoxy to reinforce the foreclosure of long unrecognized populations and groups. This is evident, I would argue, in Bell's call to Latin American peoples to forgive agents with official responsibilities in systems that long have repressed them. In this call, there is a near-complete neglect of the host of movements and texts among Latin Americans in postgenocidal settings, where "truth and reconciliation" commissions do their work, and where victims of oppression have laid foundations for a whole new approach to thinking through forgiveness.[47]

A second tendency that Walker identifies—and one very strong in current discussions of political theology in the United States—is indebted to the influential writings of Slavoj Žižek. We might term this theological tendency, "post-Christian materialism." This is my rendering of Žižek's description of his position in *The Puppet and the Dwarf: The Perverse Core of Christianity*: "My claim here is not merely that I am a materialist through and through, and that the subversive kernel of Christianity is accessible also to a materialist approach; my thesis is much stronger: this kernel is accessible *only* to a materialist approach—and vice versa: to become a true dialectical materialist, one should go through the Christian experience."[48] By materialism, Žižek means no mere opposite to "idealism," or some reference to the world of bodies and their languages over and against consciousness and thinking; rather, he means something much more complex, that is, the primacy of a social-symbolic order of practices and beliefs for understanding humanity and world. It is "materialist" in giving primacy to this complexity, instead of to something that is outside of very human practices and beliefs. It is "Christian" because he interprets the message of Christ as, above all, signaling that "the

46. Walker, "Theology and Democratic Futures," 202.

47. As one example, see *Guatemala: Never Again! REMHI Recovery of Historical Memory Project,* The Official Report of the Human Rights Office, Archdiocese of Guatemala (Maryknoll, N.Y.: Orbis, 1999), esp. "The Wrath of Injustice," 25–28, and "The Path to Social Reconstruction," 313–24.

48. Slavoj Žižek, *The Puppet and the Dwarf: The Perverse Core of Christianity* (Cambridge: MIT Press, 2003), 6. On Žižek's materialism, see Adrian Johnston, *Žižek's Ontology: A Transcendental Materialist Theory of Subjectivity* (Evanston, Ill.: Northwestern University Press, 2008).

difference between God and man is transposed into man himself [sic]."[49]
As "Christian," Žižek reads Christ's words on the cross "Father, why hast
Thou forsaken me?", as throwing all focus onto "man himself" left alone,
with, now, the "nonexistence of the big Other."[50] Žižek's fundamental
project is a materialist one, then, but it passes through Christian theological claims, and continually borrows from them. In Walker's language,
there is in this tendency a "dialectical engagement between particular
theological ideas and concepts and other theoretical frameworks and discourses . . . ," with the result that there emerges a "critical thinking in
which the theological is pressed into service for the elaboration of other
radical and subversive non-theological discourses."[51] This renders Žižek's
project not only conceptually rich and complex, but also enigmatic: it
is fundamentally nontheological, and yet at the same time Žižek drops
in theological notions on an occasional basis, often drawing upon quite
orthodox traditions, giving them fresh, and at times eccentric, twists. This
is evident especially in the way he uses G. K. Chesterton's work *Orthodoxy*. Yet this does not make Žižek a theologian of "radical orthodoxy,"
as with the above tendency. This is because he does not position orthodox theology at the center of his work, and then over and against critical and secular theoretic discourses. Indeed, he steeps himself in those,
too. At best, the theological for Žižek is a necessary passageway and an
occasionally invoked perspective, borrowed from Theology to bolster his
unfolding materialist project.

Žižek's approach is evident if we note some of Žižek's other theological points. In his *In Defense of Lost Causes,* along the way of his analysis of
Hegel's view of Napoleon in Jena, Žižek lets drop a view of "the mystery
of incarnation" as meaning that "what happened in the case of Christ is
that God himself, the creator of our entire universe, was walking around
as a common individual."[52] That view hardly does justice to Hegel's view
of the incarnation, much less to the alternative renderings of incarnation
that theologians and others have debated. Žižek can go on to invoke
substitutionary atonement theory for rebellion[53] and comment that Che

---

49. Slavoj Žižek, *The Parallax View* (Cambridge: MIT Press, 2006), 6.
50. Slavoj Žižek, ed. *Revolution at the Gates: Selected Writings of Lenin from 1917*
(New York: Verso, 2002), 180.
51. Walker, "Theology and Democratic Futures," 201.
52. Slavoj Žižek, *In Defense of Lost Causes* (New York: Verso, 2008), 133.
53. Ibid., 438.

Guevara has a "weird Christ-like aura."[54] Although this kind of discourse all portends a new seriousness given to theological discourse, Žižek keeps it subordinate to his materialist ends. The theological is pressed into service for materialist ends. Precisely this materialism makes Žižek an energizing read for many—and I count myself among them—who are eager to see critical thought address and seek to redress the systemic and political suffering that Žižek addresses throughout his work. The problem, however, is that Žižek's occasional hijacking of theological notions leaves unaddressed, and often uncriticized, the way those theological notions often underwrite a very antimaterialist ethos of transcendence, of the "big Other." In this sense, Žižek leaves strangely uninterrogated the epistemic sovereignty and theoretical imperialism of much Theology, particularly those methodologies that continually function to exclude the subaltern knowledges that seek to weigh-in upon Theology's discourse. For all his differences with radical orthodoxy, then, in this hesitance to interrogate orthodoxy there is in Žižek's work a similarity to it.[55]

The third tendency, more seemingly anti-theological, is the one in relation to which I would clarify my book's approach to the theological. Walker sees it largely exemplified by the work of Alain Badiou, particularly as this French philosopher formulates his materialist ontology with the aid of mathematics.[56] The historical ontology of my book does not pretend to deploy anything like that found in Badiou's *Being and Event* or in his *Logics of Worlds*. My work does feature, however, a key trait of Badiou's, that is, his tendency to admit to "the theoretical efficacy of certain theological concepts and constructions without admitting the entire panoply of theological claims and commitments into its discourse."[57] Although Walker doesn't mention it, a key example of his point might be Badiou's book *Saint Paul: The Foundation of Universalism*.[58] Here, among many

54. Ibid., 433.

55. For Žižek's engagement with radical orthodoxy, particularly John Milbank, see Slavoj Žižek and John Milbank, *The Monstrosity of Christ: Paradox or Dialectic?* ed. Creston Davis (Cambridge: MIT Press, 2009).

56. Alain Badiou, *Being and Event*, trans. Oliver Feltham (New York: Continuum, 2000 [French 1988]). See also Badiou's more recent *Logics of Worlds: Being and Event 2*, trans. Alberto Toscano (New York: Continuum, 2009 [French 2006]), and *Polemics*, trans. Steve Corcoran (New York: Verso, 2006).

57. Walker, "Theology and Democratic Futures," 201.

58. Alain Badiou, *Saint Paul: The Foundation of Universalism*, trans. Ray Brassier (Stanford: Stanford University Press, 2003 [French 1997]).

other interpretive moves, Badiou extracts from the "mythological core" of Paul's notion of "the Christ-event," a "formal, wholly secularized conception of grace" as "affirmation without preliminary negation," a truth, for Badiou, of "pure and simple encounter."[59] Resurrection is similarly given a meaning extracted from Paul's mythological core, emphasizing that the "event's sudden emergence never follows from an eventual site."[60] We need not trace here how Badiou puts all this together, nor compare this familiar move with those of the Heidegger-influenced New Testament scholar Rudolf Bultmann. The point is that extracts from Theology are seized upon and taken even more seriously than Žižek often does, but alongside a more vigorous disclaimer of their import. "For me, truth be told," says Badiou in his opening lines to *St. Paul,* "Paul is not an apostle or a saint. I care nothing for the Good News he declares, or the cult dedicated to him."[61] Nevertheless, Paul's thinking is theoretically efficacious, usable for promoting his philosophical meditations on a militant theory of transformative event. "For me," Badiou continues, "Paul is a poet-thinker of the event, as well as one who practices and states the invariant traits of what can be called the militant figure."[62]

Two other traits tend to distinguish Badiou from Žižek, and certainly from the Radical Orthodoxy approach to the theological in our politically weighted post-theological moment. Walker observes, for example, that Badiou and his supporters first issue a forthright rejection of any transcendental guarantee standing behind the thought they derive from certain theological concepts. Second, they reject the doctrinal matrix of beliefs and concepts that are structured into theologians' language and customary expression. These two rejections strike right at the heart of what defines much guild Theology, not only its claims to have knowledge of a sovereign god, a claim maintained by an ethos of transcendence, but also its doctrinal ordering of reflection in terms of authoritative texts and loci.

The theological developed in this book embraces both rejections. First, it can affirm Badiou's critique of the "transcendental guarantee," since this usually functions as a way to guard the privileged standpoint

---

59. Ibid., 66. Also, grace, for Badiou, "means that thought cannot *wholly* account for the brutal starting over on the path of life in the subject, which is to say, for the rediscovered conjunction between thinking and doing," 84.

60. Ibid., 71.

61. Ibid., 1.

62. Ibid., 2.

and perspective of groups that long have commanded power in guild Theology. The transcendental guarantee is usually advanced and presumed by those whose rights and powers receive regular social and ritual affirmation in the West, often without a need felt to make an argument for positions they claim to have transcendent value and truth. As already noted, Badiou's rejection of the "doctrinal matrix of beliefs" is also something that this book's view of the theological can affirm, especially given the role of those beliefs in inscribing and articulating the claims to sovereignty and transcendence that Theology usually makes.

Nevertheless, "the theological" of this book is here not positioned in mere oppositional rejection to transcendence and doctrine. The very fact that Badiou—and with him other post-theological or postsecular figures, such as Italian philosopher Giorgio Agamben[63]—find themselves laboring over a biblical and highly theological text like that of Paul's letter to the Romans, suggests that there is something more complex going on than mere rejection of transcendence and doctrine. When Badiou declares that he cares nothing for Paul's gospel, or the cult dedicated to Paul, it would be more accurate to say—and I believe close readings of Badiou bear this out[64]—that he cares nothing for a move to transcendence or to ecclesial authority. However, he does care for, and is informed by, the noteworthy and valuable militant subjectivity that Paul displays in his poetic language. Badiou may also care little for doctrine, yet he spends considerable time theorizing the relations between elements of the traditional loci of doctrines: grace, sin, resurrection, salvation, love, and more.[65]

The theological, then, has a much more complex relationship to transcendence and doctrine. In this book, there will be rejection, yes, and a repudiation, especially of claims to step outside, above, beyond world or materiality. There will be repudiation, particularly of claims to possess some fulcrum of knowledge for viewing the whole, some authoritative standpoint resting on doctrine that orders knowledge to a transcendent sovereign. These all fail. The claims to move "beyond," for all their claims

---

63. Giorgio Agamben, *The Time That Remains: A Commentary on the Letter to the Romans*, trans. Patricia Dailey (Stanford: Stanford University Press, 2005 [Italian 2000]).

64. On the very page on which Badiou says, "I care nothing for the Good News he [Paul] declares," he moves on to say that there is in Paul "no transcendence, nothing sacred, [only] perfect equality of this work with every other, the moment it touches me personally." Badiou, *St. Paul*, 1.

65. On these themes, see ibid., 42, 84, 59, 77–78, 82–83.

to have grasped a perspective or point that is other to finite humanity, remain steeped in, mediated by, and limited to the very dynamics they claim to transcend. And yet, in the aspiration and reach, in the attempt to move beyond—in these attempts that are failures—there is left a debris, a fallout from transcendental moves, past and present, in which thought and experience must labor today. Ernesto Laclau's musing at one point is both instructive and emblematic of the way of the theological, of transimmanence: "The social terrain is structured, in my view, not as completely immanent or as the result of some transcendent structure, but through what we could call *failed transcendence*."[66] The theological, in this post-theological moment, works amid this failed transcendence. This means that while there is a rejection of transcendence, there must also be an acknowledgment that the failures of transcendence partially determine the way transimmanental thought and being occur now.

A similar, not purely rejectionist, kind of thinking also characterizes the theological with respect to doctrinal conceptuality. The theological unfolded in this book does not work to accommodate doctrine, surely not that which orients theological minds to look beyond the world. The theological *does* respect a certain power of language and concept to catalyze and embody the transimmanental movement I find in spectral practice. It is precisely here that the imagistic art forms, the symbolic force mentioned above, become important. The prodigious arts of spectral imagery in practice, by which occluded, foreclosed, and oppressed peoples weigh-in from the regions to which they are often consigned and into which they are disposed, can at times find their place in doctrinal languages. What a discourse of the theological does entail, then, by way of a language, is not doctrine's conceptual ordering, but imagistic art forms' symbolic force in practice. These may be discernible in some doctrinal discussions. While there is here a repudiation of doctrine as a transcendentally ordering concept and structure, there can be an embrace of the linguistic force that doctrinal language often brings, but only *if* it stays close to the originary discourses of faith and spirit that characterize movements and communities of struggle that use the artful force of images.[67] From amid this spectral imagery in practice comes what we will

---

66. Ernesto Laclau, *On Populist Reason* (New York: Verso, 2005), 244.

67. For one of the most deft and promising proposals of a way forward for treatment of the theological in Christian traditions, see the work by South African theologian John W.

term a transimmanental world-making, which, as Pierre Bourdieu called for at the end of his life, is a way "to give *symbolic force*, by way of artistic form" to the critical ideas and analyses that patterns of foreclosure, exclusion, and oppression often generate.[68]

In short, the theological of this book, while closer to the atheistic rejections of theology manifest in Badiou and his followers, nevertheless will develop those rejections in a more dialectical way. The notion of transimmanence will emerge more dialectically in relation to transcendence, acknowledging that we must work in the ruins of transcendence, that we must not simply oppose transcendence but reconstitute ourselves amid its "failure" (Laclau). The notion of transimmanence, with respect to its primary language, will also work dialectically in relation to the distinctive language of Theology, doctrine, rejecting its functions of ordering thought and practice to the transcendent, but tracing and nurturing the artistic forms of symbolic language, the force of which enables the repressed to weigh-in for change amid the weight of the world.

---

de Gruchy, *Christianity, Art, and Transformation: Theological Aesthetics in the Struggle for Justice* (Cambridge: Cambridge University Press, 2001).

68. Pierre Bourdieu, *Firing Back: Against the Tyranny of the Market 2,* trans. Loïc Wacquant (New York: New Press, 2003 [French 2000]), 25.

Chapter One

THINKING THE THEOLOGICAL: A HAUNTING

This world—already our own—is the world of bodies. Because it has, because it is, the very density of spacing, or the density, intensity, of a place. . . . What is coming to us is a dense and serious world, a world-wide world, one that doesn't refer to another world, or to an other-world . . .

Our world has inherited the world of gravity: all bodies weigh on one another, and against one another, heavenly bodies and callous bodies, vitreous bodies and corpuscles. . . . But bodies weigh lightly. Their weight is the raising of their masses to the surface. Unceasingly, mass is raised to the surface; it bubbles up to the surface; mass is thickness, a dense, local consistency.[1]*—Jean-Luc Nancy*

You know as well as I do that people who die bad don't stay in the ground.—Toni Morrison[2]

---

1. Jean-Luc Nancy, *Corpus,* trans. Richard A. Rand (New York: Fordham University Press, 2008 [French, 2003]), 93.
2. Toni Morrison, *Beloved* (New York: Knopf, 1987), 188.

This book's discernment of the theological as a dimension of agonistic political thought and practice, and as unfolding especially in the prodigious force of artful images deployed in practice, is a discernment that is backgrounded, conceptually, by the conjoining of two recent approaches in contemporary theory. These are, first, the theories of power emerging from Michel Foucault's key theoretical moves, and, second, certain theories of specters, of haunting, perhaps "hauntology," to recall Derrida's neologism.[3] I wrote in the preface that this book is not so much a political theology as it is a political theorization of the theological. That theorization begins to take form within the intersection of Foucauldian studies of power and other critical theorists' reflections on haunting and spectrality. My turn here to "thinking the theological" is undertaken not only to make clearer the notion of "the theological," but also to situate it, to inscribe it, in the languages of theoretical discourses. Even though we may not find a single disciplinary home for the theological in the academies of the West, and certainly not alone in the discipline of Theology, this turn to theory is a way to locate the kind of disciplined discourse that the theological is. To the question, "Where is the home of a disciplined reflection on the theological?," my answer does not consist in pointing to any one disciplinary unit (say, represented by the university departments, anthropology, sociology, comparative literature, political science, certainly not Theology). Instead, a first answer is that its home is wherever there is a disciplined reflection on how theories of power and of specters (their haunting and ghostly presences) interplay.

Accordingly, this chapter will, in a first section, introduce key moves in Foucault's theories of power and also of select critical theories of spectrality. These provide the background for further theorizing of the agonistic political in the following chapter. The second section presents what "world" is, wherein both its weight and density are extended and/or concentrated, showing when and how a haunting and liberatory power is borne by sufferers of imposed social suffering. A third section argues that the world's weighing bodies includes an understanding of "sense" that challenges the "imperio-colonial sense" of Theology, a sense dramatized, for example, in the theoscopic "God sees you," referenced in the preface. In a final section, "The Theological as Theology's Hydra," I clarify further how the theological is born in the struggle of those who weigh-in with

---

3. Jacques Derrida, *Specters of Marx: The State of Debt and the Work of Mourning, and the New International,* trans. Peggy Kamuf (New York: Routledge, 1994 [French 1992]), 10.

spectral transformative practices, thus haunting Theology and its imperio-colonial sense.

Theorizing Power and Specters

Theorizing Power with Foucault

Foucault's importance to this work is already apparent from the opening lines of the preface. There he points tellingly to the agony and oppression of the cell, and yet he situates that state of confinement in the context of what can be called a networking view of power, one that can be contrasted with a notion of power as repression. This approach is evident in an oft-quoted passage from a well-known interview with Foucault:

> It seems to me now that the notion of repression is quite inadequate for capturing what is precisely the productive aspect of power. In defining the effects of power as *repression* . . . one identifies power with a law which says no, power is taken above all as carrying the force of a prohibition. . . . What makes power hold good, what makes it accepted, is simply the fact that it doesn't only weigh on us as a force that says no, but that it traverses and produces things, it induces pleasure, forms knowledge, produces discourse. It needs to be considered as a *productive network* which runs through the whole social body, much more than as a negative instance whose function is repression.[4]

Scholars who cite this passage do not always note that Foucault here is not completely rejecting the notion of power as repression. Indeed, Foucault's life of contesting with power in the streets and society, especially with police power,[5] should admonish any who would cite this passage to gloss the need for political contesting of repression. The main force of the passage, however, is to insist that the notion of power as repression, while necessary, is not sufficient. It is inadequate for grasping what makes power "hold good," or "what makes it accepted." He wants readers to

---

4. Michel Foucault, *Power/Knowledge: Selected Interviews and Other Writings, 1972–1977*, ed. Colin Gordon (New York: Pantheon, 1980), 119.

5. For one example, see David Macey, *The Lives of Michel Foucault* (New York: Vintage, 1995), 350.

see that power not only says *no* in a kind of top-down fashion, but that it also abides in a social system's microrelations and everyday interactions. It, again, "traverses and produces things," thus inducing forms of knowledge, producing discourse, inducing pleasure. Foucault's focus on the cell as a culmination of "an entire parapenal institution" is one example of his insistence on focusing on the networking of power through many relations and everyday practices. There is still domination, but it must be complexly approached through its networking.

The contrast between repressive and networking power is more fully developed across Foucault's writings as a distinction between "juridical" and "biopolitical" notions of power. The juridical model pivots around notions of law and sovereignty, with power, mainly "repressive," viewed largely as "power over," pressing upon agents and groups. As Foucault stresses at several points, there is a persistent binarism with power as sovereignty in the juridical model: the ruler and the ruled, controlling laws and the legally bound subjects—in prisons, the jailors and the jailed; in war, the victors and the vanquished; or again, in murder, the life taker and the slain victim. Foucault also sees this juridical structure at work in racism, as it still pervades the global division of labor and power in the West, marking who "legitimately" belongs among the exploited classes at risk of death, and who are to live among the more entitled and privileged.[6]

The other model of power is "the biopolitical model," often the one with which Foucault is today more readily identified. It is closer to what I identified as the networking mode of power. It is built around Foucault's notion of "governmentality," and refers to the multiplicity of ways that power develops among complex relations, the way it produces "technologies of power." Governmentality, for example, sets terms that often are conditions for indirect killing, "political death." It characteristically operates through circuitous and unexpected ways of working across many sites, folding a variety of social domains into one another. On this

---

6. Foucault, "*Society Must Be Defended*": *Lectures at the Collège de France, 1975–1976*, trans. David Macey (New York: Picador, 2003 [French 1997]), 254–55. Foucault's notion of race and racism is uniquely—some would say idiosyncratically—linked to certain acts of "counterhistory" by repressed groups suffering under juridical sovereignty (see 69–84). On the "global division of labor and power" (GLDP), which is often marked by race, see John Mittelmann, *The Globalization Syndrome: Transformation and Resistance* (Princeton: Princeton University Press, 2000), 4, 34–107.

model the negativity of killing can appear as part of the productivity of life, as "positive."[7] The complexity of racial marking and discrimination, for example, can be a complexity that is death dealing. Ruth Wilson Gilmore's study of prisons and California political economy captures this in her very definition of racism. "Racism," she writes, "is state-sanctioned or extra-legal production of group-differentiated vulnerability to premature death."[8]

As Gilmore's definition suggests, we should be careful not to view Foucault's two modes of power, the juridical and the biopolitical, as mutually exclusive. They often dwell together. The biopolitical does not supplant the juridical concerns of maintenance and protection of sovereignty. In the United States, certain post–9/11 practices—resurgent war, torture, heightened nationalism, and suspension of constitutional rights—function as a sharp wake-up call for any academic complacency that would overlook the exercise of brutal sovereign power in the name of some kind of biopolitical complexity in whose dense opaqueness all systems of repression and judicial sovereignty disappear. Considering this context, Judith Butler, in her book *Precarious Life*, thus makes a point that is more fully in keeping with Foucault's view of how the two models of power interact: "governmentality might become the site for the reanimation of that lost ground, the reconstellation of sovereignty in new form . . . the deployment of sovereignty as a tactic . . ."[9] I would go further and suggest that governmentality and its biopolitics presuppose and often stage exercises of sovereign power, especially when its more expansive and intensive technologies of power are seen to be breaking down, not securing desired power efficiently enough. This is particularly true in "states of emergency." In such a state, what Italian philosopher Giorgio Agamben has termed a "state of exception," biopolitical governmentality and juridical sovereignty merge. In fact, in states of exception, the everyday, biopolitical conditions are subject less to governmentality and more to a juridical sovereignty, one that invokes its power to "decide the

---

7. Foucault, *"Society Must Be Defended,"* 70.

8. Ruth Wilson Gilmore, *Golden Gulag: Prisons, Surplus, Crisis, and Opposition in Globalizing California* (Berkeley: University of California Press, 2007), 28.

9. Judith Butler, *Precarious Life: The Powers of Mourning and Violence* (New York: Verso, 2004), 97.

exception."[10] This is not the place to debate the complexities of Agamben's political theory of the state of exception.[11] The main point here is that much of Agamben's theory underscores the need to acknowledge that the biopolitical and the older juridical models often dwell together.

Why is Foucault's theory of power important for this book? His models of power, both the juridical and the biopolitical, as theorizations of the repressive *and* networking modes of power, respectively, structure a distinctive approach to study of human enmeshment in structures of power. Human enmeshment in structures of power is essential to understanding the being of humans in the world. Thus, the theorization of power in Foucault enables an ontology of power, a political ontology. Foucault himself referred to his writings on power as a "historical ontology of ourselves."[12] This is not an ontology of Heidegger-like fundamental structures, but a historical and social ontology.

Recent thinkers who have followed in the wake of Foucault's "historical ontology" include such figures as Ian Hacking, Judith Butler, Chantal Mouffe, Jean-Luc Nancy, Giorgio Agamben, and numerous others. For articulating my own historical ontology of the agonistic political in this book, I rely particularly on Theodore Schatzki and Pierre Bourdieu. Both of these thinkers respect Foucault's way of theorizing power, and yet, with a finer-grained theoretical vision, they articulate the historical ontology of power with respect to social practices. This will give my ontology of the agonistic political greater specificity than ontology usually displays, and also allow me to write with more concreteness about how the theological emerges as a dimension of agonistic politics. Schatzki, in particular, enables us to think the conjuncture between being and practice, while Bourdieu, building on that conjuncture, also enables us to reflect on another conjuncture, that of power and symbol. This latter conjuncture, especially, bridges to the theological's role as transimmanentally engaging power with the symbolic force of art and image.

10. Giorgio Agamben, *State of Exception*, trans. Kevin Attell (Stanford: Stanford University Press, 2005), 3, 6–7.

11. For one recent critical discussion of Agamben, see Alison Ross, ed., *The Agamben Effect*, special issue of *The South Atlantic Quarterly* 107, no. 1 (Winter 2008), esp. Ewa Płonowska Ziarek, "Bare Life on Strike: Notes on the Biopolitics of Race and Gender," 89–105.

12. Michel Foucault, "What Is Enlightenment?," in Paul Rabinow and Niklas Rose, eds., *The Essential Foucault: Selections from Essential Works of Foucault, 1954–1984* (New York: New Press, 1994), 53–57.

Theorizing the Spectral

The turn to spectral theory in Western academies has a largely poststructuralist academic pedigree, especially through Jacques Derrida's 1992 work, *Specters of Marx*. Derrida's reflections on specters, ghosts, apparitions, spirits, and conjuring make up what he termed a "hauntology," discourse about what haunts, what is absent but still unsettlingly present, to all being.[13] He calls for what has not been: scholars who dare to think the ghost—this, his "hauntology."[14]

Other poststructuralist theorists have taken up Derrida's dare. As Jeffrey Weinstock writes in his *Spectral America*, literary theorists have traced in a host of "deconstructive gestures" the shadowy realms that attend the allegedly clear and distinct theoretical arguments and programs. Derrida is not the only figure here, of course. Other texts making this theoretical turn, as Weinstock identifies them,[15] are Jean-Michel Rabaté's *The Ghosts of Modernity* (1996), Peter Buse and Andrew Stotts's *Ghosts: Deconstruction, Psychoanalysis, History* (1999), and Peter Schwerger's *Fantasm and Fiction* (1999).

There are also the nearly uncountable works of fiction that work ghostly figures and specters into their prose. In such fiction it is especially history's mountain of the systematically and unjustly slain that provokes thought about the spectral. In fact, while it cannot be my task here, the turn to spectral theory should be viewed not simply as a Western turn of theory. It is especially indigenous peoples, but also African, Asian, and other colonized peoples, whose legacies of political and cultural repression, and often genocide, have spawned memories—"re-memories," writes Toni Morrison about "the six million and more" lost to slavery and the Middle Passage—of ancestors, ghosts, and haunting presences. These traditions are freed up from the secularist strictures of much of the Western academy, thus able to forge new knowledges from seething presences. The rise of Western academic theories of haunting, then, are themselves a haunting generated by communities that have suffered epistemic and political violence by the West.

---

13. Derrida, *Specters of Marx*, 10.

14. Ibid., 11–12.

15. Jeffrey Andrew Weinstock, "Introduction: The Spectral Turn," in Weinstock, ed., *Spectral America: Phantoms and the National Imagination* (Madison: University of Wisconsin Press, 2004), 5.

In recent times, the momentous 1987 work of Toni Morrison's *Beloved* offers a story of a ghost, a fingering of the jagged edge of pain amid souls who still haunt the living. Leslie Marmon Silko's novel *Almanac of the Dead* is but one of many other texts that invoke the spectral, in her case, from the traditions of indigenous peoples. "The truth is," writes Silko, "the Ghost Dance did not end with the murder of big foot and one hundred and forty-four Ghost Dance worshipers at Wounded Knee. The Ghost Dance has never ended, it has continued . . ."[16] Those swept away by disappearance and torture in "the dirty war" in Argentina still haunt the lives, and so the stories, of Argentine writers, especially in Luisa Valenzuela's *Open Door* (1988) and *Strange Things Happen Here* (1979).[17] Argentina's dirty war also provided stories about spirits and ghosts for Lawrence Thornton, as in *Imagining Argentina* (1991) and *Naming the Spirits* (1995).

In social science, there is the eminent work of sociologist Avery Gordon, already quoted in this work. Her book *Ghostly Matters: Haunting and the Sociological Imagination* (1997) seriously engages the fictional material, but also takes its cues from earlier theorists in the West. These include Karl Marx in his *18th Brumaire of Louis Bonaparte* (1852); Walter Benjamin as he reflects on how the past weights the present and the future in his "Theses on Philosophy of History" (1923); Max Horkheimer and Theodore Adorno's short note "On the Theory of Ghosts" (1944) in their *Dialectic of Enlightenment*; and especially Raymond Williams's work on "structures of feeling" in his *Marxism and Literature*.[18]

Weinstock reads these poststructuralist interests in theorizing the ghostly as largely due to recent poststructuralist millennial anxieties.[19] To privilege a general millennial anxiety in the Euro-American West, however, is to miss the deeper roots of postructuralist critiques, that is, in their own complex resistance to the nature of Western sovereignty as a

---

16. Leslie Marmon Silko, *Almanac of the Dead* (New York: Simon & Schuster, 1988), 724.

17. See the extensive examination of Valenzuela's fiction in Avery F. Gordon, *Ghostly Matters: Haunting and the Sociological Imagination* (Minneapolis: University of Minnesota Press, 1997), 63–136.

18. Max Horkheimer and Theodore Adorno, *Dialectic of Enlightenment*, trans. John Cumming (New York: Continuum, 1997 [1944]), 216; and Raymond Williams, "Structures of Feeling," in his *Marxism and Literature* (New York: Oxford University Press, 1977), 128–35.

19. Weinstock, *Spectral America*, 5–6.

colonizing project, an awareness and struggle of the many who suffer the "modern/colonial world system."[20] Tracing spectral theory to the West's millennial anxiety credits the West with too much, slighting the way the theory has in fact emerged more from the fracture in the West's history created by its colonialism and imperialism. Spectral thought is one of those theories, a form of "border thinking," that has sprung up from that fault line between colonized and colonizer, what Walter Mignolo has also termed, "the colonial difference."[21]

Robert J. C. Young, in his historical analysis of postcolonialism, under-scores how important the "colonial difference" is to poststructuralists, pointing out that it has another politics, especially when recalling its key formative thinkers, whose key crucible and matrix for reflection was the French Algerian war. Young's words should be attended to carefully:

Many of those who developed the theoretical positions subsequently characterized as poststructuralism came from Algeria or had been involved in the war of independence. Fanon, Memmi, Bourdieu, Althusser, Lyotard, Derrida, [Hélène] Cixous— . . . None of them, it is true, were Algerians proper, in the sense of coming from the indigenous Arab, Berber, Kabyle, Chaouia or Moabite peoples that make up the population of modern independent Algeria. . . . They were, so to speak, Algerians improper, those who did not belong easily to either side— . . . *The postructuralism associated with these names could better be characterized therefore as Franco-Maghrebian theory, for its theoretical interventions have been actively concerned with the task of undoing the ideological heritage of French colonial-ism and with rethinking the premises, assumptions and protocols of its centrist imperial culture.*[22]

But what of spectrality, in particular, of haunting and the "ghostly matter"? The short answer is that the ghostly and spectral are what the

---

20. Walter D. Mignolo, *Local Histories/Global Designs: Coloniality, Subaltern Knowl-edges, and Border Thinking* (Princeton: Princeton University Press, 2000), 33–38.

21. Ibid., 24. I do not deny, and have in fact argued elsewhere, that poststructuralism can often reinforce some of the most exploitative patterns of Western globalization. See Mark Lewis Taylor, "Subalternity and Advocacy as *Kairos* for Theology," in Joerg Rieger, ed., *Opting for the Margins: Postmodernity and Liberation in Christian Theology* (New York: Oxford University Press, 2003), 23–44.

22. Robert J. C. Young, *Postcolonialism: An Historical Introduction* (London: Blackwell, 2001), 414. Italics added.

poststructuralist traces as fault lines, fissures, infiltrations operating in the colonizer's centralizing cultural and political apparatus. To trace them is to find the vestiges of the vanquished, often to highlight and strengthen long-colonized peoples, aiming to eviscerate the strength of colonizing and imperial projects.

We can summarize three key notions that are perhaps at the core of spectral theory: haunting, the specter, and ghost(s). Consider first the term, *haunting*, the active presence—better, the "presence-ing"—of something taken to be absent (erased, effaced). As Avery Gordon writes, there is a "seething" aspect to this process of being present,[23] which is all the more pronounced when the effaced ones are those who have been unjustly slain. Noting connections between the presence of the dead and writing, Margaret Atwood observes, "Having the dead return when not expected can be a hair-raising experience, especially if they are feeling slighted, and needy, or worse, angry."[24] The seething presence of the effaced— "seething" not just as filled with anger but as also turbulent, portending change—gives to the Western present a certain charge. Its "occluded and forgotten past" is heavy.[25] It weighs heavy upon, and in, the present. Morrison's words persist: "You know as well as I do that people who die bad don't stay in the ground."[26]

Haunting, as this general process of seething presence amid structural dynamics that would efface it, can then be elaborated in relation to two other notions in spectral theory. The second is that of *specter*, the central term for which the theory can perhaps be named. The specter is haunting congealed into a portentous promise or threat, one that carries and suggests an accountability, a demand upon the present to remember, often to effect a liberation for the effaced ones. Then, the third is the notion of *ghost*, a term usually used in spectral theory for specific instances and images discerned amid the haunting, which may or may not become specters in the specific sense—as portentous, potentially transformative promise, threat, demand. The character Beloved in Morrison's text is a "ghost," related to the ghosts of six million African and African-American others lost to the Middle Passage and slavery. Chinese American laborers

23. Gordon, *Ghostly Matters*, 8, 17, 21.
24. Margaret Atwood, *Negotiating with the Dead: A Writer on Writing* (New York: Anchor, 2002), 159.
25. Ibid., 195.
26. Morrison, 188.

are also ghosts; their bones resting still in the railway track beds of the U.S. West, where their labor secured the most difficult transit areas of the economically essential transcontinental railway system.[27] So also are there ghosts of the massacred in the indigenous territories of the Americas.[28] There are the dead from land theft and dispossession of Mexico in the U.S. nineteenth-century Southwest,[29] and then also those lost to "shock and awe" aerial assaults upon Iraqi lands.[30] Whether and how all of these constitute a haunting of the present such that they might also become portentous specters, transforming the present, depends on the further conceptual work of treating them and upon further strategic practices of remembrance and action. Here, however, it is important to note that the intersection of Foucault's theorization of power with key insights from spectral theory yields the conceptual background of this book. But what point of this intersection will be most important? It is here that the notion of "weight of the world" is important.

Weighted World: A Prisoner's Hurled Tray

In this section, I develop several insights from Jean-Luc Nancy's reflections on weight that also set important meanings of "world." This enables a particular way of viewing power and spectrality together. What results also is a distinctive understanding of writing and "sense," which will become significant to the style and concern of the theological as it haunts Theology.

I begin with a personal vignette to initiate reflection on the notion of the "weight of the world."[31] In 1977, when I was a theological student—in

---

27. Iris Chang, *The Chinese in America: A Narrative History* (New York: Penguin, 2003), 53–64.

28. David E. Stannard, *American Holocaust: The Conquest of the New World* (New York: Oxford University Press, 1993).

29. See Laura E. Gómez, *Manifest Destinies: The Making of the Mexican American Race* (New York: New York University Press, 2007).

30. For the first careful analysis, see Gilert Burnham, Riyadh Laftu, Shannon Doocy, and Les Roberts, "Mortality after the 2003 Invasion of Iraq: A Cross-Sectional Cluster Sample Survey," *The Lancet* 368, no. 9545 (October 21, 2006): 1421–28. For respected sources that since place the Iraqi civilian losses as high as one, or even two, million, see the Just Foreign Policy Web site, at http://www.justforeignpolicy.org/iraq, accessed September 14, 2010.

31. The fruitfulness of the metaphor is evidenced by the many meanings at play in Pierre Bourdieu's work in the English translation of the edited collection Pierre Bourdieu

fact, while first reading Michel Foucault's book *Discipline and Punish*—
I worked as an intern for the Virginia State Office of Attorney General,
investigating prisoner complaints of abuse in the Virginia State Penitentiary. On one of my first visits with officials to the prison, a man being
held in a holding cell deftly hurled his full tray of food through the bars
in my direction. The food and drink missed me but hit a prison official.
Nevertheless, after officials hustled me from the room, I knew that I, too,
had been struck—by his rage.

The rage I felt was part of a complex sensibility, and one that would
become all the more complex over years of confronting similar situations
and reflecting on the unprecedented and exponential growth of U.S. prisons after 1977.[32] Part of the complexity that day was that there was also
a rage in me, which I sensed was not separate from that of the prisoner.
Not that I was experiencing the trauma he must have faced on the way
to a most immediate and acute imprisonment. My anger was focused
more on the whole setup, a "world," which, for whatever reason, could
present one human being behind bars and another, me, outside of them.
I was enmeshed, feeling confined, not in that man's cell, but within that
"parapenal institution, which is created in order not to be a prison," as
Foucault put it in the epigraph to this book's preface.[33] I felt what I would
now call "the weight" of this world, my own enmeshment in it as well
as his. In my case, the parapenal institution was the government office
where I was an intern, but also the theological academy, as well as forces
of racialized power, economic stratification, and other dynamics of the

---

et al, *The Weight of the World: Social Suffering in Contemporary Society*, trans. Priscilla
Parkhurst Ferguson (Stanford: Stanford University Press, 2000). In it, the English translator
reflects on how the French word *la misère*, in the title *La Misère du monde*, carries a surplus of interacting meanings, not all of which would have been preserved for English readers if *la misère* had been rendered using the false cognate term *misery*. Bourdieu's entire
book plays upon the multiple meanings and resonances of *la misère*, suggesting "poverty"
in economic, spiritual, and moral terms. It invokes suffering, unhappiness, and misfortunes
of the collectivity, as well as of individuals. There are echoes of Pascal's reflections on the
misery of man without God, as there are of Marx's *La Misère de la philosophie* (*The Poverty
of Philosophy*), itself a reply to Proudhon's *La Philosophie de la misère*, and Victor Hugo's
novel *Les Misérables*. The notion of "weight," used to translate *la misère*, will also feature
a rich and polyvalent significance.

32. Michelle Alexander, *The New Jim Crow: Mass Incarceration in the Age of Colorblindness* (New York: New Press, 2010), 6–9.

33. Michel Foucault, *Discipline and Punish: The Birth of the Prison* (New York: Pantheon, 1977 [French 1975]), 294.

state apparatus of which prisons are a part and in whose tangle each one of us around that man's holding cell was enmeshed. The racialized dimension was especially strong, as I, a white man, watched another en route to incarceration in this case an African American, joining the sea of other black men and women who disproportionately make up the more than two million imprisoned in the United States today among those of other communities of color.[34] In short, I felt the weight of the parapenal institution that systemically, in different ways, pressed upon us both, and culminated in that man's cell.

This complex sensibility would be replicated later for me at other sites, during times of my meetings with survivors of torture across the Americas, with others in U.S. prisons, with those who endure sexual and physical violence in home and street, with survivors of massacres in Guatemala, Mexico, El Salvador of the 1980s and 1990s, more recently Peru and Colombia, also with Palestinians whose lives are sundered and lands plundered by "the wall" and by practices of apartheid that Israeli government officials maintain.[35] As powerful and often overwhelming as these structural violations can be, the complex sense of the world's weightedness can also be known when confronting the rage and struggle of a single mother, of a homeless man, of an immigrant community, of persons ostracized for their mode of sexual practice and identities, or of impoverished families struggling to forge dignity and survival out of unrelenting want.

I am hardly alone in this sensibility. Others share it. I do not believe that this sensibility can be dismissed as guilt over freedoms, opportunities, or entitlements that I and some may have, which others do not. Those are of course operative. But the "weight felt," I suggest, should be approached more as a sense of a persisting connection intrinsic to shared humanity being disrupted, of a copresence to one another that,

---

34. Blacks are six to eight times more likely to be in prison or jail than whites, and Hispanics three times more likely. See Bruce Western, *Punishment and Inequality in America* (New York: Russell Sage Foundation, 2007), 30–33.

35. On Israel's construction of the wall, see *International Court of Justice Reports of Judgments, Advisory Opinions And Orders: Legal Consequences of the Construction of a Wall in the Occupied Palestinian Territory* (New York: United Nations Publications, 2005). For background on the phenomena of separation of peoples in Israel, see Ilan Pappe, *The Ethnic Cleansing of Palestine* (Oxford: Oneworld Publications, 2007).

paradoxically, can be startlingly provoked by the separation worked by bars, Plexiglas walls, and slamming doors.

This "weight" I take, first, as referring to the suffering known by the most acute and direct victims of social constraints and oppressive structures, whether these be from imprisonment, war, poverty, the daily violence and burden of racial, gender, and sexual discrimination, or of the economic and military burdens of imperial and neocolonial imposi- tions. The "weight," however, is borne, second, as the different but not unrelated weight of those who know of, empathically relate to, wonder about, and reflect upon the dividing these forms of socially imposed suf- fering work. What is it about being and power that the most brutal of social divisions can impose a weight registered on both sides of a divid- ing of flesh?

These are queries emerging from my reflections on the personal vignette and other cognate experiences. We need to interrogate some of the assumptions in my recounting of this experience. Consider, first, the very notion of "world" that this kind of weightedness provokes and perhaps assumes. Philosophers have problematized the notion of "world" from the beginning. One route for reflecting on the notion of world ema- nates from Heidegger's reflections, taking world as surroundings, envi- rons (*umwelt*), in which entities around one are not only "ready-to-hand" but meaningfully so, laden with care.[36] Nancy, in querying "what world means" in the most general sense, responds in his 2007 book, *The Cre- ation of the World* or *Globalization*, with a claim typical of Heidegger's legacy: world is "a totality of meaning."[37] This totality is "of meaning" because the totality in question is not just a location that envelopes or situates us along with other people and entities; it is also something in which we are interested. There is not only sense of location in the totality, but also of belonging to it. With the sense of belonging comes interests in it, cares—it is meaningful for those in the totality. Nancy, especially

36. Martin Heidegger, *Being and Time*, trans. John Macquarrie and Edward Robinson (New York: Harper & Row, 1962), 91–95, 114.

37. Jean-Luc Nancy, *The Creation of the World* or *Globalization* [hereafter, *CWoG*], trans. and with an introduction by Francois Raffoul and David Pettigrew (Albany: State University of New York Press, 2007), 41. In spite of the similarity to Heidegger, the marked departure of Nancy from Heidegger, especially on the issue of *Mitsein* (being-with) and *Dasein* (being-there), is important to note. See Mary-Jane Rubenstein, *Strange Wonder: The Closure of Metaphysics and the Opening of Awe* (New York: Columbia University Press, 2008), 99–110.

in his recent work, distinguishes this "world" from another experience of the totality, a homogenizing one, where embraceable meaning(s) often are *not* known, where values are abrasive and excluding, turning world into "globe" (or *glomus,* as he writes), where places all too often become a "land of exile" or "vale of tears."[38] It is still a meaningful totality, but the way it means is by excluding, destroying the kind of habitation that evokes belonging.

World, then, is labile. It is a set of spacings and balancings that can shift in their character and form. It cannot be reduced in the first instance simply to some basic antagonism, but it is agonist in the sense that the world's being is tensively poised, a precarious and fragile balance, always vulnerable to the outbreak of acute struggle and along various lines of antagonism and opposition. World has the character of being a totality of meaning, but its distribution of meanings and power can easily change. Most significantly, its labile character is a proneness to alternate into globe, where homogeneity takes over, where at-homeness and basic freedoms from suffering are withdrawn. World is lost. What, we may ask, keeps us in world, as distinct from globe? Or, what marks the difference between that totality we welcome as world and that we lament as globe and glome?

Here is where the notion of "weight" comes into play, indeed, a certain distribution of motions intrinsic to weight and weighing. In Nancy's book *Corpus,* notions of weight and weighing become especially constitutive of how one has and constructs world, or maybe loses it as it becomes homogenizing globe, or *glomus.* Nancy's philosophical reflections on weight, as in all of his writings, come in the form of often cryptic and polyvalent expressions that are difficult to interpret and susceptible to diverse readings. Here, it is Nancy's notions of weight, and later transimmanence, that emerge as most significant, even though other aspects of his philosophy will need to be accessed from time to time.[39]

---

38. Nancy, *CWoG,* 41–42.

39. For fine secondary treatments of Nancy's work, in addition to Rubenstein, *Strange Wonder,* 99–132, see B. C. Hutchens, *Jean-Luc Nancy and the Future of Philosophy* (Montreal: McGill-Queens University Press, 2005); Ian James, *The Fragmentary Demand: An Introduction to the Philosophy of Jean-Luc Nancy* (Stanford: Stanford University Press, 2006); and Philip Armstrong, *Reticulations: Jean-Luc Nancy and the Networks of the Political* (Minneapolis: University of Minnesota Press, 2009).

Consider, first, his treatment of weight. It is important to stress that weight involves motion, different kinds of motions. In fact, he often writes when referring to world in ways that interchange weight and the verbal form, "weighing." Everything, he says, "ends up communicating with weighing. A body always weighs or lets itself be weighted, poised. . . . It weighs on, it presses against other bodies, right up against other bodies. Between it and itself, it's still weighing, counterweight, buttressing."[40]

The world of bodies, for Nancy, is constituted by this weighing, this always moving weight. One notes throughout his discussions that while weighing down, being heavy, is part of weighing, it is not the only kind of motion. There is also a kind of lateral movement, of bracing against, which occurs between persons and entities that are side by side. There is also the kind of movement or shifting that refers to bodies weighing lightly. "Their weight" can be "the raising of their masses to the surface. Unceasingly, mass is raised to the surface; it bubbles up to the surface; mass is thickness, a dense, local consistency."[41] So, weight is not just susceptibility to down-pressing movement, a response to gravitational pull. It *is* that, but also includes buttressing, a bracing laterally and involving multiple directions of pressure, even those directed upward in modes of rising. Think of the kinds of multiple pressures at work in an arch forged of heavy, fitted stones over a walkway, maybe secured by some adhesive, but also cut, distributed, positioned one to another so that distributed weight makes up the strength of the arch, keeping the heavy stones pressed against one another to create the arching effect. In the arch, weight is distributed between surfaces of stone—upward, outward, downward, and often along a continuum of directions. All these motions need to be thought to understand "weight" among bodies that make up "world" for Nancy. We might say that weight is a play of forces and of balancing pressures, moving in many directions to keep tensively in place the manifold and teeming bodies that make up what he so often refers to as our "singular plural world." In *Corpus*, this kind of balancing of pressures is articulated in terms of spacing that occurs as *extension*, in which there is a tense interplay of intimacy and distance between bodies. Precisely this spacing of extension is what constitutes world. "The world

40. Jean-Luc Nancy, *Corpus*, 93.
41. Ibid.

is spacing, a tension of place, where bodies are not in space, but space in bodies."[42] World, for Nancy as for this book, emphasizes an "embodied being-in-the-world *as* finite spatial existence."[43]

Now there is another kind of motion that I want to introduce, that *of shifting weight.* "Shifting," with respect to weight and how the world weighs, is not a term I know Nancy himself to use. Nevertheless, it is crucial for naming an important change that can occur when considering how the world weighs, the mode of its congealing, we might say, at particular sites. I deploy the word *shift* for a distinction that Nancy *does* make between the world's weight as distributed and "extended," on the one hand, and as "concentrated," piled up, amassed, on the other. I am aware that with this notion of shifting between extension and concentration I may be inserting a mode of antagonism into Nancy's thought that is not always easy to discern in his focus on multiple relations in his "singular plural world." Yet the distinction seems necessary, especially in light of his later works. Moreover, antagonism, though not the first thing to say about being, is nevertheless an always present possibility in the tense, agonist poise of the world's fragility.

"Shifting" names what happens when the world's weight is no longer sustained by extension, by the delicate spacing of bodies, involving both mutual intimacy and distancing of bodies.[44] Shifting names what happens when the labile extension and delicate spacing of world bodies is disrupted. The results are not extension, relation, and spacing in a singular plural world, but "masses, gatherings, crowdings, crammings, accumulations, demographic spurts, exterminations," and so on.[45] Consider again the stone arch: if its stones are cut askew, thus abutting one another awkwardly, the whole weight can shift, allowing them to tumble en masse, forming a pile. This result can illustrate what Nancy terms "concentration." With respect to human bodies losing their extension—that delicate spacing of intimacy and distance crucial to their weighing and their world—there occurs instead a deprivation of "living space." Nancy terms this "evil," even "absolute evil, a wound opened up on itself, the sign of a self so far reabsorbed into itself that it's no longer a sign, no longer

---

42. Ibid., 27.
43. James, *The Fragmentary Demand,* 110.
44. Ibid., 101.
45. Ibid., 79.

a self."[46] Elsewhere, Nancy says that especially "capital concentrates." I quote here a passage, the clarity and concreteness of which illustrates weight as concentrated and laden with suffering:

> Capital means: a body marketed, transported, displaced, replaced, superseded, assigned to a post and a posture, to the point of ruin, unemployment, famine, a Bengali body bent over a car in Tokyo, a Turkish body in a Berlin trench, a black body loaded down with white packages in Suresnes or San Francisco.[47]

It should be underscored, however, that this shift from weight as extended to weight as concentrated does not set up a strong duality of good and evil. They are instead related, almost as the same weight, differentiated only as one might know the difference between shifting one's body weight from one foot to the other. While that shifting of body weight may nicely illustrate the intimacy and closeness of connection between the delicately sustaining weight of extended bodies on the one hand, and their piling into concentration on the other, the consequences of concentration in the world are severe. In a concentrated world—what Nancy would more see as "globe" or "unworld" (*immonde*)—we know "bodies, murdered, torn, burned, dragged, deported, massacred, tortured, flayed, flesh dumped into mass graves, an obsessing over wounds."[48] Here there is an absence of that sustaining intimacy and distance of the world's bodies related in extension. There is, he writes, "no winding-cloth to define the spacing of one, and then another, death." There are instead "the cadavers in a mass grave . . . wounds heaped up, stuck in, flowing into one another, the soil tossed right on top."[49] Injustice, in fact, for Nancy, is defined as "the mixing, breaking, crushing, and stifling of bodies, making them indistinct (gathered up in a dark center, piled up to eliminate the space between them, within them—assassinating even the space of their just death)."[50]

I return to my sense of the world's weight when facing the holding cell in the Virginia penitentiary of 1977. In light of Nancy's theorization,

---

46. Ibid., 81.
47. Nancy, *Corpus,* 109-10.
48. Ibid., 77
49. Ibid.
50. Ibid., 47.

as I have distilled it above, what I felt on that occasion, was my rage intersected by that of the confined man in the parapenal entirety of an imprisoning U.S. society. What I felt, I stress, was not just a weight pressing down, but the whole conspiring of motions together that marked the shift—from a world weighted through extension of spacings that enable sustained mutual intimacy and distancing, to *immonde* or globe, of concentrated weight in the prison system. By deftly hurling his tray through the bars, the confined man marked the shifting of weight to that which piles on, instead of that which sustains. Quite actually, the prison is a place that piles bodies, stacks them, crams them, routinizes and regulates them. The prisons are sites of world's concentration—better said, they mark an end of world, a congealing of concentration, the rise of *immonde*, of globe, of an "absolute evil." Even time is concentrated to devastating effect, "becoming in prison a thick dull mallet that pounds consciousness into a coma," amid the "mind-numbing, soul-killing savaging sameness that makes each day an echo of the day before with neither thought or hope of growth."[51] It is the result of the world's weight shifting—to use Nancy's words, again—from extension to concentration. To be sure, personal agents and political forces are the immediate performers of the shift, with their diverse activities setting conditions for the shift, enabling concentrated power to hold good. But these personal agents and their activities are a part of shifting of whole structures in the delicate forming of world, in the always labile tension between the different motions of weighing. It is that shifting that I felt, sensed, as I stood before the confined man hurling his tray. As I felt weight being concentrated into *immonde*, into piled-up, massing, and cramming evil, I also mourned the loss of world (*monde*) which comes only through sustaining that delicate labile balance of mutual intimacy and spacing that constitutes living.

The Weighted World's Haunting "Sense"

Nancy's mix of the deftly turned literary phrase with conceptual rigor, as he explores the relationships between world and weight, has important implications for clarifying how it is that the theological haunts the guild discipline of Theology. Before taking this issue directly to Theology,

---

51. Mumia Abu-Jamal, "Killing Time," *Forbes* (November 30, 1999), 106.

though, we need to approach the difficult issue of how the weighted world has sense, or, as Nancy would prefer to say, is a "body of sense,"[52] for this helps to clarify how the theological has a distinctive sense.

Continue to reflect on the rage of the man in the prison cell hurling his food tray. He is part of the weighted world in yet another mode. He marks the way bodies have sense, indeed *are* a kind of sense, especially as world shifts its weight toward a concentration of bodies, and thus bodies in pain. His hurling of the tray was a gesture by which he sought to shift back from *immonde* to *monde,* from weight as concentrated and collapsed piling, to weight as extended for identity and relation in a singular plural world. As such, his hurling was a performance, a kind of sign of the way those who undergo the shift into concentrated weight nevertheless haunt that concentration, are spectral to it. They remind that the shift to concentration is a departure from that mutual intimacy and distancing of bodies that constitute world. The hurling gesture marks the fact that concentrated bodies are, as Nancy himself states at one point, a "haunting presence . . . anonymous and exponential."[53] Concentrated bodies are a perpetually suppurating wound, where bodies and beings are compressed. And yet, there is from the wound a transformative action that at least points, however desperately, to world amid "unworld." It is also a way of communicating. Key to any such transformative impact is a gesture's or action's capacity to haunt, to unsettle those concentrations of power and knowledge where weight is amassed, where injustice as the indistinction and extinction of bodies occurs through breaking, crushing, and stifling.[54]

The man's hurling of the tray is just one performed gesture of haunting arising from the wound, and, as we will trace throughout this work, it is only one hint, maybe but a tiny act that is suggestive of many such actions that become part of spectral practices bearing upon the multiple weights of concentrated power. Even in the prisons there are many other such acts, and the most effective of them may be the acts wherein rage, sadness, and fear are forged into written communications.[55] In them,

---

52. Nancy, *Corpus*, 21–27.
53. Ibid., 79.
54. Nancy, *Corpus*, 47.
55. For one collection of works by especially adept prison writers, see Joy James, ed., *Imprisoned Intellectuals: America's Political Prisoners Write on Life, Liberation, and Rebellion* (Lanham, Md.: Rowman & Littlefield, 2003).

bodies of the amassed in prisons come to expression. Bodies concentrated in such actions and communications we may identify as "exscrip-
tions," another term of Nancy's. The basic idea is not, to stay with our
prison example, simply that writers communicate "outside" prison walls.
That's part of it. But as exscription in Nancy's sense, his gesture exceeds
its action, has an excess. In Nancy's thought, it means that communication of this sort is more than the gesture, whether a meaningfully hurled
tray, or, more traditionally, the inscribed words on a page. Exscribing
is the writing out from a body. Indeed, all signifying discourse, Nancy
insists, any act of speaking or writing, especially communication through
the arts, is an exscribing, a touching (with intimacy and distancing) of
embodied existence. Nancy can even speak, as he does in *The Gravity
of Thought*, of this exscription as the "final truth of inscription,"[56] indeed,
of all thought, because writing never lacks this excess, this writing of the
body. It never escapes this touching of bodies in a weighted world. In
Corpus, Nancy summarizes the point:

> With thoughts about the body, the body always forces us to think
> farther, always *too* far: too far to carry on as thought, but never far
> enough to become a body.
>   Which is why it makes no sense to talk about body and thought
> apart from each other, as if each could somehow subsist on its own:
> they *are* only their touching each other, the touch of their breaking
> down, and into, each other. This touching is the limit and spacing
> of existence.[57]

Prisoners who write, who gesture with hurled tray or with pen in hand,
"weigh-in," I suggest, from their place amid and under concentrated
immonde. They write not only texts expressing their emotions and to
friends and family, but also legal motions as "jailhouse lawyers,"[58] or
communications to activists working with them on the outside amid
and against the present world of mass incarceration.[59] This weighing

56. Jean-Luc Nancy, *The Gravity of Thought,* trans. Francois Raffoul and Gregory Recco
(Atlantic Highlands, N.J.: Humanities Press, 1997), 79.

57. Nancy, *Corpus,* 37.

58. Mumia Abu-Jamal, *Jailhouse Lawyers: Prisoners Defending Prisoners v. the USA* (San
Francisco: City Lights, 2009).

59. See prisoners' contributions to broader activist work at the Prison Activist Resource
Center, http://www.prisonactivist.org/.

in against compressed and concentrated weight is an attempt to recreate world by writing and rewriting bodies. This weighing-in occurs
wherever weight concentrates, not just in the prison houses, but also
in the warehouses of neglect that hold our infirm, aged, and mentally
distressed—in the shanty towns of the poor, every "Gaza" where bodies are amassed, abandoned, reckoned disposable, weighed, finally, as
of no account. These bodies, though, also weigh-in and weigh against
the weight of the world that shifts into concentrated and burdensome,
crammed "unworld." They write not just for their bodies. They write
their bodies. They seek, from within a place where bodies are squeezed
and concentrated, a re-creation of world, one sustained in part by a
memory or a hope of world as that sustaining interplay of mutual relation and distance. The re-creation is a process that makes "freedom"—
and the emphasis for Nancy is on freedom as having to be *made or
created*, not something that can be presupposed or shown to have a
ground. Thus, Nancy situates his notion of freedom in the context of
his somewhat abstract views of extension, weight, and spacing: "For
freedom *is* the common nonpresupposition of *this mutual intimacy and
distancing* where bodies, their masses, their singular and always indefinitely multipliable events have their absence of ground (and hence,
identically, their rigorous equality)."[60]

Here is where Nancy's distinctive views on "sense" begin to emerge.
He plays off of what in English we might describe as meaningful sense,
on one hand, and sense as perceptibility of our bodies, sensing, on the
other. It is not so much that texts or statements have or make sense, but
they and their writers/speakers are "in sense." We are extended, spaced
as bodies with other bodies, are indeed bodies "in sense," not only as living the multiplicity of daily exchanges but also when knowing freedom
or unfreedom, justice or injustice—both of these latter weighty options
depending upon whether the world is in extension or shifted into some
state of concentration. These are all parts of belonging to world, to a
world that is a body of always circulating sense.

Let us contrast Nancy's notion of sense with others that have held
sway. "Sense," along with "reference," is usually taken as one of two ways
to speak of language's functioning, and particularly of how language
"means" or has "meaning." Sense, according to Paul Ricoeur, following

---

60. Ibid., 101. Italics added.

Gottlieb Frege, focuses "the what" of discourse, while reference concerns more the "about what" of discourse.[61] Or, in philosopher Tim Crane's terms, *sense* is a word's looking "inward" to language's other words, while *reference* is more a term looking "outward," as it were, into the world.[62] Nancy's "sense," however, is not to be identified with this "sense" opposed to "reference." He is trying to excavate and illumine another kind of meaningful presence, one crucial to interpretation amid the proliferation of meaning(s). It is an alternative interpretive movement, not one shuttling between sense and reference, between the "what" and the "about what" of discourse, but, rather, a movement that cuts across them both, and circulates in their many manifestations. The "sense" of interest to philosopher Nancy is one that combines being steeped in the sensate with human orientation toward an ever more open embrace of a totality (which, however, is never had).[63] What thinking does is to traverse, cross through, the plurality "sensed" everywhere—and especially traversing or crossing through those places where singularities[64] are overlapping and intersecting other singularities or groups of singularities. This is a "sense" far more complex than that of sense opposed to reference. The latter encourages a kind of intellectual two-step between sense and reference. Instead, with Nancy, there is a much more intricate and multiple sliding along and between passageways of a singular plural world. To think as well as to exist, then, is not simply to connect sense with what sense refers to; it is also to be caught up in a tangled, at times labyrinthine, sensate experience of singularities in multiple relations. Nancy thus can write in *Corpus* of the "veins of sense," not only intimating sense's circulating character but also its embodied way. To have a "world," and to think and interpret within it, is to be in a "body of sense" with meaning(s) continually circulating through world's extended or concentrated bodies. To clarify this further, we can turn to Hutchen's language, which is worth quoting in full:

---

61. Paul Ricoeur, *Interpretation Theory: Discourse and the Surplus of Meaning* (Fort Worth: Texas Christian University Press, 1976), 19.

62. Tim Crane, "Meaning," in *Oxford Companion to Philosophy*, new ed. (New York: Oxford University Press, 2005), 575.

63. On this combination of notions, see Hutchens, *Jean-Luc Nancy and the Future of Philosophy,* 43.

64. Ibid., 43–44.

One must be "in" sense, in the sense of this world composed of the joining, playing, speaking, sharing, intersecting and communicating of itself. Articulating itself as such along the interstitial edges of such relations, the sense of the world is not something set over against the world [as in the sense/reference paradigm, again], not a co-incidence of being with itself; it resides immanently in the articulations of all possible singular beings and events within it. Specifically, one is only permitted to speak of a world that is a totality completed by *the openness of existence to itself*.[65]

It is this kind of "sense" that is at work when Nancy writes of world as "totality of meaning." It is a fullness of sense to which we belong that is known in the weighing of bodies. They weigh against, weigh under, weigh upward, and also, as we noted, sometimes can "weigh-in" with transformative impact under conditions of concentration. Nancy can also sum up his approach to sense in a weighted world—after again repudiating the easy juxtaposition of sense and reference—by writing that "this sense depends on the in-finite swerve of the coming of the one to the other."[66] With the notion of "swerve," Nancy accents a process of securing meaning, marked by a set of departures from the straight path, but also from a single path. It is marked by an openness to the many bodies' pathways that world is.

What might this imply for interpretation, for methodologies in scholarship? Nancy is pointing to a way of finite thinking in our weighted world that is distinctive. Perhaps recent words of another thinker, Judith Butler, capture the implication best, when she writes, "interpretation does not emerge as the spontaneous act of a single mind, but as a consequence of a certain field of intelligibility that helps to form and frame our responsiveness to the impinging world (a world on which we depend, but which also impinges upon us, exacting responsiveness in complex, sometimes ambivalent forms)."[67] Sense, meaning, and hence a discourse that would make sense is "a wandering labor," one that acknowledges and lives toward an impinging world of conflicts and insights that emerge from different experiences and readings of world, especially as they emerge from various clusterings of bodies, from contexts of meaning. In

---

65. Ibid., 43. Italics added.
66. Ibid., 103.
67. Judith Butler, *Frames of War: When Is Life Grievable?* (New York: Verso, 2009), 34.

deploying the image of the "wandering labor of sense," I am borrowing an important notion Nancy uses that he, in turn, took from Jacques Ran- cière.[68] This "wandering labor of sense" is not so much a passive drifting, as it is a receptive openness that entails a labor traversing passageways, circulating insights, embodying different ways of being world. Its labor is not a work for control, but a working through the multiple. It is a con- templating of relations between bodies in extension, and, depending on context, a pondering of that shifted distortion in the world's weighing that Nancy names "concentration." Especially when the world impinges from this latter shifted weight, from the world's contextual sites of con- centration that breed antagonism and resistance, from the realms of accu- mulated, imposed social suffering—especially then the weighted world bears upon, haunts, the sense of Theology. This is because the sense of Theology is often caught up in, if not actually a constituting factor in, the world's weight as concentration.

Theology's Imperio-Colonial Sense

The thinking that tends to predominate in the guild discipline of The- ology—and often whether or not its credentialed theologians are politi- cally *or* theologically "Left" or "Right"—is often in a state of resistance to Nancy's type of circulating and contextual, finite sense. Theology is by and large still committed to another kind of "sense," which frames the way its thinkers not only approach world, but also position their bodies and subject-positions in it and shape the ways they interpret it. Theology in its interpretive stance still shows itself steeped in what I will name in this section an "imperio-colonial sense," with four distinguish- ing features.

First, Theology's imperio-colonial sense often has a sustaining pre- condition, its *projection of a transcendent outside,* a beyond, toward that which is other to world. This construct preserves the sense/reference dis- tinction in Theology, which I have already contrasted with Nancy's circu- lating through "veins of sense," in a "body of sense." Sense, in Theology, especially that guild discipline rooted in the structures of European and

---

68. Jean-Luc Nancy, *The Sense of the World,* trans. J. S. Librett (Minneapolis: University of Minnesota Press, 1997), 115, and 193 n.124; Jacques Rancière, "The Politics of Litera- ture," in *Substance* 103, vol. 33, no. 1 (2004): 10–24.

U.S. higher education, usually focuses sense as structured by doctrines or other language, which define belief in a religious community, the church, and then which have a referent to some outside, some beyond, a transcendent. Meaning is pursued, sense is developed and produced, by a credentialed cadre of academic practitioners. Even if the expertise of this cadre is not emphasized, performed with an air of humility and gentility, Theology as discourse is steeped in this kind of sense, being a community of inquiry whose meanings refer to a beyond, whose trafficking in meanings constitutes its "ethos of transcendence." In this ethos, the primary value is on a kind of sovereignty of the transcendent to which their discourse refers. The sovereign located outside and beyond is taken as necessary to guard against the sovereignties of self, or of nation and other collective forms—all of which are thought to be preserved from destructive effect (from "idolatries" of self, nation, and collectivity, for example) by continual reference to *the* Sovereign.[69]

I do not deny, as can be seen in many practitioners of Theology, that the reference to a sovereign God is a reference to a "one" that is thought as multiple and dynamic (a "triune" figuring in much Christian theology) and that the virtues of accommodation, of humility, of love in community are built into the God taken as sovereign, so that a "condescendence" is made integral to transcendence, multiplicity to sovereignty. There can be a beauty to this discourse, attempting to mitigate the supremacy and summitry at which the sovereign one is positioned, as when the transcendent is rendered as "incarnate" in the baby of a lowly manger amid shepherds of the hills in Rome-dominated Palestine, a key feature of the Christmas story for many Christians. Moreover, a God language about a sovereign one who is beyond world and history can articulate, and continues to orient, many of the religious dreams and visions at work in liberatory actions of oppressed peoples.

---

69. Perhaps a recent and most clear example of this is to be found in Jean Bethke Elshtain's 2006 Gifford Lectures, *Sovereignty: God, State, and Self* (New York: Basic, 2008), 233–45. Elshtain is careful not to set up a singular sovereign, a "God, the Father Almighty." Hers is a sovereign God that she situates in a broad tradition emanating from Augustine and readings of Christian scriptures, where the one who is sovereign is an incarnating God, who embodies humility, who is "the man for others" (Dietrich Bonhoeffer), and whose incarnating ways of intricate enfleshment in world can be traced in many ways, but especially through the poignant and earthy renderings of Czeslaw Milosz's and Albert Camus's writings.

And yet, I argue that this reference to one positioned above and beyond self and society, outside their worlds, only to enter largely as special acts of creation, intervention and as condescendence, is problematic and to be resisted. To be problematic, the reference to the transcendent need not be a theocratic reference, oriented to a radically omnipotent Other, who, projected as "God Almighty," anchors, in a very marked way, the sovereignties of state or grandiose sovereignties of self, these ordered to one another in a great chain of sovereign being. Even the "softer," nontheocratic references to transcendence are not necessarily a safeguard against the excesses of imperial and colonial domination and destruction.[70] Their references to the beyond tend to consign the livingness of nature, society, and history to a derivative and dependent status. In short, the reference "outside" is essential to that parapenal entirety of which Foucault wrote, and of Nancy's piled-up, compressed and crammed, concentrated world—and thus carries the seeds of destruction. How this is so becomes evident if we move to the second feature of imperio-colonial sense.

A second feature of Theology's imperio-colonial sense is its cultivation of *a transcendental ethos,* an elevated knowledge and practice held to be appropriate to the projected/constructed transcendent. The imperio-colonial sense, by referring to a transcendent beyond, secures for knowledge and practice a certain status of elevation above other knowledges and practices. While a sense of the transcendent may not be identical to a sense of the sovereign (sovereignty concerns more *the rule or power of* the transcendent, not just being in a direction or realm that is "beyond" or "outside" world), transcendence and sovereignty tend to blend in the emergence of this elevated knowledge and ethos. A community that refers to the transcendent beyond world tends to see its discourse of reference as participatory in that sovereign realm, and in this sense above other discourses. Sovereignty and transcendence mutually implicate one

---

70. Elshtain is, again, a case in point. She works with a supple and complex notion of the transcendent gleaned from readings of the Christian Augustinian tradition; and yet, she found herself during the George W. Bush administration's preemptive invasion and occupation of Iraq an early advocate of its war-making designs, even if she backed off later by foregrounding a more critical posture. I have analyzed her role among "liberal" thinkers and other supporters of the "war on terror," in Mark Lewis Taylor, *Religion, Politics, and the Christian Right: Post-9/11 Powers and American Empire* (Minneapolis: Fortress Press, 2005), 19–22.

another in a project of a governing knowledge. It is not surprising, then, that sovereignty has been referred to as a site in the human world of a "this-worldly transcendence."[71]

The special knowledge and its elevation may be urged upon adherents and supported by "faith." Faith's trusting in things unseen is taken here as a way to elevate a knowledge of an unseen other world, an outside realm, an unseen other whose cogency depends upon that faith. Or, the elevated knowledge may seek to raise itself upon arguments pertaining to various dimensions of world, which are taken as pointers to another world, certain "signals of transcendence," perhaps, in the immanental terrain that suggest a "something more." The language used in this knowledge, to be sure, always stresses that full or adequate knowledge is never attained. The transcendent is always some version of the *Deus absconditus,* "hidden God." And so Theology's language is always an indirect and figurative communication: analogical, symbolic, metaphorical. Minimal as the signals of transcendence may be, however, they still are taken as sufficient for creating Theology as elevated discourse pertaining to the transcendent, and this helps to shape further an ethos of transcendence in communities that routinely invoke the transcendent. Both to summarize Theology's elevated discourse oriented to a sovereign transcendent, and also to understand better the notion of sovereignty itself, I quote Nancy's reflection on "the sovereign":

> The sovereign is at the height because the height separates the top from the bottom and frees the former from the humility of the latter: from the humus, from the back bent from working the earth, from laying down in sleep, from malady or death, and from *extended things* in general. Extension holds everything at the same level, but the thing that is not extended, what looms over extensions and inspects it, is the *thinking thing* and the subject of the general government of things. In the place of a sensibility of the near, through touch, smell, and taste, it makes the organs of distance, sight and hearing, prevail.[72]

---

71. Tracy B. Strong, Foreword, in Carl Schmitt, *Political Theology: Four Chapters on the Concept of Sovereignty* (Chicago: University of Chicago Press, 2005 [German 1922, 1934]), xxx.

72. Jean-Luc Nancy, "Ex Nihilo Summum (Of Sovereignty)," in *CWoG,* 96–97.

Nancy's language points well to the rise of the imperial character of Theology's discourse, its taking a position that is on high, oriented as it is to the transcendent Other as sovereign. This tends to produce a set of scholars who enjoy a state of elevated discourse, easily entailing also a sense of entitlement to survey other discourses. This harbors a seed of control, of a "general government of things." At times this hardly seems consonant with the airs of gentility and humility that particular practitioners of Theology can exhibit, but it becomes evident especially in the failure to take with full seriousness the way references to the transcendent are mediated by very this-worldly dynamics. This becomes more evident, especially as we consider next the third feature.

A third feature of Theology's imperio-colonial sense is its *hermeneutical resistance to contextualizing Theology's language.* By this I mean a particular interpretative stance of Theology, wherein the beliefs and claims of its discourse are assessed intellectually, without considering the interplay of cognitive beliefs and claims with extradiscursive factors that come from contexts of interrelated bodies in the weighted world. The elevated discourse of Theology is akin to Nancy's "thinking thing," so intrinsic to concentrated power. Its orientation to the transcendent—even with all its insistences that the transcendent is incarnate and thus immanent—keeps it above extensions, where intimacy and distance between bodies congeal and concentrate in different modes of a weighted world. Its discourse privileges a "rationality" that is above the myriad constellations and contexts of related bodies, the "we" of the world.

Some will be quick to remind here that guild Theology's rationality is seen as related to, and even generated by, church contexts and for the sake of its various ecclesial, proclamatory, or faith practices. Thus, Theology can acknowledge that it always has its transcendent in very earthen vessels. But ecclesial forms of life and their practices are not the only way—not even the most defining ways—by which theologians and church members forge their "earthen" being in the world. More important are the multiple ways in which natural processes and social systems construct specific embodiments of the church and religious communities in the world—politically, economically, racially, sexually, and so on. If Theology attends to these latter defining forces, its theologians usually do so largely as a subsidiary concern, that is, keeping the primary focus of Theology's discourse on an ecclesial formation that nurtures and maintains the elevated discourse of the transcendent for its church communities.

It may be objected that these contexts of social, cultural, and political worlds are extraneous to the task of thinking, not as integrally connected to thought as we have seen Nancy to stress them to be.[73] It is difficult for this objection to be sustained by much more than assertion. If one has any respect at all for the role of critical reflection, especially when thinking referentially of the transcendent, then these contextual factors—the modes of the world's bodies weighing upon thinking—should not be treated as extrinsic to thinking. To my mind the power of context for being and thinking has been most forcefully put by philosopher Theodore Schatzki, in his book *The Site of the Social*,[74] and whose work later will enable our further reflection on the agonistic political.

Contexts, to summarize Schatzki, are the networks of our living, shaping our flesh, our affect, *and* our thinking. They have a surrounding, immersing aura, giving us ways of living like water does for a fish, like an electromagnetic field does for bodies (with some notable differences, to be sure). We can add to these similes further commentary on how contexts have powers of determination. Contexts' determining power may be *causative*, as when parents continually encourage a child to study hard and provide environments conducive to study, thus making likely the production of a student who excels in learning. Contexts may determine us by also being *institutive*, as when family wealth so grounds a person's life, as can happen for some, such that he or she never need worry about having a house to live in (with, perhaps also, a separate personal study well stocked with books). Concerning the affective dimension of contexts, being praised, loved, affirmed (or not) has a kind of instituting role, too, orienting one's very being toward the future in special ways. Contexts also are determinative by being *prefigurative*, suggesting not so much what our precise futures will be, but more what we will have to wrestle with, what opportunity structures we will be given or be denied. In short, contexts prefigure certain social constraints and enablements beyond those that we possess by reason of our individual differences.

Nevertheless, in spite of the persuasiveness of Schatzki's arguments, the issue of context for Theology cannot usually be settled by philosophical arguments alone. This is because the hermeneutical resistance

---

73. Nancy, *Corpus*, 37.

74. Theodore R. Schatzki, *The Site of the Social: A Philosophical Account of the Constitution of Social Life and Change* (Harrisburg: Pennsylvania State University Press, 2002).

in Theology is due less to an intellectual conundrum, and more to a desire to maintain certain privileged knowledge and subject-positions. The debate about context in Theology's thinking is often an epistemological disputation that masks the guild discipline's routinized pattern of safeguarding the subject positions and subjectivities of those who long have been taken as the primary agents of discourse in Theology. This becomes more evident when one observes, in the Theology guilds of North American or European settings, what happens when certain thinkers with their long-excluded bodies and communities, bring new contextualized discourse into Theology. They begin to name their theological discourse from the communal backgrounds that are of concern to them, as in African American or black theology, U.S. Hispanic or Latino/a theology, Asian American theology, feminist theology, gay or lesbian theology, and so on. Let us grant, as we must, that each of these adjectives attached to theology in these locutions is itself a construct, an essentializing and ontologizing of groups of people that is fraught with many of the pitfalls of so-called identity politics. Peoples and theologies cannot, nor should they, be so easily categorized. We thereby risk glossing many differences internal to those groups, and glossing, too, many assemblages of traits and interests shared between them. People have what sociologist Gordon terms a "complex personhood," beautifully rendered in her *Ghostly Matters*. I cite just one of her phrases: "Complex personhood means that even those called 'Other' are never never that." Nevertheless, the adjectives do name the results of a resistance to what Gordon terms the equally "complicated working of race, class, and gender, the names we give to the ensemble of social relations that create inequalities, situated interpretive codes, particular kinds of subjects . . ."[75] Thus, in spite of the risks of essentialization, there is warrant and need for the constructs of Asian-American theology, black theology, and so on.

Theology's interpretive resistance to acknowledging the importance of context to thought becomes all the more marked when and if long-excluded voices begin to speak of the "Western," "colonial," or "white" contexts of Theology's traditional thinkers and knowledge,[76] or of, say,

---

75. Gordon, *Ghostly Matters*, 4.
76. James H. Cone, "White Theology Revisited, 1998" in his *Risks of Faith: The Emergence of Black Liberation Theology, 1968–1998* (Boston: Beacon, 2000), 130–38.

their gendered or sexual being.[77] The usual and frequent response of Theology, in more progressive quarters, is silence, or perhaps a polite marginalizing acceptance. But when voice is found to protect the usual concerns of the decontextualized, elevated knowledge in Theology, the "subaltern knowledges" of new contexts are often dismissed as "ideological" or "reductionist." The reductionist charge usually holds that this talk of contexts "reduces" thought to the realms of society and body, and, second, "reduces" thought about the transcendent, about the Other, to world contexts of body and society, and so strips the Other of its defining transcendental character. The reasoning here is viciously circular—"circular" because the insistence usually boils down to claiming that one needs the Other to have a transcendent Other, and "vicious" because the ongoing criticism of the contextual turn, which accompanies a protection of the transcendent Other, continues to silence and exclude the already silenced and long excluded.

The resistance to contextualizing Theology's discourse, then, is another way to mask what Gayatri Chakravorty Spivak has termed "the geopolitically differentiated subject" of European discourse.[78] The subject that matters—both as "subject matter" deserving the most nuanced treatment and also as subjects most to be cherished and granted entitlements of power and wealth—is the subject of the European imperio-colonial project and its descendents. We have already noted the way Spivak carefully traces a dynamic of "foreclosure" in Kant's theorization of the subject in his *Critique of Judgment*. Here, in Theology, the construction of the transcendent Other is bound up with a process of foreclosing others whose place is deemed inappropriate, or subordinate to, the reigning discourse of Theology, as it has been pursued in most of the West's philosophy and Theology. Similar foreclosures are operative in Hegel and in Marx, even if in Hegel "foreclosure" often seems too gentle a term for his "deeply offensive" dismissals and "radical racist separation" that he advises for African subjects, who are so lacking in history and spirit that he need not speak of them when giving his accounts of world history.[79]

---

77. Marcella Althaus-Reid, *Indecent Theology: Theological Perversions in Sex, Gender, and Politics* (New York: Routledge, 2000).

78. Gayatri Chakravorty Spivak, *Critique of Postcolonial Reason: Toward a History of the Vanishing Present* (Cambridge: Harvard University Press, 1999), 27, 31, and throughout.

79. George W. F. Hegel, *The Philosophy of History*, trans. J. Sibree (New York: Dover, 1956), 93, 99. The quotes are from Spivak, *Critique of Postcolonial Reason*, 43 and 94,

Yet, I suggest *foreclosure*, as Spivak draws the term from Lacanian and Freudian discourse, is an excellent term for naming an act of studied nonchalance. It occurs when the ego of philosophy or Theology "rejects [*verwift*] the incompatible idea *together with the affect* and behaves as if the idea had never occurred to the ego at all."[80]

It needs to be acknowledged that in Theology, recent decades have seen the discipline of guild Theology displaying various turns to the contextualization of its language. Not surprisingly, this is done most by thinkers coming from foreclosed and oppressed communities. Especially those who understand their reflection as an embodiment of liberating struggle have cognitively embraced diverse contextualities, among them Eleazar Fernandez in his *Reimagining the Human: Theological Anthropology in the Face of Systematic Evil*, in which he begins with the variable of class identity and then relates it to others (such as gender, race, nation, and more).[81] James Cone's work is renowned for focusing on his own life story and on the struggle of black empowerment in the United States in theological reflection.[82] He is less known for the equally impressive way he articulates connections between that struggle and those working out of consciousnesses shaped by gender and sexuality, class and nation.[83] Similarly, Peruvian theologian Gustavo Gutiérrez, after beginning his theological reflection from his context as a priest among the poor in Latin America (in particular, the Rimac district of Lima), then rendered his contextual starting point more complexly by examining issues of race, gender, and environment.[84] Women of all backgrounds, as in the formative work of Kwok Pui-lan's *Postcolonial Imagination and Feminist Theology*,[85] have

---

respectively. On her criticism of Marx, and particularly of his construct, "the Asiatic mode of production," see Spivak, 67–111.

80. Spivak, *Critique of Postcolonial Reason*, 4, citing Jean Laplance and J.-B. Pontalis, *The Language of Psycho-Analysis*, trans. Donald Nicholson-Smith (New York: Norton, 1974), 166–69.

81. Eleazar S. Fernandez, *Reimagining the Human: Theological Anthropology in Response to Systemic Evil* (St. Louis: Chalice, 2004).

82. James Cone, *The God of the Oppressed*, rev. ed. (Maryknoll, N.Y.: Orbis, 1997).

83. James H. Cone, *For My People: Black Theology and the Black Church* (Maryknoll, N.Y.: Orbis, 1988).

84. See the new introduction to the fifteenth anniversary edition of Gustavo Gutiérrez's *A Theology of Liberation: History, Politics, and Salvation*, rev. ed. (Maryknoll, N.Y.: Orbis, 1988), xxi–xxv.

85. Kwok Pui-lan, *Postcolonial Imagination and Feminist Theology* (Louisville: Westminster John Knox, 2005).

been crucial in keeping guild Theology cognizant of contexts—and again, not just contexts of gendered or sexed bodies, but also those stereotyped, subordinated, and repressed by race and class as well.[86] These writers cited here are mainly the theologians who have inaugurated early challenges to Theology's occlusion of subordinate communities' contributions. Since then, many others have complexified further the identities and interests of theological writers and their knowledge, working in Asian American, U.S. Hispanic and Latino/a, and African American contexts, and in indigenous Christian settings.[87]

Theology is often quick to cite all this as progress. As Miguel De La Torre has pointed out, however, most professors who wish to teach Theology in the United States from a perspective other than white male European traditions are forced to transform the subject of their courses into an adjective—as in "Black Theology" or "Asian Theology." Such courses he notes—and my experience would confirm this—are usually only offered as electives. Required courses in the "introduction of Theology" rarely teach a parity of import between European white male theologies and others. If "others" are listed among required readings, they are often fewer in number, presented as "recent alternatives," and rarely made the subject of rigorous examination. The primary cognitive action and theological forms taught are the heavily doctrinalized traditions of the European "malestream" West. As De La Torre also observes wryly, the courses that lean in this way, however, are rarely, if ever, named "Eurocentric Male Theologies."[88] De La Torre's criticisms of the European male citadel in Theology are amply extended and reinforced by others in liberation theology, as well as in postcolonial or decolonial theologies that see in the foregrounding of this geopolitically differentiated subject not only a

---

86. For key early texts in theology by women addressing contexts of sexism, patriarchy, and "kyriarchy," as well as more recent formulations, see Susan Frank Parsons, ed., *The Cambridge Companion to Feminist Theology* (Cambridge: Cambridge University Press, 2002). For exemplary reflection on complex feminist reflections on contextualized bodies, see Laurel C. Schneider, "What Race is Your Sex?," in *Disrupting White Supremacy from Within: White People on What We Need to Do,* ed. Jennifer Harvey, Karin A. Case, and Robin Haeley Gorsline (Cleveland: Pilgrim, 2004), 123–41; and Jasbir K. Puar, *Terrorist Assemblages: Homonationalism in Queer Times* (Durham: Duke University Press, 2007).

87. For one critical display of the diversity of the present theological period, see Finnish scholar Veli-Mati Karkkainen's *Doctrine of God: A Global Introduction* (Grand Rapids: Baker Academic, 2004).

88. Miguel A. De La Torre, ed., *Handbook of U.S. Theologies of Liberation* (St. Louis: Chalice, 2004), 1–2.

foreclosing of "others," usually of non-Euro-American voices and perspectives, but also a hiding from critique that comes from many thinkers in the world South whose wealth and power are curtailed by global powers of the North.[89] It should be noted, too, to push De La Torre's points further, that a certain hegemonic masculinism in Theology—among white *and* nonwhite scholars—can function to neglect or "minoritize" the theological work carried on by all women, especially women of color.

One way to sum up this third feature of Theology's imperio-colonial sense, this hermeneutical resistance to the contextual turn, is to say that the Euro-American male subject-position often fails to meet the intellectual responsibility of what Pierre Bourdieu has termed "reflexivity," rendered most clearly in his *Pascalian Meditations*:

> To practice reflexivity means questioning the privilege of a knowing 'subject'. . . . It means endeavoring to account for the empirical 'subject' of scientific practice in the terms of the objectivity constructed by the scientific 'subject'—in particular by situating him [or her] at a determinate point in social space-time . . .[90]

Bourdieu remarks further what this reflexivity means for the study of *homo academicus*:

> Nor can one be satisfied with seeking the conditions of possibility and the limits of objective knowledge in the 'subject,' as the classical (Kantian) philosophy of knowledge recommends. . . . One has to look into the object constructed by science (the social space or the field) to find *the social conditions of possibility of the 'subject' and of his work of constructing the object* . . . and so to bring to light the social limits of his act of objectification.[91]

There is precious little space in the academic institutions of guild Theology to practice this kind of exposure. And so, the imperio-colonial sense includes the following fourth feature.

---

89. This has been an emphasis of various liberation theologians and especially by postcolonial and decolonial critics in theology. As one example, see R. S. Sugirtharajah, *Postcolonial Criticism and Biblical Interpretation* (New York: Oxford University Press, 2004).

90. Pierre Bourdieu, *Pascalian Meditations*, trans. Richard Nice (Stanford: Stanford University Press, 1997), 119.

91. Ibid., 120. Italic added.

In a fourth feature, Theology is involved in *maintaining the subject-position and subjectivities of Euro-American, predominantly white and male, discourse and thinking.* I do *not* mean that there is an abundance of administrators and theologians in Theology and its institutions who intend to maintain this, although there are some. What I do mean is that there is a failure, along with the failure of reflexivity, to make the structural changes necessary to foreground the bodies and lives of long-occluded and foreclosed peoples in positions of classroom and institutional control in Theology. To be sure, there is much talk—almost as a kind of mantra, invoking "diversity" and "otherness." Rarely, however, is there the sustained commitment to make changes that would actually empower those whose lineages are traceable to the undersides of imperio-colonial history. Rarely found, for example, are commitments by institutions to set specific goals for the future faculty's racial/ethnic or gender make-up, to create functioning parity of opportunity and power among racial/ethnic groups, between men and women.[92] The maintenance of privileged subject-positions, then, is not so much a matter of persons' intentions and beliefs, but more as sociologist Howard Winant defines the working of racism: a "routinized outcome of practices that create or reproduce hierarchical social structure."[93] This routinizing of outcome often is sustained by essentializing stereotypes, fears, and discrimination that long have circulated in colonizing cultures and that long have been imposed upon colonized others, as men or as women, almost always as marked by the construct of race, and for the purpose of exploiting their lands, resources, and bodies for empowerment of the colonizing power.[94]

The distribution of faculty positions in major Christian theological institutions of the United States gives some evidence of the slowness of change, if change there be at all, in the way Euro-American and white

92. One exception about which I know is Episcopal Divinity School in Cambridge, Massachusetts, whose case is summarized in "Case: Preparing the Ground," in the Association of Theological Schools 2002 Folio *Diversity in Theological Education,* www.ats.edu/Resources/Documents/DiversityFolio.pdf, accessed September 14, 2010.

93. Howard Winant, *The New Politics of Race: Globalism, Difference, Justice* (Minneapolis: University of Minnesota Press, 2004), 126.

94. On race as the "ultimate version of the difference axiom" in colonialism, see Jürgen Oesterhammel, *Colonization: A Theoretical Overview* (Princeton: Markus Wiener, 2002). On gender and sexuality at play with race in imperio-coloniality, see Anne McClintock, *Imperial Leather: Race, Gender, and Sexuality in the Imperial Contest* (New York: Routledge, 1995).

subject-positions have been maintained in the institutions of Theology. Among all member schools in the Association of Theological Schools (ATS), faculty of color make up some 15 to 17 percent of all faculty.[95] The figure can often be lower, if one looks at only U.S. institutions, and certainly is lower at select major institutions.[96] In U.S. theological institutions as a whole, of all tenured professors in ATS schools (where the power of a faculty resides, usually), a full 84 percent of them are white, 15 percent being African American, Asian American, or U.S. Hispanic/ Latino/a. Only 25 percent, one quarter, of all tenured faculty members are women. Among just the full professors, the highest-ranked and most credentialed group, 87 percent of them are white, with African Americans, Asian Americans, and U.S. Hispanics-Latinos/as together making up 12 percent. Only 21 percent of all full professors in the U.S. ATS schools are women.[97]

In short, while there has over the last decade been greater production of thinking out of often foreclosed communities, in the form of different kinds of contextual theologies, and even though there has been some rise in the percent of racial/ethnic representation on faculties (from 4 percent to 12.7 percent between 1980 and 2001[98]), this has not yet marked a shift in power within guild Theology, which remains centered largely around the discourses structured by and for Euro-American white and male subjectivities and subject-positions. Even if the numbers at times show increases in racial/ethnic faculty, that numerical growth by itself is not an indicator of the mitigation of white power in those settings, unless the regime of instruction also changes (in curriculum, text usage, classroom, and campus ethos), with faculty of color, both women and men,

95. Daniel O. Aleshire, "Gifts Differing: The Educational Value of Race and Ethnicity," in *Race and Ethnicity*, special issue of *Theological Education* 45, no. 1 (2009): 1–18, at 12.

96. At Princeton Theological Seminary, of all faculty (at assistant, associate, and full professor ranks), 88 percent are white, with racial/ethnic members (African American and Asian American, no U.S. Hispanics-Latinos/as) being 12 percent.

97. I am deriving these percentages of women and racial/ethnic groups at ATS schools, and those that follow, by using my calculator on data gathered by the ATS in its "2009/2010 Annual Data Tables," at http://www.ats.edu/Resources/Publications/Docu ments/AnnualDataTables/2009-10AnnualDataTables.pdf, accessed September 14, 2010.

98. "Full-time Racial/Ethnic Faculty in ATS Member Schools," in *Diversity in Theological Education* (see n. 85, above).

significantly present in the upper ranks and with authority to teach basic introductory courses.

In sum, the imperio-colonial sense of theology circulates in a discursive formation that has these four features. First, it has its condition in its orienting projection of a transcendent Other, an outside, a realm beyond. Then, second, it constructs, maintains and nurtures others in an "elevated knowledge" (based on "faith" or perceived "signals of transcendence") that is thought to point to that transcendent Other, adapting the sense of Theology's statements and claims to this Other to whom it refers. Third, it often resists, in its hermeneutical *habitus,* a disciplined turn to contexts, either to affirm them as necessary sources for foreclosed and repressed thinkers themselves, or enabling and limiting the social conditions of their own entitled thinking. And then, all too often this yields a preferential maintenance of the bodies, subjectivities, and subject-positions of Euro-American faculty and administrators in the positions of greater power in Theological institutions.

Conclusion: The Theological as Theology's Hydra

"The theological" of this book thus haunts the discourse of guild Theology as usually practiced. It unsettles and haunts not only by the presence of oft-excluded persons in Theology, but also by posing a challenge to largely decontextualized reflection in Theology. Neglect concerning import of context and mediation in Theology, and of its references to the transcendent is, to my knowledge, widespread in U.S. theological education especially. Because the theological traces and theorizes ways that persons and groups who are traditionally rendered subordinate under the concentrated weight of the world are able, nevertheless, to haunt, unsettle, and perhaps dissolve the structures of those systems of knowledge and power, the theological also haunts the Theology whose effects often participate in the world's weight as concentrated.

In this sense, the theological, as well as the struggles of those whose work and resistance it traces, poses as Hydra with respect to Theology. I deploy the image of the Hydra here intentionally. It provides one way to contextualize the dis-ease of the academy today with the spectral wandering labor of sense, Theology's resistance to continual contextualizing that is intrinsic to the body of sense. The Hydra, in Greek myth, was a

many-headed venomous serpent whose heads would grow back whenever cut off; also, when cut into sections, each could regrow into a whole
new creature. It is a fitting image for the resilience of the theological in its
engagement with Theology.

Theological and colonizing architects of Western expansionist projects, whether under the banners of Christian mission, civilization, or
development, also took interest in this Greek mythic story. They reveled
especially in the figure of Hercules whose task was to destroy the Hydra.
In Greek narratives, Hercules's second labor was to slay the Hydra, which
he achieved by sealing off the neck of each head, severing each with a
lighted torch, and then using arrows dipped in the serpent's own poi-
son to vanquish it. According to historians Peter Linebaugh and Marcus
Rediker, the "Hydra" was the mythic term used by Western commercial
and educated elites to symbolize the multitudinous and resilient forces of
workers, which had to be tamed, shriveled, punished, and, perhaps also
exterminated.[99] Intrinsic to Kant's "foreclosure" of non-European subjects
as worthy of consideration was also his view that the nonwhite races will
be eradicated, "stamped out" (*Alle racen warden ausgerottet warden*).[100]
Francis Bacon often deployed the Hercules/Hydra myth, suggesting that
architects of the global market perform their "labor of Hercules" against
the enemies of civilization: "West Indians, Canaanites, pirates, land rov-
ers, assassins, Amazons and Anabaptists."[101] Sir Walter Raleigh, Thomas
Hobbes, William Shakespeare, and a host of others deployed the Hydra
symbol in similar ways. Thomas Edwards, a seventeenth-century British
writer, made a catalog of the many heads of heresy that constituted a
"Hydra, ready to rise up in their place."[102] He also portrayed John Cal-
vin as a "Christian Hercules" because he triumphed over the monstrous
papists, Anabaptists, and libertines.[103] These are just a few of many examples in the history of this symbolism of the Hydra in the West that could

---

99. Peter Linebaugh and Marcus Rediker, *The Many-Headed Hydra: Sailors, Slaves,
Commoners, and the Hidden History of the Revolutionary Atlantic* (Boston: Beacon, 2000),
3–6, 331.

100. See Kant's *Reflexionen 1520*, as discussed by J. Kameron Carter in his *Race: A Theological Account* (New York: Oxford University Press, 2009), 89–90.

101. Linebaugh and Rediker, *The Many-Headed Hydra*, 39.

102. For additional information on the Hydra/Hercules mythology, and its importance,
see my discussion in *Religion, Politics, and the Christian Right*, 120–23.

103. Linebaugh and Rediker, *The Many-Headed Hydra*, 39.

be given.[104] It continues into the present, with "Hydra" being a symbol invoked to describe the West's grappling with the network today of
pirates, terrorists, and other perceived insurgencies against the West. An
article late in the administration of George W. Bush in 2007, for example,
urged that new U.S. energies be mobilized for campaigns in Afghanistan.
The article was entitled "Revitalizing U.S. Efforts in Afghanistan," with
key sections on the mix of unruly agents described as "Hydra-headed
Insurgency."[105]

Rather than tame the Hydra in the name of some Herculean exercise
of sovereignty, the way of the theological is to trace the body of sense
that is the weight of the world, particularly as those struggling amid its
concentrated weight seek to weigh-in to create a world with a more just
spacing. The theological foregrounds, traces, and thinks along the way of
the Hydra and, in the midst of hermeneutical complexities, affirms even
the uncertainty of outcome, theoretical and practical, that will accompany
a wandering labor of sense through many contexts. The theological does
not give up on all criteria of adjudication between the claims of different
contexts, but it undertakes any such adjudications amid the shifting and
delicate interlacing of bodies that sense traverses, in its wandering and
laboring across contexts, historical, personal, social, economic, political.
As a theological venture, this will take thought and practice not into a
space of transcendence, but more, as Nancy theorizes, into a "transimmanence," a continual opening of existence to itself.[106] Again, that transimmanence is the critical space for clarifying the notion of "the theological"
proposed for this work.

Being "in sense," valuing especially the proliferation of meaning(s)
among those suffering the concentrated weight of the world, and their
interpretive gestures and thinking, will mean foregrounding and exploring in disciplined ways their contextual worlds. Exemplary are the writings of Tat-Siong Benny Liew in Asian American biblical hermeneutics

---

104. For discussion of the image, see historian William Kidd, "Marianne: from Medusa
to Messalina—Psycho-Sexual Imagery and Political Propaganda in France, 1789–1945,"
Journal of European Studies 34 (December 2004): 333–48.

105. Lisa Curtis and James Phillips, "Revitalizing U.S. Efforts in Afghanistan," The Heritage Foundation, Backgrounder Paper # 2076, October 15, 2007, http://www.heritage.org/
Research/MiddleEast/bg2076.cfm, accessed September 14, 2010.

106. Jean-Luc Nancy, *The Muses*, trans. Peggy Kamuf. French 1994 (Stanford: Stanford
University Press, 1996), 34–35.

in the United States,[107] Emilie Townes in ethics, who theorizes the concrete worlds of diverse African American women and others, or Naim
Ateek, writing out of the Christian struggle from Palestine.[108] These and
other explications and struggles to present singular contextualities (Asian
American, African American, and so on), especially because these have
long been rendered invisible or foreclosed, must become not only efforts
of the marginalized themselves, but also a struggle of all theological interpreters. Members of dominant groups in North America should begin
wrestling with greater emphasis on the constructed notion and force of
"whiteness" and their own participation in it.[109] All these individual and
group singularities are as important to "sense" as are the pluralities. In
fact, there is no simple choice here between the singularities and plurality
as two options. What is before us as interpreters, in Nancy's language, is
the "singular plural." Moreover, being *in* sense does not mean eschewing
comparisons and debates between the various contexts, between individual writers and group dynamics, and entering into the play of critique
between them. But being "in sense" does mean giving up on the hope
that sovereignty, and an imperio-colonizing sense of transcendence of
meaning, rests within any one or few of them, or with any single group of
interpreters. It means resting, wandering, working in the always/already
closeness of the bodies of world, their "brushing up against . . . distanced
proximity."[110] With this language of Nancy's we are back to that world of
"extension," of spacings and distances that constitute freedom and life,
which is alternative to the world as "concentration."

The wandering labor of sense includes "an unappeasable and always
unsettled" quality. For creation of justice, and working toward it with
an unappeasabilty and unsettled quality, has what Nancy risks naming
a strange "sovereignty of meaning." Note, however, it is the unsettling
quality of the unappeasable meaning that is "sovereign," not a meaning
secured by a group referring to the transcendent. That unappeasable

107. Tat-Siong Benny Liew, *What Is Asian-American Biblical Hermeneutics? Reading the
New Testament* (Honolulu: University of Hawaii Press, 2008).

108. Emilie Townes, *Womanist Ethics and the Cultural Production of Evil* (New York:
Palgrave Macmillan, 2006); and Naim Stifan Ateek, *Justice and Only Justice: A Palestinian
Theology of Liberation* (Maryknoll, N.Y.: Orbis, 1989).

109. Exemplary here, still, is the work of theologian James Perkinson, *White Theology:
Outing Supremacy in Modernity* (New York: Palgrave Macmillan, 2004).

110. Jean-Luc Nancy, *Being Singular Plural,* trans. Robert D. Richardson and Anne E.
O'Byrne (Stanford: Stanford University Press, 2000 [French 1996]), 98.

and unsettled quality is crucial to both truth and justice, as we shall see in subsequent chapters, a point often viewed as counterfactual to many working in imperio-colonial paradigms of scholarship today, those who see truth and justice as more threatened than aided by the unappeasable and unsettled intellectual traditions of our times.

In short, what we have before us, beckoning toward a sense of the theological, is not just the dissolution of imperio-colonizing sovereignty as an interpretive ideal for Theology, but also the birth of a sensate/sensing of what Hutchens helpfully terms "a multiply reticulated and irreducible singularity."[111] The thrust of our hermeneutical endeavor, then, for articulating the theological, is a mode of wandering. But this is not only a wandering in and for wandering itself. It is a wandering *through* sensate and sensed "reticulations, and especially as these bodies of sense are susceptible to the shift from extended to concentrated weight of the world. The challenge to theological interpretation, as indeed for all truly complex interpretive endeavors, is to grapple with this complexity, commit to the "wandering labor of sense," to circulate meaningfully the incomprehension and difficulty of thought presented by proliferating meaning across historical and present contextual singularities.

---

111. Hutchens, *Jean-Luc Nancy and the Future of Philosophy,* 43, following Nancy's early language in Jean-Luc Nancy, "Sharing Voices," in *Transforming the Hermeneutic Context: From Nietzsche to Nancy,* ed. G. Ormiston and A. Schrift (Albany: State University of New York Press), 211–59.

Chapter Two

THE AGONISTIC POLITICAL

> . . . *the political cannot be restricted to a certain type of institution, or envisioned as constituting a specific sphere or level of society. It must be conceived as a dimension that is inherent to every human society and that determines our very ontological condition.*[1]—Chantal Mouffe

> *I have put forward the notion of necropolitics and necropower to account for the various ways in which, in our contemporary world, weapons are deployed in the interest of maximum destruction of persons and the creation of deathworlds, new and unique forms of social existence in which vast populations are subjected to conditions of life conferring upon them the status of living dead.*[2]—Achille Mbembe

While all humans may be described as the "living dead," and also be subject in some way to what Mbembe names above as a necropolitics, the politics to which he refers is one that instrumentalizes life so that certain

---

1. Chantal Mouffe, *The Return of the Political* (New York: Verso, 1993), 3.
2. Achille Mbembe, "Necropolitics," in *Public Culture* 15, no. 1 (2003): 40.

conditions of being are a suffering that is not the lot of all.[3] I have already articulated this difference between what Mbembe calls the living and the living dead, by way of Nancy's notion of a weighted world. The world is a continual weighing, and yet there are shifts that make a difference, especially the shift from weight extended, with spacings and balancings that make for life and world, to weight concentrated, piled on, "cramming," isolating and organizing humanity and world into a repressive structure. Mbembe presents the organized occupation of Palestine by Israel and the United States as the quintessential example of "late-modern colonial occupation," in which sacral narratives of national identity underwrite state strategies of division and fragmentation and, especially, a "politics of verticality" that offers almost a perfect picture of what Nancy described in more abstract terms as the world's weight compacted, piled up, in a state of "concentration."[4]

To describe a shifting of the world's weight, from extension to concentration, as I did in the previous chapter, is the most abstract and fundamental way of referencing the agonistic political that is the human ontological condition.[5] There is an agonistic striving between extension and concentration that is a kind of labor, a struggle in the weighing of bodies to hold the delicate singular pluralities of world in their life-giving relations, remaining creative in collision with the brutal concentrations of weighing, of which late-modern colonial occupation is but one mode. The previous chapter's discussions of U.S. mass incarceration are another. In all this there is no simple binary opposition of dynamics of good and evil, but antagonism between good and evil is a part of the complex, delicately structured world, within which weight can shift from extension to concentration and its destructive effects.

This chapter foregrounds and explains more fully the notion of the agonistic political by developing theories of human practice that show more concretely how weight "shifts." This is a political ontology, but again, recall that in the orbit of Foucault's theory of power and practice we are not seeking dehistoricized, asocial "fundamental structures of being." To the contrary, the emphasis is on the historical and social *practices* in which human being is enmeshed and so constituted. "Ontology," as I use

3. Ibid. 14, 40.

4. Jean-Luc Nancy, *Corpus,* trans. Richard A. Rand (New York: Fordham University Press, 2008 [French 2006]), 77–79.

5. Chantal Mouffe, *The Return of the Political* (New York: Verso, 2005), 3.

the term in this work, refers to discourse about the conditions of being in which humans live, which are always historical and social. Because they are about managing, contesting, and embracing strife within the labile agonistic world, those conditions of being, our ontological conditioning, are political. Turning to the agonistic political as practice not only guards against the universalizing and totalizing moves of ontology, it also prepares the way for seeing the kinds of practices carrying the haunting power of those seething presences that are the hallmark of the theological. As Avery Gordon reminds her readers repeatedly in *Ghostly Matters*, the imaginative moves of the haunting, the spectral and the ghostly, are made not through disembodied spiritual media, but through practices, the ways humans collectively inhabit action through practices, especially of remembrance ("re-memories"), a doing in the present that connects with the past of the unjustly slain and with the bearers of imposed social suffering.[6] Gordon cites Michel de Certeau to underscore this point, who, in his *Writing of History*, suggests that "taking the dead or the past back to a symbolic place is connected to the labor aimed at creating in the present a place (past or future) . . . 'something that must be done'."[7] Note in de Certeau's phrasing the need for "labor," for a "creating," for reflection on "place," and on "something that must be done." This is the terrain of the theological: human practices that effect haunting and seething presences.

This chapter's theorization of the agonistic political draws primarily on two major practice theorists, Theodore Schatzki and Pierre Bourdieu. They are selected for three reasons. First, they each articulate an understanding of practice as constitutive of being, tracing human ontological constitution in the distinctive ways humans organize action in practices. Second, the understanding of practice developed by each facilitates reflection on a political dimension that concerns not only power, but also power worked out agonistically under conditions of domination (Bourdieu is more successful here than is Schatzki). Finally, both are selected because while they develop theoretical rigor when reflecting on practice, they also draw substantially from empirical worlds of their own and

6. Avery F. Gordon, *Ghostly Matters: Haunting and the Sociological Imagination* (Minneapolis: University of Minnesota Press, 1997), 168, 174, 182–83.

7. Michel de Certeau, *The Writing of History*, trans. Tom Conley (New York: Columbia University Press, 1988), 101.

others' field research into living communities—Schatzki from studies of
the Shakers and contemporary economic NASDAQ day traders, Bourdieu
from fieldwork among the Kabyle of Algeria, as well as among "the tribe"
of *homo academicus* in the dominant Eurocentric West.

The chapter begins with Schatzki's social-site ontology of human
practice. Schatzki's theory provides us an understanding of how practice
constitutes human being, and what, precisely, practices are. In a second
section, I turn to Bourdieu's dispositional theory of practices, which deepens an understanding of practice's agonistic quality, especially because
Bourdieu shows how the agonistic powers make dominance and its various modalities part of practice and, hence, again constitutive of human
being. The third section draws together the implications of Schatzki's and
Bourdieu's theories of practice for understanding the agonistic political
and some of its major traits. In a conclusion, I show how key elements
of Bourdieu's notion of symbolic capital, although fruitful, neglect the
ways symbolic functions contribute to the seething presence of transimmanence *as practice.*

A Social-Site Ontology of Practice

One value of journeying toward "the theological" through social-site ontology is that it enables us to navigate our way through some of the most
important debates about the social order and about the ways humans
live with one another in it, as well as about the more-than-human orders
of organisms and things. Thinking through these dynamics at social sites
is crucial to taking context seriously, for discourse of the theological or
any other discourse. This becomes clearer if we clarify social-site ontology in relation to social ontology more generally. Schatzki himself introduces social ontology within a "tale of two ontologies."[8] The two are
individualism and socialism, or elsewhere he simply writes of "individualist" and "non-individualist" ontologies, substituting "non-individualist"
for "socialist."

The formulas, individual/social, or individual/society, he sees as
striking a venerable distinction, in accord with which social ontologies

---

8. Theodore R. Schatzki, *The Site of the Social: A Philosophical Account of the Constitution of Social Life and Change* (Harrisburg: Pennsylvania State University Press, 2002),
124.

have organized themselves and debated key issues since their nineteenth-century origin.[9] By "socialist" or "non-individualist" he means an ontology that views social facts, events, and formations as "distinct but not independent from" facts, events, and developments accruing to interacting individuals. Hence, socialist ontologies are prone to discourses on the powers of "culture" and "society" for shaping individual behavior. What Schatzki calls "the burden of these socialisms" is their continual defense of "a difference in being between individualist stuff and some distinct, irreducible component of the social."[10] "Individualism" does not deny the reality of social affairs, or the importance of the category of the social, but does seek to affirm that social life is primarily "a labyrinth of individuals" in interaction. The social, according to individualists, is not ignored, but it tends to be focused through the dynamics, structures, and processes attributed to individuals. The "social" usually becomes only a name attached to interactions between individuals. Is it more than a name? The individualist responds to that question usually with a studied (or sometimes unstudied) "nominalism," that is, holding that the social is only a name not having a reality that rivals that of individuals.

In this book's political ontology, and the understanding of the theological that rises with it, I follow Schatzki in holding that both nominalist individualism and nonindividualism ("socialism") are problematic. It is important, though, to grasp the criticism advanced against each. Against individualism, Schatzki argues that it is "contravened"[11] by its inability to account for individual beliefs, actions, and experiences as embedded in some milieu or medium. In all those beliefs, actions, and experiences, there is almost always a "further factor" that points to individual experience's entailment in some shared, social interaction that cannot be accounted for simply by reference to another individual's beliefs and actions. Analyzing some intersubjective, social collectivity becomes necessary. On the other side, nonindividualism's tendency to reify a social whole as outside, other than, or having qualities or dynamics distinct from individuals and their interactions is also contravened, this time by the inability on the part of nonindividualists (and Emile Durkheim is the

---

9. Ibid., 125.
10. Ibid., 140.
11. Ibid., 134 and 141.

primary representative with whom Schatzki jousts[12]) to give much more than a stubborn assertion of reified "social facts." Socialist ontologies stumble, he argues, particularly in that their "proven irreducibility of the social" almost never makes room for, or renders with full complexity, the actions of individuals that individualists have been better at expositing.[13] If individualists tend to gesture incompletely to the social, often merely projecting individualist dynamics onto the social, socialist ontologies feature a contrary limitation, that is, they may admit the reality of individual force and presence, but fail to get all the way back "down to" the complexities of individuals' active living.

Even though Schatzki is fairly evenhanded in his criticism of the two ontologies, he nevertheless rightly locates his own site ontology on the side of the social, nonindividualist category. The reason he does so is this: even though his site ontology will allow for individualism's "insight that individuals and constellations thereof are causally responsible for the progress of social affairs,"[14] a full understanding of that insight itself requires a profound respect for what he often calls the "mesh of orders and practices" in which both individual and social life are embedded. The nonindividualist, socialist ontologies, even if erring in their holism and reification of the social, nevertheless respect the power and enveloping character of that "mesh." The preexistence of the mesh gives the social the edge in determinative power in shaping the nature of outcomes in human action. Schatzki's social-site ontology, as a theory of the mesh of orders and practices of social life, enables his rigorous analysis of contexts, but also enables him to honor the insights of both individualist and socialist ontologies.[15] In short, the argument is that you can better theorize the uniqueness of individual action and practice through a nuanced theory of the social than you can theorize the fullness of the social from the complexities of individual experience. The "social site" is the particular mode of the social that best enables this.

---

12. Ibid., 135–38.

13. Ibid., 140.

14. Ibid., xi.

15. A brief word on Schatzki's theory of "orders" is important. Another of the virtues of his theory of practice is that this human endeavor is theorized as also enmeshed in nonhuman phenomena. Practices, for Schatzki, are partnered with orders in the total mesh of factors that set the scene of human co-existence. Ibid., 6–17.

What Is a "Social Site?"

Sites, for Schatzki, are the particular meshes of life's relational complexity in which humans live. They are the contexts within which humans live and move and so are articulated as belonging to "the involuted lacing of human and other phenomena into extensive arrangements that determine as well as bind together their characters and fates."[16] This is a further development, through practice theory of Jean-Luc Nancy's singular plural world. Things and people, as Schatzki says elsewhere, "hang together as clusters of inter-related determinant stuff,"[17] and this can be affirmed without denying the indeterminacies, instabilities, and irregularities that also pervade those interrelated clusters of order. Social sites are important because they enable our theorizing of those relational orders, as orders ("clusters of inter-related determinant stuff") while also allowing for their complexity and susceptibility to change.

I can clarify further the notion of social site by distilling four points from Schatzki's analysis. First and most generally, *a social site is a context*, what Schatzki terms a "contexture." This notion must be understood in contrast to "textures." A texture refers to the larger setting that a scholar might give to a text, say, Ha Jin's *War Trash*, a novel about a Chinese immigrant in the United States recalling his war years fighting for China in the Korean War against the United States, and this immigrant's liminal dwelling between at least four worlds (his native China to which he cannot return because of the shame of defeat in Korea, the Korea to whose residents he has built some ties, the Taiwan where he was once offered exile by his South Korean and American captors, and the United States to which he ended up immigrating).[18] Some might think that one contextualizes when placing this novel in the setting of other texts and writings, for example, in a tradition of Asian, Chinese, Asian American, or Chinese American literatres. This, however, is not what a context properly is. This would be, in Schatzki's language, only a "textural" setting, just a further elaboration of the same, that is, texts situated in relation to other texts. To be a contexture, that which does the enveloping or surrounding must be different in nature from what is enveloped. Thus, context as contexture would mean, in the case of our example, the various activities, events,

---

16. Ibid., xiii.
17. Ibid., 1.
18. Ha Jin, *War Trash* (New York: Vintage, 2005).

identities, and histories that envelop the novel *War Trash*. This would entail focus on the historical, political, personal, and social experiences of Chinese and Korean soldiers at war with one another, and both in different ways with U.S. military forces in the Korean War from 1950–1953. For knowledge of that contexture, of that war and its period, it would mean turning to another kind of text, based on fieldwork and notes about the period, such as Bruce Cumings's *The Origins of the Korean War*.[19] The different quality of contextures, or their difference in kind, distinguishes them from textures. In the language of Michel Foucault, one might say that the contexture involves "nondiscursive" affairs and not just "discursive" ones.

Therefore, the first key point about social sites is that they are contexts, not just as textures of ever-widening textual collections, something individualists or social theory nominalists often do recognize, but contextures, as ever-widening domains of a different quality, usually activities, events, identities, and histories. Sites are where things exists and events happen. Thus sites are a type of contextual relation. The next three key points about a social site elaborate the kind of context a social site is, addressing different aspects of the kind of "where" that a site is.

My second point thus preserves Schatzki's important claim that "social sites are locations in space." Their focus is usually on a specific location, and they reference a spatial domain—a space, place, field, or region[20]—as proper to the context. There are relatively simple and more complex ways of designating a social site's located quality. Place is often avoided by merely topical treatments. For example, to return to *War Trash*, I could suggest that its social site concerns war, the legacy of war's psychic and physical wounding and trauma, the displacement and émigré status it forces upon so many. But this topical approach, by itself, can miss the elements of place. It overlooks the physicality and sociality of China, Korea, and the United States, all of which interact and construct place in

---

19. Bruce Cumings, *The Origins of the Korean War—Volume 1: Liberation and the Emergence of Separate Regimes, 1945–1947* (Princeton: Princeton University Press, 1981); and *Volume 2: The Roaring of the Cataract, 1947–1950* (Ithaca: Cornell University Press, 2004).

20. On theories differentiating "space" and "place" see Yi-Fu Tuan, *Space and Place: The Perspective of Experience* (Minneapolis: University of Minnesota Press, 1977/2003), 19–33; and Michel de Certeau, *The Practice of Everyday Life,* trans. Steven Rendall (Berkeley: University of California Press, 1984), 117–18.

distinctive ways. *War Trash*'s social site, properly speaking, is not simply a group of topics and themes, important as they are. A social site comes into being when there is a foregrounding of location and place and their complexities, as a setting for considering those themes and topics.

Third, *social sites are also the wider scenes* within which their located phenomena are enveloped and by which they are determined. To understand an event named "the Korean War," especially as context for understanding a literary piece like *War Trash*, wider matrices warrant analysis and constitute the being of its social site. Thick descriptions of local sites, then, by themselves do not constitute analysis of a social site. Examination also needs to be made of the wider scenes enveloping local places, the interrelations of structures and processes of other places and powers: in Korea and China, but also in and by Russia and the United States, perhaps also the history of colonial and imperial powers more generally.

The fourth, and for Schatzki the most important, sense of social site is that "at least some of the *entities that occur in it are inherently components of it*. That is to say, for something to be or to occur in a social site it must occur *as* a constituent part of its context."[21] Hence, those entities and persons that belong to a social site are inherently and constitutively part of it. Schatzki admits that this is a "more rarified" and difficult sense of social site. His key point here is that even though a social site may have an extensive matrix, not everything in that matrix belongs to the social site. To refer to the example of discerning the social site of *War Trash*, we can observe that as crucial as the United States is to its social site, a young baseball player in Middleton, USA, is not a constituent part of the novel's social site in the way that actions in 1945 of a young U.S. Army major, Dean Rusk (later U.S. Secretary of State under President John F. Kennedy), were when he helped to set the dividing line between North and South Korea at the 38th parallel, a wholly U.S. action related to it geopolitical interests and designs for Korea in the aftermath of the Japanese surrender at end of World War II.[22] The action by Rusk and fellow officers is, of course, not the only constituent part of the social site of *War Trash*, but it is exemplary of the kind of development that is. With this fourth sense of context, together with the previous one, we

---

21. Schatzki, *The Site of the Social*, 65.
22. Cumings, *Origins of the Korean War*, 1:120–21.

have a social site, Schatzki emphasizes, the "strongest and most interest-ing type."[23]

These features of a social site make it a unique way of enmeshing humans. These four qualities at work at social sites characterize "human coexistence." Description of such a social site is intrinsic to a social-site "ontology," because it limns the being-in-coexistence of humans in it. This enmeshment, as we have noted above, is simultaneously one that mediates between, and acknowledges insights of, both individualist and socialist ontologies. A social site is where the uniqueness of individual intention, subjectivity, and actions are at work but always as inherently parts of contextures that envelop and determine individual life. Indi-vidualism is challenged by this social-site ontology because individual actions require analysis as inherently belonging to social contextures. Most socialist ontologies are also challenged and qualified because the many lines and particular processes at the site will usually insist on a theorization of human action that cannot be reduced to some "social fact," a social totality, as often reified by socialists above or beyond individuals.

What Is a "Practice?"

In turning now to practice and practices we are taking up what is argu-ably the most important aspect of Schatzki's theory of what human coex-istence is. As we have seen, and which will become still clearer in this section, practices are social, entailing participation with other persons, directly or indirectly. For Schatzki, the organization of this sociality, this being-in-relation of persons, occurs through human practices' structuring of action and interaction. Human practices are important because they are what structures this social action, providing action's distinctiveness at social sites.

In general terms, as we have seen, Schatzki means by "practice" the organizing of action by humans, or better, "organized nexuses of actions." These are the packets or bundles crucial to practice's organization. But each packet or bundle, whether we are talking about moral practices, reli-gious practices, or cooking practices—all of them hang together because

---

23. Ibid.

of four linking phenomena. Each linking phenomenon makes a distinctive contribution to constituting a practice, developing distinctive social experiences at social sites.

The first linking phenomenon is "practical understanding." This is not mere know-how, the ability to execute a skill. According to Schatzki, it is more like what Bourdieu has described as a *habitus* or practical sense ("having a feel for the game"), or Anthony Giddens's "practical consciousness" ("tacitly grasping a rule"). We can give an example from youth video gaming. A teenage boy may be highly skilled in using the plastic box of buttons and levers and have great hand-to-eye coordination; that's the know-how. But if he also has the ability to approach a new game, even when it features a control box he's never seen before, if he can sense his way forward, to participate in the game, play it, discern even perhaps how to master it, then he has demonstrated "practical understanding," that elusive "feel for the game" that is more than technical know-how. By contrast, an older adult may read the directions and achieve technical know-how, but still lack the essential "feel for the game."

The second linking phenomenon is a set of rules. As Schatzki defines rules, these are neither tacit understandings nor the making explicit of something previously hidden and assumed. He reserves the words *rule* and *rules* explicitly for a community's formulations that are interjected into social life to guide and orient its activities.[24] Thus, for Schatzki, rules are "explicit formulations, principles, precepts, and instructions that enjoin, direct, or remonstrate people to perform specific actions."[25] Cooking practices in a pizzeria would feature rules in the form of recipes given out to cooks, schedules regulating labor times, health standards, and other responsibilities, perhaps a pizzeria manager's prohibitions on circulating the contents of a widely admired recipe to cooks at other restaurants, and so on. Note, especially with respect to theorists who would take rule-governed behavior as the central feature of practices,[26] that for

---

24. Typically, adds Schatzki, these are interjected into social interaction by authorities who can enforce them; Schatzki, *The Site of the Social,* 79–80.

25. Ibid., 79.

26. Schatzki thus engages in extensive critical dialogue with Robert Brandom, "Freedom and Constraint by Norms," *American Philosophical Quarterly* 16 (1979): 187–96, as well as Brandom's major book, *Making It Explicit: Reasoning, Representing, and Discursive*

Schatzki, rules constitute only one linking phenomenon, and they are, on his theory, limited to those that are explicitly formulated.

The third linking phenomenon is perhaps Schatzki's most complex. He names it "teleoaffective structure." Practices, he suggests, also link activities together by means of a structure, a "range of normativized and hierarchically ordered ends, projects, and tasks to varying degrees allied with normativized emotions and even moods."[27] Teleoaffective structure is not only one of the linking phenomena that forms a practice; it is itself a complex, internally structured set of links. It brings into various degrees of interaction or alliance two features: first, the end-oriented or project-oriented strand of this structuring (its teleological aspect), and second, the emotional or mood-oriented part of the structuring (its affective aspect). Some practices, writes Schatzki, privilege more the teleological normativity, as in cooking practices. Others, such as child-rearing practices, may give more weight to the affective dimension.[28] It should be noted that again contextual sensitivity is paramount, since, to return to my example of the pizzeria, a given pizzeria might have an extraordinary commitment to its employees, guaranteeing remarkable benefits packages and personal care that convey unusual respect, such that a kind of family feeling of belonging is maintained at the labor site. Or, perhaps the pizzeria is a family-run operation with managers and staff related by kinship in various ways. In this case, affective structuring will be strong and not just the teleological, which is focused on the end of producing pizzas. Note that this particular linking phenomenon of practices knits together normatively mandated ends and projects *with* emotionally weighted normative expectations. Thus, teleoaffective structure is often just as crucial a way to establish normativity as is the explicit formulation of rules. Schatzki here displays the consonance of his practice theory with Foucault's thought, particularly with Foucault's thinking on "governmentality," in which, bio-politically, there is a continual constructing/disciplining of social structure normatively creating life as lived at the social site. This normative force operates in the intricacies of planning projects and affective modalities, and not just in the mandates of officials and authorities, of states and

---

Commitment (Cambridge: Harvard University Press, 1998). In Schatzki, *The Site of the Social,* 71–72, 84–85.

27. Schatzki, *The Site of the Social,* 80. Italics added.
28. Ibid.

subordinate systems within states, all of which entail implicit and explicit rules.[29] To use Judith Butler's language, the framing of activity and of affective sensibilities are always in mutual interaction.[30]

These "teleoaffective structures" are exceeding complex and variant.[31] They are not to be identified with properties of the individual subjects, however much subjects participate in them. Nor are they to be identified with the "collectively willed ends and projects" of a certain group.[32] Teleoaffective properties belong to a practice, to the organization of activity. Thus, in a cooking practice this structure is to be discerned in a whole cultural style of acting, not so much in the attitudes of any of the actors or in the collective statements of authorities. Again, these latter are not irrelevant. But the teleoaffective structure belongs to a dimension of practice, a style or way of practicing where ends and affects are always interplaying. As operative at social sites, they are also a human order related to other orders of human actions and things in the world. We might say that "teleoaffective structure" is a normativizing ethos that permeates ends and affects and then binds them together to make a distinctive contribution to the other linking phenomena of a practice.

The fourth linking phenomenon is what Schatzki terms "general understanding." This is closely articulated with teleoaffective structures, but takes on a role as a distinctive fourth component of a practice's organization. General understanding concerns the infusing "regime" marked usually by some "sense of community" or "religious conviction."[33] The nineteenth-century Shaker community Schatzki studied experienced outcomes of steadfast determination in its workers, a mutual care and courteousness of interaction, and a respect (usually) for leadership due to the infusion of "sense of community." Their religious convictions, especially those which held that the earth was to be sanctified through their labor, produced qualities of work marked by tenacious dedication and zealous

---

29. On "governmentality" in Foucault, see Michel Foucault, *Security, Territory, Population: Lectures at the Collège de France, 1977–1978* (New York: Palgrave Macmillan, 2007), 108–9, 115–16, 342–43.

30. Judith Butler, *Frames of War: When Is Life Grievable?* (New York: Verso, 2009), 6–12.

31. See, for example, Schatzki's discussion of what happens when there are disagreements, as there can be, about teleoaffective structure; Schatzki, *The Site of the Social,* 82–84.

32. Ibid., 81.

33. Ibid., 86. For more on "general understanding," see 242–43.

perseverance. In NASDAQ culture of today, Schatzki finds its infusing regime to be what day traders describe as a "sense of the wonder and goodness of free pursuit of individual gain." In contrast to nineteenth-century Shakers, this results in much more unstable life-ways and attitudes, either a "delicious satisfaction" when gain accrues to day traders or "hollow despondence" over their losses.[34]

What Schatzki discusses as sense of community and religious conviction are somewhat blandly, and vaguely, named when designated as "general understandings." The latter phrase is not without significance, however. It is clear that the notion *general* here signifies the way a communal and/or religious sensibility pervades and infuses the whole of a practice's structure in ways that the other linking phenomena (practical understanding, set of rules, and teleoaffective structure) do not. Teleoaffective structuring and general understanding may seem quite similar, but as Schatzki presents them the difference is that, with general understanding, the teleoaffective becomes something more than end-oriented affect, as comprehensive as that affect may be. It becomes also an "infusing regime," a way of organizing the whole practice or set of practices, giving it a distinctive shape and character. Beyond this infusion, Schatzki stresses that these infusing regimes also create intensification (zealousness, dedication, joyous celebration, remarkable despondence) in the practice. Accompanying this intensification is often also a formation of aesthetic expressiveness (Schatzki references Shaker song-life during labor) and a mutual care for the community expressed in joint building projects. The "regime" quality of general understanding lies in the power it takes on as gathering up the whole of a practice, infusing it, giving it force in its organizing of human activity.

This fourth linking phenomenon at work in practice could be helpfully explicated by notions of other theorists. Raymond Williams's notion of "structure of feeling," for example, articulates it well, by which he points in human practice to sets of internal relations, of diversely structured patterns, mixing affect and belief. These relations do not quite sediment, he notes, to create social forms like institutions and traditional patterns that are publicly discernible. A structure of feeling is always in process, inchoate, infusing, and though difficult for practitioners themselves to name, it is often, nevertheless, determinative of social practice and its intensity.

---

34. Ibid., 166.

It is most powerfully resonant and alive, argues Williams, in the arts, "the aesthetic," and in "imaginative literature"—both "low" (popular) and "high."[35] Williams, in a particularly elegant formulation, summarizes the "structure of feeling":

> We are talking about characteristic elements of impulse, restraint, and tone; specifically affective elements of consciousness and relationships: not feeling against thought, but thought as felt and feeling as thought: practical consciousness of a present kind, in a living and inter-relating continuity.[36]

To move to the social sites of colonial history, we might also recall Edward Said's notion of a "structure of attitude and reference," operative in practices where "ideas about dependent races and territories were held both by foreign-office executives, colonial bureaucrats and military strategists, and by intelligent novel-readers educating themselves in the fine points of moral evaluation, literary balance, and stylistic finish."[37] Whether Williams's "structure of feeling" or Said's "structure of attitude and reference," both notions have an advantage over Schatzki's term *general understanding*, in that they include more forthrightly the role of affect as well as belief, of emotion as well as idea, in the infusing regime that Schatzki himself sees as binding up the bundle of a practice as it shapes human being.

With this explication of Schatzki's theory of practice amid his social-site ontology, we may turn now to Pierre Bourdieu. Schatzki has given us a rendering of human being as always an interplaying conjuncture of being and practice. Human being, we might say, is always "practice-being." It is in the milieu of *this* being that the agonistic political can be discerned, and then the theological as dimension of the political. We first need to identify, though, another conjuncture at work in social ontology, that of power and symbol. It is here that Bourdieu's contribution is particularly striking.

---

35. Raymond Williams, *Marxism and Literature* (New York: Oxford University Press, 1977), 133.

36. Ibid., 132.

37. Edward W. Said, *Culture and Imperialism* (New York: Vintage, 1993), 95.

Dispositions and Domination: Symbolic Capital in Practice

> *There is an economy of practices, a reason immanent in*
> *practices, whose "origin" lies neither in the "decisions" of*
> *reason understood as rational calculation nor in the deter-*
> *minations of mechanisms external to and superior to the*
> *agents.*—Pierre Bourdieu

Bourdieu's words above are a fitting introduction to his approach to practice theory. His is a theory of the "practical sense" that defines and drives
human actions.[38] This sense in human actions is an "economy of practice."
His views of the economy of practices were developed across his many
works, from the pages of his *Outline of a Theory of Practice* (French
1972/English 1977), to *The Logic of Practice* (French 1980/English 1990),
and to *Language and Symbolic Power* (French 1984/English 1991). Some
of the most succinct and clear delineations of symbolic power, especially for this book's need to theorize the agonistic political, are found in
such later writings as *Pascalian Meditations* (French 1997/English 2000),
and *Masculine Domination* (French 1998/English 2001), and *Firing Back:*
Against the Tyranny of the Market (French 2001/English 2003).[39]

Across these works, however, what is the nature of this "economy
of practice," or of the practical sense? It is, as he also writes in the epigraph, a "reason immanent in practices." This "reason," however, is to be
confused neither with calculating reason nor with the mandated "reason"
of external determinations impinging upon agents of practices. In other
words, it is determined neither by a calculative sort of costs/benefits consciousness, nor by external forces like "class consciousness" or the psy-
chological forces of the unconscious. All of these are involved, but what
is fundamental to the practical sense, as I shall emphasize, is the way
symbolic processes of recognition and misrecognition mediate between
subjects' bodies and their social and natural environments. Bourdieu's

---

38. Pierre Bourdieu, *Pascalian Meditations* [hereafter, *PM*], trans. Richard Nice (Stanford: Stanford University Press, 2000 [French 1997]), 64; see also 182–88.

39. For critical assessments of Bourdieu's oeuvre, see Craig Calhoun, Edward LiPuma,
and Moishe Postone, *Bourdieu: Critical Perspectives* (Chicago: University of Chicago Press,
1993); David Swartz, *Culture and Power: The Sociology of Pierre Bourdieu* (Chicago: University of Chicago Press, 1997); and Deborah Reed-Danahay, *Locating Bourdieu* (Bloomington: Indiana University Press, 2005).

work, even more than Schatzki's, enables us to reengage Jean-Luc Nancy's notion of the "body of sense" and the way bodies are spaced in an extended world, or concentrated by shifting weight. With Bourdieu, we have an account of how the shifting toward dominative concentration occurs, and, as with Nancy, it involves examining how bodies interplay, are ordered and weighted relative one to another. "Each agent has a practical, bodily knowledge of her present and potential position in the social space, a 'sense of one's place' as [Erving] Goffman puts it, converted into a *sense of placement* which governs her experience of the place occupied, defined absolutely and above all as a rank, and the way to behave in order to keep it ('pulling rank') and to keep within it ('knowing one's place', etc.)."[40] To understand the workings of this, we need to turn to Bourdieu's dispositional theory of practices. Recall that what I am presenting here by way of these practice theories, is an explication of the agonistic political at work in the singular plural world (Nancy), as a way of understanding, too, how the labile world is tensively vulnerable to shift into concentrated weight and its suffering.

A Dispositional Theory of Practices

We begin with Bourdieu's notion of the "socialized affect,"[41] which can be described as a socially constructed and historically conditioned emotion or desire. The primary term that Bourdieu uses for this socialized affect is "disposition," and so important is this latter notion that Bourdieu can refer to his practice theory as "a dispositional theory of practices."[42] Elsewhere, he stresses that "dispositions are the true principle of the acts of practical knowledge."[43] As socialized affects, dispositions cannot be consigned only to domains internal or external to human individuals. Again, as with Schatzki's social-site ontology, this practice theory begins in a place where individual and collective domains are in interaction. The disposition as socialized affect can be studied simultaneously through both "socio-analysis" and "psychoanalysis." Bourdieu explicitly calls for both analytic approaches, urging theorists in sociology and psychology to transcend

---

40. Bourdieu, *PM*, 184.
41. Ibid., 164.
42. Ibid., 166.
43. Ibid., 169.

their mutual suspicions of one another.[44] In this, Bourdieu's methodology in the human sciences, and his overall philosophical approach, continue the call Foucault made at the conclusion of his *The Order of Things* for seeing psychology and ethnology as not just two of the human sciences, but as two interpretive analytics that span the entire domain of those sciences.[45] Bourdieu holds those analytics together.

It is by tracing Bourdieu's notion of dispositions, these socialized affects, in socially elaborated desire,[46] that we journey into the heart of Bourdieu's practice theory. As affect and desire are socially elaborated in the original field, the domestic field, different dispositions and affects tend to develop in relation to one another, especially as young bodies experience in the domestic field a socialization of the sexual body and a sexualization of their social bodies. This working and interplay of the dispositions occasion complex transferences of dispositions from the domestic field to agents, groups, and institutions in other fields of social life. The dispositions as *libido* in the domestic field, for example, are transferred and transformed into specific dispositions that place individuals in society in different ways, enabling them to influence and be influenced variously. Just how complex this transformative process of dispositions can be is signaled by a passage we do well to quote at length. Note particularly how individual and social aspects interplay in the transference of dispositions across various fields, which then define place and position:

> The process of transformation through which one becomes a miner, a farmer, a priest, a musician, a teacher or an employer is long, continuous and imperceptible, and, even when it is sanctioned by rites of institution (such as, in the case of the academic nobility, the long preparatory separation and the magic trial of the competitive examination), it normally excludes sudden, radical conversions. It starts in childhood, sometimes even before birth (since, as is particularly clear in what are sometimes called "dynasties"—of musicians,

---

44. Ibid., 172; and Pierre Bourdieu, *Masculine Domination* [hereafter, *MD*], trans. Richard Nice (Stanford: Stanford University Press, 2001), 40.

45. Michel Foucault, *The Order of Things: The Archaeology of the Human Sciences*, a translation of *Les mots et les choses* (New York: Pantheon, 1970 [1966]), 373–87, especially 379.

46. Bourdieu, *PM*, 165.

entrepreneurs, academics, etc.) it involves the socially elaborated desire of the father or mother and sometimes a whole lineage.[47]

Because this process of transformation occurs by the socialization of affect and the social elaboration of desire, there is much more going on than mere journey through time, or mere accumulation of experience.

Of particular importance to this interplay of dispositions across various fields—say, from domestic to professional ones—is Bourdieu's important notion of *habitus*. By *habitus*, Bourdieu names the way dispositions are inscribed in people's bodies, again, not only in their bodies individually, but their bodies as interacting with nature and society. One of Bourdieu's ways of describing this interactive domain of *habitus* is to relate it to bodily *hexis*, the body's style of gesturing in usually small but sometimes grand ways, or of holding oneself in relation to others. This is reminiscent of Nancy's notion of bodies' intimate spacings and weighing relative one to another. *Hexis* might be described as the aura or subtle arrangement or positioning of oneself in relation to others. It is usually not intentional, but more a reflexive carriage of the body, marking ways of one's socialization of being and unconscious. In *The Logic of Practice*, Bourdieu stresses, "Body *hexis* speaks directly to the motor function, in the form of a pattern of postures that is both individual and systematic, being bound up with a whole system of objects, and charged with a host of special meanings and values."[48]

With this notion of *habitus*, Bourdieu is able to position himself against what he sees as the two predominant, fallacious views of practical action: a mechanistic view holding that practical action is mainly a mechanical effect of the constraints of external causes, and a "finalist" view, by which rational action theory holds that subjects act freely, choosing their practiced actions as a result of calculation of chance and expected profits. Against both of these, Bourdieu positions the notion of *habitus*. The very multiplicity of dispositions in any socialized subject creates a complexity of the subject that, however influenced it may be by external causes, prevents it from becoming a mere automaton. On the other side, the multiplicity of dispositions at work in the subject also

47. Ibid.
48. Pierre Bourdieu, *The Logic of Practice* [hereafter, *LP*] (Stanford: Stanford University Press, 1990 [French 1980]), 74.

means that "the agent of a practice is . . . 'never completely the subject of his [or her] practices.'"[49] Consequently, Bourdieu participates in that tendency of poststructuralist and postmodern thought of "dissolving" the subject. Bourdieu comes close to this in the following passage:

> The "I" that practically comprehends physical space and social space (though the subject of the verb *comprehend*, [the "I"] is not necessarily a "subject" in the sense of philosophies of mind, but rather a *habitus*, a system of dispositions) is comprehended in a quite different sense, encompassed, inscribed, implicated in that space.[50]

Note, what keeps this dissolution of the subject more concrete than the vanishing subject often touted by poststructuralist thought is Bourdieu's associating the dispersed "I" with a bodily *hexis*, a socially created way of positioning and being positioned in interaction with others and world.

Bourdieu's move here is not simply that of questioning the autonomy of subjects. Nor is Bourdieu merely challenging naïve realist notions that take world as having an impact on the senses and minds of subjects in some unmediated fashion. Nor, still again, is he simply arguing that subject and world, mind and being, are mediated by one another. His main concern is this: the distinctive work of socialized bodies that mediate the practice of *habitus* and *hexis*, of subjects and their worlds.[51] Bourdieu is thus making a more materialist move, yet one that seeks to take account of both psychoanalytic and socioanalytic approaches, a combination not adequately effected, as Bourdieu sees it, by those approaches that claim a Marxian pedigree and invoke the mantle of "materialist."[52] His is a "materialist theory of the economy of symbolic goods,"[53] where "materialist"

---

49. Bourdieu, *PM*, 138.

50. Ibid., 130.

51. When this is done with respect to scholars' practices, i.e., when scholars' intellectual processes and products are related to their social conditions of existence, one usually transgresses one of "the fundamental taboos of the intellectual world." Bourdieu, *MD*, xiii.

52. For Bourdieu on Marx here, see *PM*, 177, and *LP*, 112–13. We will return to the nature of the "materialism" of Bourdieu's theory of symbolic exchange in the subsequent chapter.

53. Bourdieu uses this phrase to describe the kind of theory "I have been trying to build up over many years," in *MD*, 34.

refers to his penchant for continual reference to the body's socialized affect that then socially reconstellates its symbols across different social fields. But what is the notion of symbol, for Bourdieu, in this material economy of practice?

Symbolic Capital and Symbolic Violence

Of central importance to Bourdieu's notion of the materialist character of power and "practical sense" is his notion of symbolic capital. Here, too, is Bourdieu's primary contribution to my notion of the agonistic political. This is the primary mode of capital with which he is concerned. His reflections on different modes of capital (economic, political, cultural, symbolic) are ways to theorize power in social life. His language of "symbolic capital" may seem an unusual use of the term *capital*, in view of those who would link it mainly to economic power. What Bourdieu is claiming is that the symbol is part of capital—taking "capital" as the concretized realization of a force relation by an individual, group, or institution vis-à-vis other individuals, groups, and institutions in the continual interplay of dispositions. This is "capital" in the most basic sense of the word, as ability to be the head, to take a lead, to stand over. If we are used to deploying the term mainly with respect to the economic field, as wealth or "wealth that circulates" in the economic or financial fields, that would be acceptable given that economic conditions often do function as the primary means by which power is maintained, by which force relations are concretely realized. But by speaking of "symbolic capital," and also elsewhere of cultural and social capital,[54] Bourdieu reminds that the attainment or experience of disproportionate power vis-à-vis others is not only economic. In fact, paraphrasing Foucault again, economic capital cannot "hold good, be accepted"[55] without looking at the functioning of other modes of capital, other modes of gaining advantage, of being overpowered or overpowering vis-à-vis others, being dominating or dominated.

What more precisely is this "symbolic capital"? To answer that question it is necessary to return to his notions of the socialized affects, the

---

54. Bourdieu, *PM*, 242.
55. Michel Foucault, *Power/Knowledge: Selected Interviews and Other Writings, 1972–1977*, ed. Colin Gordon (New York: Pantheon, 1980), 119.

dispositions. Bourdieu's psychoanalysis and socioanalysis come together in his claim that these affects lead children in the domestic field, the social field of their first bodily engagement, "to take the point of view of others on him-/herself, to adopt their point of view so as to discover and evaluate in advance how s/he will be seen and defined by them." And again, the socialization of being is at work here, since in this situation children's being is a being perceived, "condemned to be defined as it 'really' is by the perception of others."[56] There is here both an egoistic pursuit of self-love and a fascination with, and need to secure, approval of others. Glory, honor, credit, praise, fame—these make up the currency of symbolic capital. Here the notion of recognition enters, playing on the tension between "being recognized by others" and "having being as recognized." Social practice, particularly the symbolic construction of the body in social interaction, is constitutive of human being.

It is with this notion of symbolic capital that Bourdieu's social theory becomes Pascalian meditation. He recalls Pascal, from *Pensées* 404: "The greatest baseness of man [sic] is the pursuit of glory. But that is the greatest mark of his excellence; for whatever possessions he may have on earth, whatever health and essential comfort, he is not satisfied if he has not the esteem of men." And again, from *Pensées* 151: "Admiration spoils all from infancy. Ah! How well said! Ah! How well done! How well-behaved he is! Etc. The children of Port-royal, who do not receive this stimulus of envy and glory, fall into carelessness?"[57] This "search for recognition," as Bourdieu calls it, is at work in the *habitus,* the system of dispositions carried in the bodily *hexis* since childhood. From its first forging in childhood, it continues through other domains of social interaction, work, and play. The various "rites of institution" sponsored by academies, guilds, and state offices are designed to continue to nurture (or not) this drive for recognition.

It may be objected that this is simply a socio-psychoanalytic theory for the privileged, for those who receive the praise, and that it thereby fails to account for the many who do not receive that recognition. Bourdieu, however, explicitly distinguishes what he calls "positive" and "negative" symbolic capital. This is the "ambiguity of symbolic capital" and what makes it, for some, the enabler of various forms of domination as

---

56. Bourdieu, *PM,* 166.
57. Ibid., 166–67.

well as, for others, of their subordination. Human need for symbolic capital, the need to satisfy a search for recognition, leads to different kinds of domination. Note how both recognition, and also the domination often created by the struggle for it, are both intrinsic to human being. I cannot take up here a survey of all social worlds to ask whether there are settings in which social recognition, and the search for it, unfold apart from experiences of domination. But even if generous giving of recognition occurs in certain social contexts, these, too, would experience, negatively or positively, the effects of the many other searchers for recognition who are less generous, always competitive, seeking to maintain their place in a world of domination. The world of recognition/domination is the one into which we are born, and with which all must struggle, even if we might glimpse or hunger for a world of recognition *without* domination.

Bourdieu writes poignantly of those who are "the losers in the symbolic struggle for recognition, for access to a socially recognized social being, in a word, to humanity."[58] What Bourdieu terms "the curse of a negative symbolic capital" often involves the translating of hierarchies of greater and lesser worth into hierarchies of fair and unfair treatment, as when care of the dying in hospitals is shown to vary according to peoples' perceived social importance.[59] In *The Weight of the World*, Bourdieu recounts one person's struggle for recognition, who articulates her need for visits from those outside the hospital, a fifty-year-old hospital patient who said, "Yes, because otherwise you're really not very important anymore, you're really just a piece of straw, completely placed in the hands of people, and of a certain kind of cruelty, especially at night, even sadism."[60] Bourdieu's work is replete with stories of those bearing a negative symbolic capital through failure to know recognition.

A still more systemic experience of negative symbolic capital is evident in the searches for recognition that come up against various stigmata—especially of race and gender, but also of language (pronunciation) or nation. Bourdieu writes an entire volume on gender injustice and the

---

58. Ibid., 241.
59. Bourdieu, in *PM,* 241, cites the somewhat dated works of B. B. Blaser and A. Strauss, *Awareness of Dying* (Chicago: Aldine, 1965), and *Time for Dying* (Chicago: Aldine, 1968). See, however, Francois Bonvin, "The Sick Person as Object," in Bourdieu's *The Weight of the World: Social Suffering in Contemporary Society* (Stanford: Stanford University Press, 2000), 590–99.
60. Bourdieu, *Weight of the World*, 598.

complexities of "masculine domination." He also gives regular attention to race and racism[61] in various works and throughout the published collective research project called *Weight of the World*.

Concerning the more specific workings of symbolic capital, as it exploits the search for recognition for securing domination, it is crucial to identify in Bourdieu's work three commingling dynamics. He returns to these dynamics that generate suffering throughout his work. A first dynamic concerns *value-laden oppositions*. There is the structuring of particular social sites so that oppositions are set up, which not only organize communal life at those sites, but also link that communal life to nature and cosmos, thus endowing aspects of social structure with different meanings and value. Bourdieu's studies of the Kabyle peasant society of Algeria function throughout his work as a way to exemplify how the opposed structure of man/woman, for example, is linked to cosmic principles, to the division of labor, and then to an ordering of virtuous being. Bourdieu has extrapolated from these studies to analyses of other cultures, even Western ones where women's emancipatory "progress" is often said to be exemplary. He writes that, still,

> . . . in the present state of the division of labor between the sexes, symbolic prizes such as honor, glory, or celebrity are still offered mainly to men; boys are the privileged recipients of the pedagogic action aimed at sharpening sensitivity to these prizes; they are especially encouraged to acquire the disposition to enter into the original *illusio* of which the family universe is the site, and are therefore more susceptible to the charm of the social games which are socially reserved for them and in which the prizes are one or another of the various possible forms of domination.[62]

A second dynamic of symbolic capital is its *naturalization*, or essentialization, of the social oppositions mentioned above. This essentialization of social oppositions is also, writes Bourdieu, a "dehistoricization," one that renders them almost unquestionable. The oppositions are made

---

61. Bourdieu, *PM*, 170, 238, 241.

62. For one notable study of the way gender/sex generates discursive regimes, see Judith Butler, *Gender Trouble: Feminism and the Subversion of Identity*, 1999 ed. (New York: Routledge, 1999 [1990]). Neither Bourdieu nor Butler analyze closely the way race and racism intersect with these powerful constructs of sex and gender.

to seem—and not just cognitively, but in social actors' reflexive and spontaneous understandings—"natural," part of the order of things. They are seen as givens. Historical analysis would remind that social oppositions are rooted in very contingent and complex historical actions. Social history, for Bourdieu, is what could subvert essentializing myths. Such needed subversive history, however, can never be done, first, amid one's being structured by symbolic capital. The oppositions are given first as essential, natural. Again, citing the Kabyle social context, he references the near inevitability of the naturalization of male/female, with women positioned in the social structure as homologous with such traits as "magical, ordinary, bottom, wet, home, darkness," and men with such alternative traits as "official, exceptional, top, public square, light, sun," and so on.

> The social order functions as an immense symbolic machine tending to ratify the masculine domination on which it is founded: it is the sexual division of labor, a very strict distribution of the activities assigned to each sex, of their place, time, and instruments; it is the structure of space, with the opposition between the place of assembly or the market, reserved for men, and the house, reserved for women, or, within the house, between the male part, the hearth, and the female part—the stable, the water and vegetable stores; it is the structure of time, the day and the farming year, or the cycle of life, with its male moments of rupture and the long female periods of gestation.[63]

Symbolic capital's naturalizing function has consequences throughout the body social and the body politic, and in these ways, both structure human being.

The third dynamic of symbolic capital develops a notion of *"(mis) recognition."* Here we are taken back to the importance of the *habitus,* that system of dispositions and socialized affects. With this third dynamic, the first two dynamics of symbolic capital—setting up value-laden oppositions and then naturalizing them—are ratified and appropriated from within the *habitus* of the dominated themselves. Instead of recognizing themselves, they "misrecognize" themselves by responding through their bodily affects to the way they are viewed, recognized, by the socially

---

63. Bourdieu, *MD,* 10–11.

powerful—in families, social systems and economic fields. Commentators have sometimes described this misrecognizing dynamic as Bourdieu's notion of "the complicity" of the dominated. That is an unfortunate
rendering, implying a collusion or willful acceptance of domination by
subordinated persons and groups. Bourdieu himself rarely uses the term
complicity.[64] More often he speaks of the ratification of domination in
one's own *habitus* as a coercion, one that is "set up only through the
consent the dominated cannot fail to give to the dominator (and therefore to the domination)." Clearly this is something far more complex
than mere complicity. Still, it is a dynamic of practice in which subjects
participate in, and even strengthen, their own subordination. "The effect
of symbolic domination . . . is exerted not in the pure logic of knowing
consciousnesses but in the obscurity of the dispositions of *habitus*, in
which are embedded the schemes of perception and appreciation which,
below the level of the decisions of the conscious mind and the controls
of the will, *are the basis of a relationship of practical knowledge, and
recognition that is profoundly obscure to itself.*"[65] In short, as subjects are
recognized by others, especially those with greater power to shape bodily
life in everyday exchanges, there is a misrecognition, a misrecognition
that marks their entry into not just profound obscurity, but also often into
inequality and subordination.

Bourdieu provides numerous examples in his book *Masculine Domination* of the ways the bodily *hexis* of women (and of men[66]), of their
somatized social relationship to dominant men, is part of their own domination. This relationship persists in spite of whatever suffering, disso-
nance, and inbuilt critique and resistance to their domination they may
also have. He explores, through an interpretation of Virginia Woolf's *To
the Lighthouse*, for example, how women avoid being caught up in the
male games of privilege, yet still are "almost always condemned to participate, out of an affective solidarity" with men.[67]

Bourdieu gives another, particularly revealing, example in his reference to another writer, James Baldwin, in Baldwin's *The Fire Next Time*.

---

64. For an exception, see Pierre Bourdieu, *Language and Symbolic Power* [hereafter,
LSP], ed. and intro. John B. Thompson, trans. Gino Raymond and Matthew Adamson (Cambridge: Harvard University Press, 1991), 23.

65. Bourdieu, *PM*, 170–71.

66. Bourdieu, *MD*, 49–50.

67. Ibid., 75–76.

The passage Bourdieu treats describes how an African American boy—and, we could insert, with different aspects of meaning, other nonwhite children in the United States—comes to know and internalize the difference between whites and nonwhites, and the limits that are set for the latter. The Baldwin text Bourdieu foregrounds is this:

> Long before the black child perceives this difference, and even longer before he understands it, he has begun to react to it, he has begun to be controlled by it. Every effort made by the child's elders to prepare him for a fate from which they cannot protect him causes him secretly, in terror, to begin to wait, without knowing that he is doing so, his mysterious and inexorable punishment. He must be "good," not only to please his parents and not only to avoid being punished by them; behind their authority stands another, nameless and impersonal, infinitely harder to please, and bottomlessly cruel. And this filters into the child's consciousness through his parents' tone of voice as he is being exhorted, punished, or loved; in the sudden, uncontrollable note of fear heard in his mother's or his father's voice when he has strayed beyond some particular boundary. He does not know what the boundary is, and he can get no explanation of it, which is terrifying enough, but the fear he hears in the voices of his elders is more frightening still.[68]

Bourdieu's gloss on this text is to treat the fear here, what generates timidity, as not caused by the parents or by any one object behind the parents. The causative force is more an ethos or network of fear, and this is what is felt. A passage from *Language and Symbolic Power* clarifies Bourdieu's point: "the cause of the timidity lies *in the relation between* the situation of the intimidating person (who may deny any intimidating intention) and the person intimidated, or rather, between the social conditions of production of each of them. And little by little, one has to take account thereby of the whole social structure."[69] There is an entire matrix of fear, a dominating network, which the Baldwin passage vividly dramatizes for Bourdieu.

---

68. Bourdieu, *PM*, 170, citing James Baldwin, *The Fire Next Time* (New York: Vintage International, 1993), 26.

69. Bourdieu on "the distinctiveness of symbolic dimension," in Bourdieu, *LSP*, 51. Italics added.

In his treatment of the Baldwin text—a treatment that I later examine as deficient in significant ways—Bourdieu notes how small everyday experiences (the tone of a mother's or father's voice, the setting of a boundary for a child, and so on) work as triggers. There is a "triggering" by these means of the socially elaborated dispositions, such that the schemes of perception and appreciation—determining what and how things are ("perception") and who and which entities are worthy ("appreciation")—set off and consolidate in the *habitus* of dominated persons, a matrix of domination that envelops them from both without and within. To recall Foucault's language, this role of *habitus* is what allows power "to hold good," to be accepted. When this occurs in the structuring of domination, writes Bourdieu, it is a "symbolic violence" a coercion, and "the form par excellence of symbolic violence is the *power* which . . . is exercised *through rational communication*, that is, with the (extorted) adherence of those who, being the dominated products of an order dominated by forces armed with reason, . . . cannot but give their acquiescence to the arbitrariness of rationalized force."[70]

Guardians of Symbolic Capital

Although Bourdieu gives much attention to the "acquiescence" of the dominated, it should not be missed that for him this is always but one important part of a matrix of domination, within which repressive agents are also operative, identifiable, and accountable. In structures of symbolic capital, Bourdieu describes these agents, who are often understood as benefactors—as also guardians of the capital that enables them to maintain the matrix of domination to which others acquiesce. Repressive power, then, and the guarding of it, is not absent in Bourdieu's work, however much he traces the intricacies of that repression as it winds its way through the "misrecognitions" of the dominated *habitus*.

Hence, when theorizing the various dominations, especially masculine domination, four main repressive social groups are repeatedly discussed in Bourdieu's work. There is, first, *the family*, that domestic field which usually organizes division of labor around structures of male and female, with hierarchy and values distributed between them. Second, Bourdieu discusses *the religious field*—in the West, the church—often

---

70. Bourdieu, *PM*, 83.

authorizing and reinforcing, in symbiotic relation with the family and other fields, the hierarchy of structures and meanings. The church also extends those structures and meanings so that they reflect and are imbricated in larger cosmological frameworks. Religious systems thus play a crucial role in naturalizing and "essentializing" the hierarchical structures of meaning and different experiences of power, often compounding the great suffering generated by those hierarchies and differences.[71]

Bourdieu, third, does not fail to point also to the agency of *educational systems*, not only to the array of teachers and aides who meet any one person along the way of her pedagogical journey, but especially the "scholastic reason" of higher academe. Just on masculine domination, Bourdieu is especially clear on this point:

> In fact the whole of learned culture, transmitted by the educational system, whether in its literary, philosophical, medical, or legal variants, has never ceased, until a recent period, to convey archaic modes of thought and models (with, for example, the weight of the Aristotelian tradition, which makes man the active principle and woman the passive principle) and an official discourse on the second sex to which theologians, jurists, doctors, and moralists have all contributed and which aims to restrict the autonomy of the wife, especially as regards work, on the grounds of her 'childish' and feeble nature, each period drawing on the 'treasures' of the previous one.[72]

Bourdieu's notes on the agency of the educational system in domination could be further developed by tracing ways that educators and their perspectives have variously reinforced and thus helped to sustain processes of colonization, imperial power, even issuing approvals for removal and extermination of indigenous peoples.[73] Similarly, the legacies of "scientific racism" that legitimized slavery and colonialism,[74] and economic exploitation of various sorts, all give further testimony to the importance of Bourdieu's treatment of educators as guardians of symbolic capital.

---

71. Bourdieu, *LSP,* 39–42.

72. Bourdieu, *MD,* 86.

73. Jonathan I. Israel, "Race, Radical Thought and the Advent of Anti-Colonialism," in his *Enlightenment Contested: Philosophy, Modernity, and the Emancipation of Man, 1670–1752* (New York: Oxford University Press, 2006), 591–614.

74. David E. Stannard, *American Holocaust: The Conquest of the New World* (New York: Oxford University Press, 1993), 179, 244–45.

Bourdieu references, fourth, *the state* as a key agency in structures of oppression and guardian of symbolic capital. Indeed, he refers to it as "the site par excellence of the imposition of the *nomos*, the official and effective principle of construction of the world."[75] The reason for this lies in the state's expansive organizational structure, which usually impinges in some manner on all levels of a polity. Even if all sorts of parastate relations and groups exist, the character and mode of organizing by the parastate group is usually limited by how the state is structured. The state, according to Bourdieu, "does not necessarily need to give orders and to exert physical coercion, or disciplinary constraint, to produce an ordered social world, so long as it is able to produce incorporated cognitive structures attuned to the objective structures and so secure doxic [pre-reflective, trusting and believing] submission to the established order."[76] What it imposes are not simply rules and laws, but also, more influentially, modes of classification—sex, age, competence, census categories like white and black, or "Caucasian," "Hispanic," "Asian American," "African American," and so on. The state posits and sets up various divisions that, when taken in by family, religious, and educational groups for use in daily language and practice, become all the more powerful. The state also gives special force to the various "rites of institution" ongoing throughout a national society. Even in the United States where "church" and "state" are said to be separate, large numbers of officiating ministers still intone at church wedding ceremonies, "By the powers of the state invested in me, I pronounce you . . . ." Even in states that would not be identified as totalitarian, then, the state operates as powerful guardian of symbolic capital.

So pervasive is the state's power to infuse dispositions and *habitus* with the structures and meanings of domination that Bourdieu sees his sociological discernment of state power to be something like what Kant said of the "divine *intuitus originarious*": it "brings into existence by naming and distinguishing." On the basis of this analogy, state power can be described as having a theologico-political function through its institutions and its rites. With state power it is possible to say, with Emile Durkheim, Bourdieu suggests (musing with Kafka, too), that "society is God."[77]

---

75. Bourdieu, *PM*, 186.

76. Ibid., 128.

77. Bourdieu's observation, in this form, occurs in *PM*, 245. Elsewhere, speaking of institutions and their rites more generally, he refers to "Society, the secular substitute for God" in *MD*, 112.

Another feature of the state's special power lies in the fact that its field of force includes domains within the nation-state as well as without. Especially, if we are to think across the "colonial difference," as Mignolo names the difference between the modern/colonial world system and worlds that have been colonized, one would need to analyze how the state's disciplining powers, its structures of domination, both within and without, aid in its powers of expansion. This would mean building the axiomatics of imperialism abroad into an overall view of state power. Marxist thought, of course, as evident in Rosa Luxemburg's writings, has long explored the ways colonial and imperial acquisition of colonies was crucial to the state's accumulation of capital, and hence to its power of rule in the homeland also.[78] Less remarked upon by the Marxists is the racial marking of dominated groups, another site at which state rule is exercised, whether in a particular nation-state or in the transnational matrix of state power.[79]

The guardians of symbolic power, then, are not singular figures; they are conduits of the networks of social conditions and institutions, particularly as they cluster in familial, religious, educational, and state orders. These networks do not simply constitute a matrix with labyrinthian capillaries of power. Indeed, there is a labyrinth of powers, but they also congeal continually as domination, designing repression in ways that wrench compliance from the breasts of the repressed, and often so deftly that the repressed themselves seem to accept it as natural. Thus has Bourdieu written domination into the very heart of his social ontology of practice.

Being and the Agonistic Political

How do Schatzki's social-site ontology of practice and Bourdieu's practice theory of dispositions and domination advance our understanding of the agonistic political? It is crucial to recall that the notion of "the political" is not to be identified with "politics." In the French philosophical

---

78. Rosa Luxemburg and Nikolai Bukharin, *Imperialism and the Accumulation of Capital*, ed. K. J. Tarbuck (London: Allen Lane, 1972).

79. For a contemporary analysis of the power of race in capitalism, see David Theo Goldberg, *The Racial Threat: Reflections on Racial Neoliberalism* (London: Wiley Blackwell, 2009).

discussions, which are especially helpful here, the distinction is cast as a contrast between *la politique* (politics) and *le politique* (the political).[80] Claude Lefort has perhaps given one of the clearest definitions of the political in this sense, suggesting that "the political" designates "those principles that generate society, or, more accurately, different forms of society."[81] This meaning of the political features a scope closer to that of the social in general, to the full array of social complexity. Indeed, it is often difficult, in the present state of discussion, to differentiate the political from the social, so mapped onto one another have they become. Yet, careful scrutiny of Lefort's language will show that the *discrimen*, that which marks the distinctiveness of the political, is not simply its sociality but also, and more particularly, its generative principles of and for society. The political, we might say, is that which has a force that generates and animates society. We are here back to Chantal Mouffe's reminder that the political has to do with a sociality which touches "our very ontological condition."[82] This is to reaffirm the broad scope of the political, to take it out of some public sector or realm of the social and direct us to seek it in the way human being is constituted. But what of that distinctive quality of the political, which we have highlighted from the beginning, its agonistic quality?

Schatzki's and Bourdieu's theories of practice are crucial because they provide an understanding of being's politicality, and of that politicality as distinctively agonistic. In short, both theorists enable us to identify a notion of *the political as human organizing, through practices, of agonistic striving in society.* This becomes evident if we note carefully the agonistic features of both Schatzki's and Bourdieu's practice philosophies. Let me identify first the agonism of being enmeshed in practices, and then the agonism of being (mis)recognized. Both modes of agonism are ways in which practices can effect the shifting of world weight from extension to concentration.

---

80. Simon Sparks, Editor's Preface in Philippe Lacoure-Barthe and Jean-Luc Nancy, *Retreating the Political* (New York: Routledge, 1997), xi.

81. Claude Lefort, "The Permanence of the Theologico-Political?" in Hent de Vries and Lawrence E. Sullivan, eds., *Political Theologies: Public Religions in a Post-Secular World* (New York: Fordham University Press, 2006), 148–87, esp. 152.

82. Chantal Mouffe, *The Return of the Political* (New York: Verso, 2005), 3.

The Agonism of Being Enmeshed in Practices

In his social-site ontology of human practices, Schatzki's fundamental contribution is describing human being as enmeshed in practices. Being does not just express itself in practices, as if it could be described prior to practice. Practices constitute being. Insofar as we have being, we practice and are practiced. Where, though, is the agonism in human being as practice? From Schatzki's work, we can identify three crucial ways in which the very structure and dynamism of human practice is agonistic, thus structuring and effecting a shift of the world's weight to concentration.

First, as human practices organize action at social sites, the agonistic political emerges with the *constraint and enablement* that are intrinsic to human practice. In Schatzki's social-site ontology, "constraint and enablement" are two of the more salient of social practices' effects.[83] Activities that constrain are those that limit certain further actions. Enabling actions are those that make possible future actions. The organizing of activity by humans into social practices apportions constraint and enablement across contexts in different ways and with respect to different individuals and groups. Schatzki treats human experience of constraint and enablement as modes of prefiguring activity.[84] Thus, Schatzki stresses that it is the constraining and enabling powers of practices, and the ways they organize social arrangements, which "mediate the causal relevance of materiality for social life."[85] The materiality in question may include what are often seen as purely natural events—"acts of God," for certain minds—such as solar flares, earthquakes, tornadoes, viruses, hurricanes, and poisonous snakes. These impinge upon social life and definitely work changes in human social practices, even exhibit a certain "annihilative potency," writes Schatzki. He is equally firm in stating, however, that "even here . . . humans remain the masters in one regard, however trite to some and redemptory for others, namely, in the significance these events hold for them."[86] He concludes his commentary on this point, claiming that "nonhuman agency is a distinct facet of the social site . . . but in the present context this is a rearguard action that only limits what humans can do.

83. Schatzki, *The Site of the Social,* 212–19.
84. Ibid., 45–46, 98–99, 214–15.
85. Ibid., 118.
86. Ibid.

The asymmetry remains. The contingency of the connections between practices and orders lies in human hands."[87]

The agonistic political shows itself in the always constraining and enabling traits of human practice, traits that persist even when in dramatic events of apparently nonhuman and "natural" disasters the nonhuman orders seem to have determinative power. Although this point about practice is mostly Schatzki's, both he and Bourdieu could point to numerous examples of the constraining and enabling quality of practice. There are the obvious examples in practices wherein licenses, credentials, diplomas, and other certifications given through ceremony and bureaucratic transaction both constrain and enable. Less obvious, but all the more forceful, are practices like those Bourdieu lifts up, which "naturalize" sexual divisions of labor in the domestic field, thus prefiguring certain constraints and enablements in other fields (academic, political, economic). The construction of a notion of "race," naturalizing inequality among groups of people, making likely a set of constraints and attendant suffering for nonwhite groups, and then routinizing outcomes of enablement for those who pass as white, is another example of practices' constraining and enabling roles. The agonistic political abides in the way being in practice is always constraining and enabling.

Second, the agonistic political is present as *an asymmetrical power of social forces vis-à-vis individual action.* We have already emphasized that Schatzki's social-site ontology is no mere embrace of socialist ontologies, of reified social organisms that override individual contributions. "Hence, an account of the progression of the social site that leaves out the creative contribution of individuals . . . overlooks an absolutely crucial site of innovation, rearrangement, and reorganization."[88] Jacqueline Rose's emphasis on the resiliency of an individual's psychic life to resist socially imposed identities, even and especially sexual identities for women and men, confirms Schatzki's point: ". . . there is a resistance to [socially constructed] identity at the very heart of psychic life."[89]

---

87. Ibid., 122. For a more concrete discussion of Schatzki's emphasis on human practice amid natural disaster, with reference to the "natural disaster" of Hurricane Katrina along the U.S. Gulf Coast in 2004, see Jeremy I. Levitt and Matthew C. Whitaker, *Hurricane Katrina: America's Unnatural Disaster* (Lincoln: University of Nebraska Press, 2009).

88. Schatzki, *The Site of the Social,* 253.

89. Jacqueline Rose, *Sexuality in the Field of Vision* (New York: Verso, 1987), 90–91; as

Nevertheless, this resistance, and its limited achievement in working certain "failures" of socially constructed identities and processes, is itself testimony to the asymmetrical power of the social. Again, it is a social matrix that is present before individuals would resist that social. It is constitutive of egos or selves who would resist or comply. Even if world is not "concentrated," in Nancy's sense, against a given subject, it is the power of a social matrix that comes prior to the individual, transforming, say, a particular subject's eye-blink into a "wink," or her wave into a calling out to someone. Take a subject's dreams, those eruptions usually seen as coming from the depths of the interior life. It is a theoretical commonplace to stress that they are nearly always conditioned by the sociality of the dreamer, even if only by the most daily of encounters with parents, family, and friends. The asymmetry of this powerful sociality vis-à-vis subjectivity lies in the fact that social practices are usually given with and preexist the emergence, or birth, of individuals and, further, continually envelop and set the field for individual action. This asymmetry of power between subjects and the action understandings carried in sociality is particularly evident in the ways subjects (their thoughts, beliefs, and various sayings and doings) are dependent on the organization and availability of wealth. In present U.S. culture, for example, almost any subject's creative innovation, or his contribution to anything having to do with himself, family, and society, is dependent upon some degree of access, directly or indirectly, to funds from a paycheck, a friend or relative's provisioning of funds, an automated teller machine, a credit card, or some other outlet that provides him the capital needed for eating, health, and well-being. None of this, again, should lead us to discount or overlook just how powerful are the resilient responses of self and subjectivity even amid such dependency, but neither should we forget that social practices' organization of economic activity has asymmetrical power vis-à-vis the self, thus creating, often, something like a "class unconscious."[90]

The asymmetry of the social with respect to the subject is eloquently summarized in a gloss on Kierkegaard that Butler provides in her book *Giving and Account of Oneself*, which I must cite at length. After citing

---

cited in Judith Butler, *The Psychic Life of Power: Theories in Subjection* (Stanford: Stanford University Press, 1997), 97.

90. See Stanley Aronowitz, "Class Matters," in his *How Class Works: Power and Social Movement* (New Haven: Yale University Press, 2003), 12–37.

what she takes as Kierkegaard's appropriate reference to the "I," Butler writes:

> Yet there is no "I" that can fully stand apart from the social conditions of its emergence, no "I" that is not implicated in a set of condition-ing moral norms, which, being norms, have a social character that exceeds a purely personal or idiosyncratic meaning.
>
> The "I" does not stand apart from the prevailing matrix of ethi-cal norms and conflicting moral frameworks. In an important sense, this matrix is also the condition of the emergence of the "I," even though the "I" is not causally induced by those norms. . . . When the "I" seeks to give an account of itself, it can start with itself, but it will find that this self is already implicated in a social temporality that exceeds its own capacities for narration; indeed, when the "I" seeks to give an account of itself, an account that must include the conditions of its own emergence, it must, as a matter of necessity, become a social theorist.[91]

The agonistic political features this asymmetry of the social vis-à-vis the individual, one that generates and shows resistance between the indi-vidual and the social.

Third, the agonistic political—as its practices constrain and enable human action through practices, and as its force is felt through the asym-metrical power of the social—also features a *clustering in contextures*. I have already introduced Schatzki's notion of context and contexture in chapter 1,[92] since it was there so consonant with Nancy's understanding of how bodies are "in sense" in a singular plural world. Recall, a "context" or "contexture" has four aspects: (a) surrounding or immersing that of which it is a context; (b) having causative, determining powers vis-à-vis the entities and persons in a context; (c) instituting persons and entities said to be in a context, and (d) being not just a "diaphanous atmosphere or medium" in which things take place, but a complex enveloping set of dynamics, the features and forces of which are different from the entities or persons enveloped. These aspects of a contextual relation should not be confused with the four aspects of a social site. A social site is one type

---

91. Judith Butler, *Giving an Account of Oneself* (New York: Fordham University Press, 2005), 7–8.

92. See the section above in chap. 1, "Theology's Imperio-Colonial Sense," 54.

of context, one mode of inhabiting the contextual relation. In particular, a social site is the kind of context involving "*where* things exist and events happen."[93] It is that "where" that is structured by human practices, which bundle actions together in unique ways to create the particular context that a "social site" is. An individual written text, for example, theologian Paul Tillich's *The Socialist Decision*, has as its context not just the textural corpus of his or others' works, and also not so much the play of ideas relative to his interests, but more the worlds of politics, economic production, society, and interpersonal engagements that envelop and pervade the social sites of his personal life and production.[94] These latter enveloping dynamics make up the context of his work.

I emphasize this clustering of human activity into contexts (contextures) to remind that the agonistic political is always differentiated, congealing, as it were, into groups in relation. The agonistic political is not found as a homogeneous force. Although agonistic power pervades all social life, it does so with a cluster effect, we might say, creating and elaborating practice in terms of different kinds of group behavior, with their unique cultural traditions, languages, modes of living, different ways of accessing power, and so on. The boundaries between these, of course, are always shifting and being renegotiated, constructed and reconstructed, but this clustering of power in contexts at distinctive social sites needs to be foregrounded in an understanding of the agonistic political. It is in the always shifting, often tensively structured, interplay between groups that additional conflict and antagonism is encountered, another crucial feature of the agonistic political.

The agonistic political, then, is a constitutive animating power of the social, of the asymmetrically powerful social, but it is never a a homogenous organic whole that impinges on individuals; instead, it is a social phenomenon that comes in clusters, in groups, and differentiated as economic, sexual, or national. It is differences within and between these that generate agonist strife and tension. Class conflict is but one important mode of this tension. Citing Foucault, Schatzki stresses that "power must be understood in the first instance as the multiplicity of force relations

---

93. Schatzki, *The Site of the Social*, 63.

94. Paul Tillich, *The Socialist Decision*, trans. with intro. by Franklin Sherman (New York: Harper & Row, 1975 [German 1933]). On the context of this work, see John Stumme, *Socialism in Theological Perspective: A Study of Paul Tillich, 1918–1933* (Missoula, Mt.: Scholars, 1978).

immanent in the sphere in which they operate and which constitute their own organization."[95] Schatzki himself follows up by saying: "'Power' thus designates the reticular force relation of particulars in the social. Indeed, the social *is* this reticular organization of particulars."[96] It is amid this kind of sociality that the agonistic political works, and within which the shifting of the world's weight can occur, from the extension that makes for life to the concentration that is intrinsic to a necropolitics (Mbembe) or *immonde* (Nancy).

Curiously, Schatzki himself provides little direct analysis of how contextual clustering generates human experiences of social inequality. He does not write with a sense of what is at stake when world is concentrated, when the agonistic political and social life become a necropolitics. Schatzki has the resources for doing so, as in his theorizing of contexts as having powers of determination and in his frequent emphases, as we have seen, on practices' "constraints and enablements." But even when Schatzki becomes very focused, empirically, on the contexts of the Shakers or of day traders in North American capitalist market economy—even then, he rarely attends to group's practices as dominating or dominated, as equal or unequal to others, regarding the various groups he analyzes.

This failure to analyze inequality and domination makes it difficult to use Schatzki alone when theorizing what we have been discussing from the beginning as that concentration of weight, and socially imposed human suffering, against which those of a seething presence may "weigh-in" with transformational import. With Bourdieu, however, the agonistic political bodies forth with greater attention to domination and inequality.

The Agonism of Being (Mis)Recognized

The agonistic political as we view it through the lens of Bourdieu's work is marked above all by the agony of being in a state of "misrecognition." It is an agonism of being misrecognized as constitutive of one's own mode of social being. Again, there is an element of antagonism here between recognized and recognizing subjects, but because that relation is so complex, as we have seen, with (mis)recognizing subjects accommodating,

---

95. Schatzki is citing Michel Foucault, *The History of Sexuality*, vol, 1: *An Introduction*, trans. Richard Hurley (New York: Vintage, 1980), 93.

96. Schatzki, *The Site of the Social*, 66.

often, to that dominating (mis)recognition, it is best to see it as agonist or agonistic, a relation of tension and struggle, but not one always of outright opposition and antagonism. Domination is, again, a complex relation. This approach to agonistic being comes with three points that need to be made about the agonistic political in Bourdieu.

First, the agonistic political is *somatized sociality*. The body is important to Schatzki, too, since he routinely emphasizes that the "doings and sayings" of practices are *bodily*, and that it is bodies in motion whose doings and saying constitute the practices that organize action.[97] Bourdieu, however, since his early fieldwork days in Algeria[98] through to his more recent commentary on masculine domination toward the end of his life, is even more mindful of the body as site of practice.

Bourdieu especially analyzes how the body's positioning and carriage is at work in practice, especially as the dispositions are shaped by interaction with others. The political, in other words, must be thought not just institutionally and socially, but also as inextricably somatic, mediated and enacted by the body. The key concepts for Bourdieu's emphasis on somatized sociality are those of *habitus* and bodily *hexis*. Through *habitus*, recall, social practices operate, "perform," to deploy Judith Butler's theory,[99] through the embodied subjectivity of an agent's socially created dispositions. Better said, subjects are performed by the culturally inscribed dispositions carried in social practices. This is especially evident in *hexis*, the subtle (sometimes blatant) aura of the body, as it positions itself in relation to others, as it achieves a certain "stylistics of existence" (Foucault).[100] "Body *hexis* speaks directly to the motor function, in the form of a pattern of postures that is both individual and systematic, being bound up with a whole system of objects, and charged with a host of special meanings and values."[101]

Perhaps one of the clearest examples of bodily *hexis* as somatic inscription of social power lies in what has been analyzed as "the cool

---

97. Ibid., 72, 260–61.

98. Pierre Bourdieu, "The Attitude of the Algerian Peasant toward Time," trans. Gerald E. Williams, in *Mediterranean Countrymen: Essays in the Social Anthropology of the Mediterranean*, ed. Julian A. Pitt-Rivers (Paris and the Hague: Mouton, 1963), 55–72.

99. Judith Butler, "Performative Acts and Gender Constitution," in Carole R. McCann and Seung-Kyung Kim, eds., *Feminist Theory Reader: Local and Global Perspective* (New York: Routledge, 2003), 415–27, esp. 417–18.

100. Foucault, cited in ibid., 417.

101. Bourdieu, *LP*, 74.

pose" of African American youth, displaying in bodily movement a social
navigation of the power fields of racialized power in the United States.[102]
That movement is both resistance to and expression of a vulnerability
created by white racism. It is a stylistics of existence as a way of protecting, holding, and projecting a self amid a force field that ultimately is one
of "social death," a notion that Orlando Patterson has used to characterize slavery, but also that others have used for conditions imposed in Jim
and Jane Crow existence in nineteenth- and twentieth-century America
and for systems of ongoing vulnerability to death from racism.[103] Today's
"new Jim Crow" conditions, as seen in U.S. mass incarceration and other
structures, present racialized cultural power in a new way.[104] The *hexis* of
black and other youth, their *habitus* amid spirals of social death, not to
mention the host of other ways that youth and adults respond somatically
to oppressive power, exemplify how bodies register the agonistic political. It is a way to fight reduction to what philosopher Agamben has called
"bare life."[105] In times of severe repression, of lynching and rampant discrimination, it is a fight against being reduced to a social death of trembling flesh, to be warehoused and dispensed with as mere "meat."[106]

The political, in short, concerns not just those whose bodies have
been put on the front lines of vulnerability to death due, for example,
to racialized power, but all of us whose experiences of enablement and
constraint in social life respond to domination by the way we carry our
bodies along the journey from the body's birth to its decay. Bourdieu
traces this in the carriage of women in Algerian society, and in the way

102. Richard Majors and Janet Mancini Billson, *Cool Pose: The Dilemmas of Black Manhood in America* (New York: Touchstone, 1992). One could compare the social and political functions of this "pose" to Octavio Paz's much earlier discussion of the stylistic self-presentation of the *pachuco*, the Mexican male youth whose attitude and body aesthetic is part of a *habitus* of being "instinctive rebels" to North American racism. See Octavio Paz, "The *Pachuco* and Other Extremes," in his *Labyrinth of a Solitude*, trans. Lysander Kemp, Yara Milos, and Rachel Phillips Belsh (New York: Grove, 1961), 13–28.

103. On "racist America," see Joe Feagin, *Racist America: Roots, Current Realities, and Future Reparations* (New York: Routledge, 2000). On social death, see Orlando Patterson, *Slavery and Social Death: A Comparative Study* (Cambridge: Harvard University Press, 1982); and Abdul R. JanMohamed, *The Death-Bound Subject: Richard Wright's Archaeology of Death* (Durham: Duke University Press, 2005), 1–44.

104. Michelle Alexander, *The New Jim Crow: Mass Incarceration in the Age of Colorblindness* (New York: New Press, 2010).

105. Giorgio Agamben, *Homo Sacer: Sovereignty and Bare Life*, trans. Daniel Heller-Roazen (Stanford: Stanford University Press, 1998 [Italian 1995]), 1–29.

106. JanMohamed, *The Death-Bound Subject*, 1–44.

that carriage not only reflects a sexual division of labor in that society and a position in a masculinist family structure, but the way it also articulates a relation between women's bodily comportment and the structure of the cosmos, all conjured in ways that weave suffering for them.[107] The agonistic political's inseparable relation to somatic sociality touches almost every aspect of social life and practice.

Second, the agonistic political is for Bourdieu marked by *a struggle for recognition*. Often he writes of a "search for recognition," but "struggle" is more appropriate, since the search is often a negative one, implicated as it is in practices that involve domination. The practices he has in mind are those that entangle the infant and the young, who hear continually, from other social actors, "Ah! How well said! Ah! How well done!" Or maybe this praise is withheld. Bourdieu, as we have noted, refers to this socialization as "the baseness of man" in its collectivity, because it is especially this recognizing that prompts a search that cannot help but press on toward domination. Indeed, the very excellence held up as the ideal is always a constructed ideal, one constructed in terms of a system of dominations rooted in many prior occasions of unequal distributions of hierarchical power.[108]

I acknowledge that this is a particularly controversial aspect of Bourdieu's thought, which perhaps also attends my notion of the agonistic political more generally in this book. There remains what I mentioned only briefly in the introduction, what we might call "JanMohammed's query": Is not this agonistic search a very limited view of the politicality of the human in the world, one that is inordinately competitive, and overly negative in its view of human sociality? Maybe it is a predominantly Western projection onto human sociality in general, which hardly takes note of what ethnographies might show of indigenous societies' "social provisioning of mutual and abundant recognition."[109] Or maybe it is only a predominantly male, patriarchal competitive dynamic that operates here, such that we need to analyze other, less patriarchal responses and structures of care. It might even be possible to interpret the "Ah!

---

107. Bourdieu, *MD*, 5–53.

108. Bourdieu, *PM*, 166–67.

109. JanMohammed, *The Death-Bound Subject*, 267–68. Again, among indigenous literatures' extensive bearing on this question, see historian Donald Fixico, *The American Indian Mind in a Linear World: American Indian Studies and Traditional Knowledge* (New York: Routledge, 2003), esp. 142–79.

How well done!" in less agonistic terms, as more admonition and encouragement. Why take it in the negative sense as a call to achieve power over others?

Again, we must recall JanMohammed's own response to such a query, which focuses on a tendency to idealize certain other contexts—indigenous societies and so on. While there are genuine alternatives to Western socialities and competitive dynamics, and they are resources not only for alternative ways of organizing human community but also for resisting the dominative structures of the West, they are not without their own agonistic processes. The alternative, more "generous and abundant giving of recognition" that some cultures may render is held against the backdrop of a consciousness of *not* doing so. Precisely in that consciousness is a persisting element of agonism.

Moreover, even if one were to say that the alternative modes of generous recognition have the status of an ideal to be implemented and aspired to, one still has not escaped agonistic struggle. Any such implementation—and often the aspiration, too—almost always is done within the conditions of subordination and agonistic constitution of one's being. Even in the projection of ideals of a more generously given recognition, especially for subordinated peoples, there is struggle. As Butler reminds us, nearly every effort by subjects to secure the most basic agency, not to mention some freedom from systemic subjection, involves deploying the conditions and terms of the dominating system.[110]

Third, and most importantly, the agonistic political is marked by Bourdieu's key notion of *symbolic misrecognition*. In *The Logic of Practice*, Bourdieu can term this misrecognition as an "alienated cognition," because the agent's being and practice is conditioned to look at its world through categories that the world imposes, pulled into apprehending the world as constructed for them, as if it were a natural world, when in fact it is constructed to achieve their domination. This "alienated cognition" is built up into *mis*recognition through countless acts of recognition, by means of a symbolic process that shuttles across social fields. The dominated subject "does not want to know," writes Bourdieu, "that what makes the most intrinsic charm of its object, its charisma, is merely the product

---

110. Judith Butler, *The Psychic Life of Power: Theories in Subjection* (Stanford: Stanford University Press, 1997), 1–2.

of the countless crediting operations through which agents attribute to the object the powers to which they submit."[111] Again, the dominated are not faulted for this misrecognition; the powerful are the ones most held responsible, having "an interest in perpetuating misrecognition."[112] The collective self-deception "is only possible because the *repression* from which it arises . . . is inscribed, as an *illusion*, at the foundation of the economy of symbolic goods."[113]

The many acts of recognition that create collective symbolic misrecognition create what Bourdieu terms the *doxa* of a society, the usually "undisputed, pre-reflexive, naïve, native compliance" built up from domination's socially elaborated affects. When symbolic process is discussed as *doxa*, the Marxian notions of "false consciousness" and "ideology" would seem to be close at hand.[114] Bourdieu seems to abstain from making much of these notions, fearing perhaps that these determinative *doxa* would be too economistic. What symbolic power secures as *doxa* is a "state of *the body*"—again, a somatized social practice in society.[115] It is a "pre-verbal taken-for-granted" response that is developed in the body through symbolic misrecognition.

This misrecognition worked by symbolic process is situated for Bourdieu in a distinctive materialism, "the economy of symbolic goods."[116] The materially determinative force, "capital," is both economic and symbolic. As he argues against all "economism" in *The Logic of Practice*, the real "economic rationality of conduct" includes the symbolic.[117] Both symbolic *and* economic production belong to the material base,

111. Bourdieu, *LP*, 140–41.
112. Ibid., 140.
113. Bourdieu, *PM*, 192 (emphasis in the original).
114. For discussion and critique of this, see Swartz, *Culture and Power*, 89–90, 289.
115. Bourdieu, *LP*, 68.
116. Bourdieu, *Masculine Domination*, 96.
117. Bourdieu, *LP*, 153. Bourdieu gives several examples of how opportunities to use economic wealth are often dependent upon symbolically constituted prestige (built up across many fields—gendered and racialized in family, community, profession, and so on). Thus, in spite of the importance of having money, political power is not lodged in that alone. Referencing his fieldwork, Bourdieu writes, "The collective judgment which makes the 'market man' (*argaz nasuq,* among the Kabyle) is a total judgment on the total man which, like such judgments in all societies, involves the ultimate values and takes into account—at least as much as wealth and solvency—the qualities strictly attached to the person, those which 'can neither be borrowed nor lent.'"

that is, the determinative forces that most shape behavior and constitute practice, and hence human being. The symbolic process that works in tandem with the economic does not work along a vertical axis, as religious symbols often mediate elements of world and those thought to transcend world, or as symbols in psychology are said sometimes to mediate between the "deep" inner life and more surface, exterior relational processes. Bourdieu's economy of symbolic goods works more laterally, or horizontally, across a differentiated social terrain, across the various "fields" of social life: domestic, labor and business, sexual, geographic, cosmological. It is this process by which "symbolic goods" or values, created by oppositions at work in one or more fields, are then exchanged across other fields and so produce a latticework of domination. Again, the creation of a patriarchal order in the domestic sphere, reinforced by cosmological symbols that naturalize masculine domination, is one key example.

The "misrecognition" worked by the economy of symbolic goods can be exemplified by the nonwhite children in white racist societies who almost inevitably are led to internalize the construct of "race" (and often, too, its meanings for gender and sexuality), and then internalize also the disparaging traits attributed to them because of their nonwhite status.[118] White children "misrecognize" very early, too, being socialized from infancy into their senses of racial entitlement.[119] Women's naturalization of their subordinate status, which the "material economy of symbolic goods" often fosters, is another example. Even if there is consciousness of this construct and of the hierarchy, and especially if consciousness generates resistance, it is evident that there is an agonistic situation. The basic point concerning this final trait of the agonistic political in Bourdieu—and it is the culminating one for him—is that *by symbolic process*, force and dominance are intrinsic to what shapes human dispositions and *habitus/hexis*, and so also human practical life and being.

---

118. Rosalind S. Chou and Joe R. Feagin, "Racism as 'Elementary,'" in Chou and Feagin, *The Myth of the Model Minority: Asian-Americans Facing Racism* (Boulder: Paradigm, 2008), 56–62.

119. Debra Van Ausdale, *The First R: How Children Learn Race and Racism* (Lanham, Md.: Rowman & Littlefield, 2001).

Conclusion: Agonistic Politics, Sovereignty, and Symbolic Force

In this concluding section of the chapter, we can sum up the kind of ontological condition that is the agonistic political. In short, it is a condition in which human being is so situated amid historical and social practices that a situation of sovereignty can now be said to characterize our ontological condition, set up especially by routinized exercises of symbolic force, often a symbolic violence. Allow me to unpack these connections more particularly.

In what sense is this a kind of sovereignty? If the agonistic political is so much a part of our being and life, as structured by practices at social sites forging human being, it would seem strange to call this a condition of sovereignty. As we might recall from Foucault's contrast of juridical and biopolitical notions of power, sovereignty pertains mainly to the juridical, a realm and way of power that is largely top-down, attributable to demarcated realms of kings and power holders. Sovereignty does not thrive so much in the play of being and life that Foucault demarcates as the *bio*political. There, power and disciplinary control are more a matter of a more dispersed "governmentality." And yet, as we must emphasize again, the juridical and biopolitical models, sovereignty and governmentality, cannot be so neatly separated. They often overlap so as to reinforce one another, especially when power holders see crises threatening their hold on power. In those cases, the everyday, mundane interplay of life forces of relation, the biopolitical, become subject to exercises of sovereign control. In fact, from the perspective of the agonistic political, we can now propose that the reason the sovereign can reinsert itself into the biopolitics of life in times of crisis is that the governmentality always has the structure of sovereignty in it, functioning in its background, ready to be activated more explicitly. In short, the biopolitical, situations of governmentality, are always tense with an agonism, with conditions for reconstellating sovereignty. Human beings' agonistic politics is always a complex fusion of governmentality and sovereignty, and especially when we examine the routinized symbolic violence at work shaping dispositions and affects of the body.

In the religious field, when guild Theology's imperio-colonial sense maintains its references to a transcendent as basis for an elevated knowledge, with its governing singularity of sense, then it is enhancing the flow of symbolic capital as it constructs sovereignty. The fact that many of the references to the transcendent include an affirmation of the transcending divine figure as also a sovereign figure underscores the point of the persistence of sovereignty in the discourses of Theology. The violence of this exercise in symbolic capital is evident not simply when the transcendent as sovereign God is taken to undergird warfare and domination by a sovereign state. It is also evident in the continuing institutional life of guild Theology that protects the subject-positions of power and leadership—among faculty and administrators—for geopolitically differentiated subjects who have the marks of a European pedigree, and usually also of a hegemonic white and male identity. These are expressive of and are markers of the modern/colonial world system.[120] Again, although it is true that thinkers from long-subordinated and excluded communities have entered the Western guild, they still do so largely at its margins and in the realms of least power, and, more tellingly yet, their discourses are difficult to contain in guild Theology. Instead, they gravitate more toward interdisciplinary sites in the academy and in public life. In other words, they begin to find their place and placement pursuing a discourse of "the theological," undertaking that wandering labor of sense in a singular plural world, which seeks to become resisting and liberatory, especially when working to include "the part that has no part."

What is of note here, however, is that even when those marginalized and subordinated in guild Theology do their work, tentatively within Theology or, increasingly, at the more interdisciplinary sites of the theological, a notion of the symbolic is still relevant, but not in the violent sense Bourdieu emphasizes. Here an important criticism of Bourdieu must be registered, and it prepares the way for our transition from the agonistic political of this chapter to transimmanence in the next chapter.

The violence in symbolic misrecognition that Bourdieu generalizes, and which includes his claim that there is a forced consent extracted from the subordinated, has often been seen as the weak spot in his theory. The usual criticism, as developed by C. Jason Throop and Keith Murphy as

---

120. On these features of "the modern/colonial," see Walter D. Mignolo, *Local Histories, Global Designs* (Princeton, N.J.: Princeton University Press, 2000), 33, 49.

well as by several others,[121] is that Bourdieu insufficiently theorizes human agency. Bourdieu would reply that it is precisely human agency that he *has* theorized when showing how agents are circumscribed, limited, also dominated, even in the moments when they most assume they are exercising their own power. Nevertheless, the rarity of his commentary on how agents might themselves become conscious of their internalized domination does tend to make it hard to see Bourdieu's view of human agency as being much more than a ratification of socially constructed dominators' wills. There is little respect in Bourdieu for the emancipatory power of the symbolic function in the agency of the dominated themselves.

Bourdieu, to be sure, recognizes and values the resistance mobilized by dominated peoples, but he sees this as generated largely by what he terms the "subversive action" created by those equipped by conceptual analysis to "raise consciousness," those who can "bring to consciousness, and so modify, the categories of thought which help to orient individual and collective practices."[122] If we recall brief comments from his early work, *Outline of a Theory of Practice*, it would seem that such symbolic weapons are only modes of "sincere fiction,"[123] which he muses stand a chance of success during times of crises but to which he attributes little force in securing critique and resistance in such times.[124] Bourdieu's views here, making resistance dependent largely on intellectual exercises of critique, seem perilously close to privileging the very "scholastic reason" he elsewhere criticizes in *Homo Academicus*.[125]

In the remaining chapters, I will push this undeveloped sense of the symbolic in Bourdieu toward a more liberatory understanding of the symbolic function. Bourdieu himself, later in life, began to write of a more positive role for symbols and art, and after further criticism of Bourdieu in the next chapter, I will have freed a more positive view of symbols and

---

121. C. Jason Throop and Keith M. Murphy, "Bourdieu and Phenomenology: A Critical Assessment," in *Anthropological Theory* 2, no. 2 (2002): 185–207, esp. 198–99. See also Deborah Reed-Danahay, *Locating Bourdieu* (Bloomington: Indiana University Press, 2005), 9, 35–36.

122. Bourdieu, *LP,* 141.

123. Pierre Bourdieu, *Outline of a Theory of Practice*, trans. Richard Nice. French 1972 (Cambridge: Cambridge University Press, 1977), 171.

124. Ibid., 168–69.

125. Pierre Bourdieu, *Homo Academicus,* trans. Peter Collier (Stanford: Stanford University Press, 1988).

the arts than his studies of symbolic capital allow. We will then be able to turn to "symbolic force by way of artistic form," as Bourdieu put it in a later work, which will enable me in this book to develop the power of art as it works through images, literature, music, poetry, sculpture, textile designing—all as ways to engage and critically counter symbolic capital's violence. This liberatory artistic force amid the agonism of political being, however, is not to be found primarily in guild Theology, nor in the realms of transcendence in which Theology works. It is encountered, to the contrary, in the passings in realms of transimmanence, a notion to which we must now turn. Within this realm, the artful images of those bearing the concentrated weight of the world are enabled to weigh-in to create world anew, world extended, as Nancy emphasizes, with intimacies and spacings that facilitate living.

Chapter Three

TRANSIMMANENCE

There seems to hover somewhere in that dark part of all our lives, in some more than in others, an objectless, timeless, spaceless element of primal fear and dread, stemming perhaps, from our birth . . . , a fear and dread which exercises an impelling influence upon our lives all out of proportion to its obscurity.—Richard Wright[1]

The image is the prodigious force-sign of an improbable presence irrupting from the heart of a restlessness on which nothing can be built.—Jean-Luc Nancy[2]

One of the major reasons that Bourdieu underestimates and so leaves symbols undeveloped is that he sees them tied up with the logics of transcendence. For him, symbols work violence in practice because they usually invoke notions of a sovereign One who anchors a variety of hierarchies and

---

1. Richard Wright, "How 'Bigger' was Born," in *Richard Wright: Early Works* (New York: Library of America, 1991 [1940]), 871–72.

2. Jean Luc-Nancy, *The Ground of the Image* [hereafter, *GI*], trans. Jeff Fort (New York: Fordham University Press, 2005), 23.

domination.³ Nevertheless, Bourdieu, in spite of failing to articulate a function of resistance and survival by symbolic function, hints in his later works that he might be open to such a function. In the preface to *Masculine Domination*, for example, he articulates a hope that he shares with "the organizations that have sprung from the revolt against symbolic domination . . . to invent and impose forms of collective organization and action and effective weapons, *especially symbolic ones* capable of shaking the political and legal institutions which play a part in perpetuating their subordination."⁴

It is in Bourdieu's later writing about turn-of-the-century Neoliberalism, though, where he more forthrightly calls for a scholarship that looks to "a new manner of doing politics," one that would "*give symbolic force, by way of artistic form*, to critical ideas and analyses."⁵ These statements can be read as a kind of new birth of respect in Bourdieu for symbolic power as a positive resource for resistance. It is true that this respect enters late in his career, seemingly only to "give force" to ideas and analyses, often to dramatize the negative consequences of neoliberal ideology that are exposed by conceptual critique. In the same essay, however, he cites the performative creativity of symbolic actions by resisters at the November 1999 antiglobalization protests in Seattle, Washington, and urges that the success of these actions be carefully studied "to uncover the principles of what could be the means and ends of a new form of international political action."⁶

This new deployment of the artful image, to which Bourdieu gestures, requires our thinking outside the ethos of transcendence. Nor will it suffice simply to deploy a reversal of references to the transcendent and speak of pure immanence. Usually such speech reverts to a surreptitious new reference to the transcendent. Thus, Gilles Deleuze and Félix Guattari observe, "whenever immanence is interpreted as immanent *to* Something, we can be sure that this Something reintroduces the transcendent."⁷

---

3. See especially Bourdieu's commentary on the "alchemy of representation," by which structures of governance, particularly in the churches of the Christian West, secure their states of domination, in Pierre Bourdieu, *Language and Symbolic Power* (Cambridge: Harvard University Press, 1991), 105–26, esp. 106.

4. Pierre Bourdieu, *Masculine Domination,* trans. Richard Nice (Stanford: Stanford University Press, 2001), ix.

5. Pierre Bourdieu, *Firing Back: Against the Tyranny of the Market 2*, trans. Loïc Waquant (New York: New Press, 2003 [French 2001]), 25. Italics added.

6. Ibid.

7. Gilles Deleuze and Félix Guattari, *What Is Philosophy?*, trans. Hugh Tomlinson and Graham Burchill (New York: Verso, 1994), 45.

We need to move, then, beyond transcendence and immanence; yet this is not simply a matter of having done with both, declaring a pox on both their houses. It is more a matter of going more deeply into this space that immanence is felt to be "immanent to," and which the transcendent has claimed to be "transcendent to." That space, really a pluriform process, similar to what in Hegel scholarship is often termed a "sublation," is a form that overcomes while preserving what it supercedes. Transimmanence, vis-à-vis transcendence and immanence, is beyond them both in this complex meaning. How are we to think our way into transimmanence in this sense?

The procedure for doing so structures the unfolding of this chapter. In a first section, I will make a first move "beyond transcendence and immanence," introducing transimmanence by surfacing a kind of liminal space in the agonistic political. Such liminal space is especially evident in those who struggle with the world's weight concentrated against them, particularly by dynamics of economic exploitation and racialized and sexualized othering. This takes us into the heart of the agonistic political, into the nucleus of sovereignty, within which, as we shall see, there is a critical resistance to sovereign control. The second section of the chapter is an extended meditation on one difficult passage in Jean-Luc Nancy's *The Muses*, which allows a fuller description of this liminal space as one of "transimmanence." In a third section, I follow Nancy further in articulating the kind of force that the sacral image has, its art-force as mode of contestation amid the agonistic political. In a concluding section, I summarize the relation of the theological to transimmanence as this chapter has rendered it in greater detail.

Beyond Transcendence and Immanence

What we need, therefore, is a change of terrain. This change, however, cannot consist in a return to a fully-fledged transcendence. The social terrain is structured, in my view, not as completely immanent or as the result of some transcendent structure, but through what we could call failed transcendence.—Ernesto Laclau[8]

---

8. Ernesto Laclau, *Populist Reason* (New York: Verso, 2005), 244.

If, indeed, going beyond transcendence and immanence means not merely having done with both, but discerningly entering into a new way in which they remain entangled, in a "sublation" of one another, I propose that we take our first cue about what that entanglement is from the modes of survival taken up by those struggling at the heart of some of the most conflictive sites of the agonistic political, where the weighing of the world concentrates as imposed social suffering. In so doing we will see the operations of the "failed transcendence" of which Laclau speaks, yet we will also have exposed a terrain that is "not completely immanent" either.[9] My claim in this section is that modes of survival among those bearing the concentrated weight of the world are at work at another kind of terrain, a space in society and world where it becomes possible, often necessary, to resort to a form of art, one that has symbolic force. As symbolic, however, it should not be seen as identical to the dominative workings of symbolic capital theorized by Bourdieu. It is forged amid that violent working of capital, but engages it and works in a more liberatory way from a space that points us to the transimmanental.

We can actually find this resort to art-force, first, by returning to one of Bourdieu's own examples, James Baldwin's *The Fire Next Time*, where Baldwin comments on an African American child sensing fear in the context of white power structures that steep his family in the curse of negative capital. This is, for Bourdieu, an example of how symbolic violence emanates from "the magic of symbolic power," a largely negative presentation by Bourdieu of symbolic power.[10] Much of what Bourdieu affirms through Baldwin's discourse can hold good—that the young boy of color raised in a white racist culture will often react with a sense of being controlled, wait in dread "without knowing that he is doing so," confronting something "bottomlessly cruel," sensing the encroachment of an "uncontrollable note of fear" from the nature of parental warnings. But Baldwin's

---

9. Ibid. The transcendences that are "failed," according to Laclau, are not only those that give succor and structure to dominating forces, but also those that constitute a transcendental prioritizing of "one struggle over all others" (241), transfer the transcendent signifier to the "transcendental level of a social a priori" (242), or again, all those approaches that refuse to acknowledge that the political organizing we need can only come from a "constitutive lack" around which the social is organized (244).

10. Pierre Bourdieu, *Pascalian Meditations,* trans. Richard Nice (Stanford: Stanford University Press, 2000 [French 1997]), 169–71.

language has a dimension to which Bourdieu does not advert. True, the child may be in a state of unknowing about the object of his fear (perhaps not perceiving imposed racial difference, in all likelihood not understanding it; why *should* a child "understand" so vicious a construct?). Still, there is nevertheless a discernment in fear, amid the sense of peril, that something is wrong, however unnameable. In the context of racism's toll on parents, the black child knows because of racism's felt threat, if nothing else, a parental authority that is "infinitely harder to please," as Baldwin says. In Bourdieu's own terms, the parents are guardians of symbolic capital to the boy. As much as the fear they telegraph is dominative, it can also become the genesis of a resistance—a resistance to the symbolic and social order of racism that is done along with parents, perhaps without them, sometimes even against them. From this can emerge symbolic forms of artful force as a kind of resistance.

This is confirmed in a passage of *The Fire Next Time* not treated by Bourdieu, just a few pages before the segment he does lift up. In it Baldwin highlights an agency for the black child to which Bourdieu has not attended. It is a passage in which Baldwin is reflecting on his own youthful discernment of the fear, the threat posed by being in a racist republic, and he emphasizes the possibility of mustering resolve to resist, rather than to accept, one's "place" in it. "Every Negro boy," Baldwin writes, "who reaches this point realizes, at once, profoundly, because he wants to live, that he stands in great peril and must find, with speed, a "thing," a gimmick, to lift him out, to start him on his way. *And it does not matter what the gimmick is.*"[11] This reach for a "thing," amid a sense of peril, is what drove Baldwin as a boy to the church. Although he later left the church, Baldwin's embrace of it was a symbolic resistance to the peril posed by his racist world. This places Baldwin's "every Negro boy" within a site of peril, yes, but it is also one of at least potential resistance. In fact, there are numerous studies of oppressed groups' awareness of their suffering, and of what might be called a *habitus* of resistance, a somatized relationality of struggle, to adapt Bourdieu's notions, all in contrast to a mere *habitus* of acquiescence. This somatized relationality of struggle is at odds with, even if never completely free from, a "misrecognizing" process of domination. Such exercises in resistance are not only the traits

---

11. James Baldwin, *The Fire Next Time* (New York: Modern Library, 1995 [1962]), 23.

of children wrestling with racialized environments, but also complexly at work, too, in adult modes of resistance.[12]

An irony of his failure to see this aspect of resistance in Baldwin's text is that Bourdieu's own notion of *hexis*, by which those coerced to "consent" to their own domination through symbolic violence, can nevertheless be used to theorize the very resistance about which Baldwin writes. As I noted earlier, this *hexis* can be evident in the "cool pose" studied as at work in the bodily carriage of young black youth; indeed, also in diverse youth of color—Asian American, Arab American, U.S. Latino/a—who adopt the dress, stylistics, music, and art of youth hip-hop culture.[13] In these cases, their resistance is not dependent only upon a cognitive work of consciousness raising and scholarly critique, as Bourdieu seems to assume in his social theory of practice and in his treatment of the Baldwin text. To the contrary, the resistance is constituted in deploying symbolic, artful gestures and participating in them.

To fully understand the importance of such gestures, I must turn to Giorgio Agamben's theorizing of sovereignty as he treats it in his books *Homo Sacer* and *State of Exception*. These can aid our understanding of the space in which "the gimmick," or the art forms, are wielded for survival. Agamben stresses that the sovereignty that does not just "rule over," but which rules through being disseminated through our life practices, is distinctive in its capacity to determine what living is, by marking and deciding among humans who is to live, who not. The sovereign has power to take life for the founding and integrating of orders, but also for marginalizing, excluding, expelling certain life-forms from the structures of power that sustain life. Dread and fear are brewed for those who are included/excluded, the dynamics on which Baldwin and Bourdieu remark. The more Agamben probes sovereignty's process of including and excluding life, mining the West's history of the state and of power, from Rome's legal/imperial context on up to the present, the more he finds that sovereignty is defined by constituting and ruling over a particular kind

---

12. Examples of these modes of resistance can be found in James C. Scott, *Weapons of the Weak: Everyday Forms of Peasant Resistance* (New Haven: Yale University Press, 1987), and *Domination and the Arts of Resistance: Hidden Transcripts* (New Haven: Yale University Press, 1995).

13. Jeffrey Chang, *Can't Stop, Won't Stop: A History of the Hip Hop Generation* (New York: Picador, 2005); and Imani Perry, *Prophets in the Hood: Politics and Poetics in Hip Hop* (Durham: Duke University Press, 2004).

of life-form, one hovering between life and death, one included within the sovereign's state of ordered beings, but only as a life-form ready to be excluded, easily dispatched to realms and camps of the nonliving, to "zones of abandonment"[14]—ultimately, to death. This is the power to perform an exception, an *exceptio*, the removal of some living forms from the sphere of life, even while constituting them for rule.[15] Those whom sovereign power places in this "state of exception" Agamben refers to as steeped in the state of "bare life." Hence, the English subtitle of his book *Homo Sacer* is, appropriately, *Sovereign Power and Bare Life*.

The history of sovereignty in the West, Agamben argues, points to this bare life with the figure of *homo sacer*. *Homo sacer* is the one who is sacred, set apart, with a life that is not secure in any community. *Homo sacer* "lives" but is marked as killable, "the subject who according to Roman law and belief, can be killed by anyone without that act of killing being condemnable as a homicide, on the one hand, or rationalized and excused as meaningful sacrifice, on the other."[16] Bare life exists as this killable figure, unprotected by state penalty or religious sacrality. When killed there is no murder. Neither is there a sacrifice given, nor a sacrilege committed. It has life, but barely—a bareness, and perhaps barrenness, that signals its delicate position between life and death. Agamben takes this to be the nature of *homo sacer*, the West's "originary political structure" at the nucleus of its practice of sovereign power.[17]

A more dramatic and clarifying example of sovereignty's distinctive power as one deciding on and shaping "bare life" can be found in Abdul R. JanMohamed's interpretation of Richard Wright's literature. JanMohamed deepens still further our understanding of the importance of the symbolic, artful gesture. He finds Agamben's notion of bare life in the

---

14. On the concept of "zones of abandonment," see anthropologist João Biehl, *Vita: Life in a Zone of Social Abandonment* (Berkeley: University of California Press, 2005), 35–44, 282–91.

15. This view of sovereignty, as Agamben himself notes, is a development of Carl Schmitt's familiar definition: "Sovereign is he who decides on the state of exception." Carl Schmitt, *Political Theology: Four Chapters on the Concept of Sovereignty* (Chicago: University of Chicago Press, 2005 [German 1922, 1934]), 5.

16. Agamben's work is a theoretical elaboration of the figure *homo sacer* that long has been commented on by classics scholars. See, for example, Carl Kerényi, *The Religion of the Greeks and Romans* (New York: Dutton, 1962), 108.

17. Agamben, *Homo Sacer: Sovereignty and Bare Life,* trans. Daneil Heller-Roazen (Stanford: Stanford University Press, 1998 [Italian 1995]), 74.

kind of subject that Wright, and black bodies generally, when struggling amid white racism's ritualized threats of violence in the form of lynching and other such acts.[18] JanMohamed's focusing Agamben's theory around these experiences is an important corrective, since so many have rightly criticized Agamben for neglecting "the way bare life is implicated in the gendered, sexist, colonial, and racist configurations of biopolitics."[19] Jan-Mohamed brings to his study of Wright's battle with racialized and sexualized politics his previous research into the colonial struggle of peoples in Africa, drawing on a wide knowledge of the "politics of literature" under the agonistic conditions of entrenched colonialism and imperialism.[20] His thought, then, has a distinctive power and value, interweaving as it does both global and U.S. local analyses.

JanMohamed explores Wright's literary work as a struggle with the intensification of "bare life" faced by subjects living through the U.S. Jim Crow era. Thus, JanMohamed writes of the "death-bound subject," one who "is formed, from infancy on, by the imminent and ubiquitous threat of death." The analogy to Agamben's notion of bare life is clear. The death-bound subject has his or her life as killable life. Here, JanMohamed is intensifying Agamben's image of bare life, by suggesting in his treatment of black subjects in the era of widespread lynching, that bare life was a more severe reduction to "trembling flesh," amid the always present specter of being "raped, castrated, mutilated, abused, etc. at will." When you know yourself to be among a people treatable in this way, writes JanMohamed soberingly, you know there is a force to reduce you to something to be stackable, burned, and then shoveled. Thus, he suggests that the reduction to bare life can be known horrifically as a reduction to "meat."[21]

Let us return now to the meaning and function of the symbolic, artful gesture. Facing the kind of threat JanMohamed delineates, with the world's weight concentrated against one in that way, what is the symbolic

---

18. Abdul R. JanMohamed, *The Death-Bound Subject: Richard Wright's Archaeology of Death* (Durham: Duke University Press, 2005), 8–10.

19. See the excellent critique by Ewa Płonowska Ziarek, "Bare Life on Strike: Notes on the Biopolitics of Race and Gender," in Alison Ross, ed., *The Agamben Effect,* special issue of *The South Atlantic Quarterly* 107, no. 1 (2008): 89–106, at 93.

20. Abdul R. JanMohamed, *Manichaean Aesthetics: The Politics of Literature in Colonial Africa* (Amherst: University of Massachusetts Press, 1998).

21. Ibid., 10–11.

"thing" that can be deployed? The child might deploy a "gimmick," but that is but one example of the child's reach for a form of art to wield amid deep-running dread and fear. Across a wider array of people's struggles with weight concentrated against them amid the agonistic political, various art forms are utilized. They can be exceedingly sophisticated. To stay with the case of Wright's struggle amid the threats of lynching in the era of Jim/Jane Crow, JanMohamed gives special attention to the kind of overcoming Wright sought through his literature, across his many works of fiction and poetry. As I mentioned in the introduction, the perspective of the lynched man's skull in Wright's poem "Between the World and Me" presents "my face a stony skull staring in yellow surprise at the sun" as artful exorcism of the death that haunts him, and that can work, argues JanMohamed, as a fulcrum for liberatory possibility. The plight of the well-known character Bigger Thomas, in Wright's *Native Son,* is another example of Wright displaying in his art a black man's facing of social death, wrestling with it.

I stress that Wright's narrative art is not just a display of suffering. Actually, JanMohamed interprets Wright's larger literary creation as a "series of dialectical overcomings." These overcomings are dependent upon a strategy of *defying* "bare life," not merely living it out as the dominators would prefer. Instead, the deathbound subject intensifies his status of bare life by risking his "actual death." This risking is done by meditating upon how bare life entails a death, is precursor to actual death. This meditation, with the aid of the art form (in a poem like "Between the World and Me," or of a novel like *Native Son*), will foreground fear, rage, dread, amid an accompanying defiance. As a result of this risking, actual death may come (as it does for the lynched in the poem, and for Bigger Thomas when executed in *Native Son*). But what matters is that one achieves what JanMohamed terms a "symbolic death," the subject birthing a "capacity to be in conscious possession of the political meaning of his death." This is what the subject, Bigger, achieves in *Native Son,* and it is what Wright achieves by his entire literary vocation. Wright's activity has "the form of *symbolic work*; precisely through writing he articulates and externalizes the terror, the power, and the value of death."[22] What is worked for Wright is a narrative "meditation on the socio-political influences that

---

22. Ibid., 37 (italics are Wright's).

determined him as a deathbound subject"[23] It is a look back from the present, and thus has an anterior quality, but it also opens a way forward, has future potentiality. I will explore this in the final chapter as a form of anamnestic solidarity—a remembrance of the dead that indicates a future collective project—all of this being crucial to the discourse of the theological as a specter of change. The stony skull in Wright's poem, a "face . . . staring," is the past entering the present and the future, where readers and hearers are confronted with a seething presence from the oft-occluded past. JanMohamed's analysis could be traced here at greater length, as he brilliantly unpacks the place to which Wright's narrative art brings him, a state of liberating remembrance that JanMohamed unpacks as a "future anterior" (borrowing a phrase from Jacques Lacan), or as achieving a "metaleptic reversal" (adapting another concept, this time from Judith Butler[24]), wherein the subject has turned on itself to see itself as formed by power *but in such a way* that it understands itself as a new founding power. This is how "Wright overcame his own devastating racial and political formation by submitting that very formation to a systematic deconstructive, destructive scrutiny and his affirmation of himself consisted precisely in negating the negation inherent in his own formation."[25]

This is complex discourse that we could continue to unpack and explicate. Enough has been articulated here, however, to indicate, contra Bourdieu, that subjects have a much more complex relation to symbolic capital and its violence than Bourdieu recognizes, and that the artful image—in Wright's literature and poetry, but for other subjects using more of art's full set of genres (perhaps especially music, painting, dance, fashion, and so on)—is wielded by such subjects with a sense of agency, complex though it may be.

Moreover, it is this "liminal space of social death," in what Wright terms that hovering "dark part of all our lives" where a primal fear and dread abide, and wherein this wielding of art forms takes place. It is this liminal space that gives us a clue about the space and time we would call transimmanence. It is a place of overcoming not to be found just in the state of things (immanently), nor by appeal to realms beyond the worlds

23. Ibid., 130.

24. Judith Butler, *The Psychic Life of Power: Theories in Subjection* (Stanford: Stanford University Press, 1997), 15–16.

25. JanMohamed, *The Death-Bound Subject,* 288.

of social and historical practice. It is found in the liminal regions of the agonistic political, in which deathbound subjects wield the arts with symbolic force, bearing the concentrated weight of the world as they do.

On Transimmanence

> *One could also put it this way: art is the transcendence of immanence as such, the transcendence of an immanence that does not go outside itself in transcending, which is not ex-static but ek-sistant. A transimmanence. Art exposes this. Once again, it does not "represent" this. Art is its ex-position. The transimmanence, or patency, of the world takes place as art, as works of art.*—Jean-Luc Nancy[26]

Analysis of this difficult passage from Jean-Luc Nancy enables us to go more deeply into this hovering place of dread and fear, in which arts creatively wielded resort neither to pure transcendence nor to pure immanence. Here we must mediate at length on transimmanence. The Nancy extract above comes at the climax of the first essay in his book *The Muses*. It constitutes a multileveled set of reflections on the plurality of art forms, inspirations (one meaning of "muses"), and of sense. In *The Muses*, Nancy circles around the notion of the singular plural character of the world, setting up a conversation between Plato, Schelling, and Hegel; concerning the latter he engages in a creative reading of Hegel's vision in the *Aesthetics, The Phenomenology of Spirit*, and *The Lectures on the Philosophy of Religion*. An entire volume could be devoted to his interpretation of these figures and the way his analysis of them yields a view of what art is, and how art is, today. Here, however, we must limit ourselves to a distillation of Nancy's key insights in order to advance the argument of this book. In this section, I distill four key aspects of transimmanence, each of which builds toward an understanding of the power of the spectral image and illumines its place in a discourse of the theological.

---

26. Jean-Luc Nancy, *The Muses*, trans. Peggy Kamuf (Stanford: Stanford University Press, 1996 [French 1994]), 34–35.

A Dialectical Relation of Transimmanence to Transcendence

Note first the dialectical relation of transimmanence to transcendence. The very notion of transimmanence is broached, given place, treated in the first instance by Nancy in relation to "transcendence." Before saying that art is "a transimmanence," Nancy has to deploy a discursive tack that says art is "the transcendence of immanence as such," and immediately afterward in the same sentence, "the transcendence of an immanence . . ."[27] Transimmanence, thus, according to these constructions, emerges against the backdrop of previous discussions, contestations built around the contrasting terms *transcendence* and *immanence*. One might say that the relation of transimmanence to transcendence is dialectical; it emerges through (*dia-*) and in development with transcendence.

Nancy's notion of transimmanence is a broken and dialectically developed notion of transcendence, but one that breaks that transcendence in a fundamental way, indeed "refuses" transcendence as Michael Hardt and Antonio Negri advise.[28] As we shall see, however, Nancy does so without embracing their Deleuzian immanentalism.[29] Moreover, as we will also note, Nancy preserves, by way of the notion of transimmanence, a philosophical respect for the artful image. In the process he is engaged in a complex reinterpretation of Hegel on the question of how important art is to religion and to philosophy. Again, our primary concern here will be to show how Nancy's view of art in transimmanence is significant to the plight of those laboring under the concentrated weight of the world.

Nancy is not alone in developing his counterposition *to* transcendence as a dialectical engagement *of* transcendence. Ernesto Laclau, when considering the political in populist reason, also relates his political and practical program to transcendence in a way that recognizes that the latter cannot simply be demonized and exorcised. In looking at the social and political character of the present, Laclau criticizes many of the radical immanence theorists of the day. He particularly focuses his critique

---

27. Ibid., 35.
28. Michael Hardt and Antonio Negri, *Empire* (Cambridge: Harvard University Press, 2000), 92.
29. On the "refusal of transcendence, see Michael Hardt and Antonio Negri, *Empire* (Cambridge: Harvard University Press, 2000), 90–91. See also Mark Lewis Taylor, "Empire and Transcendence: Hardt's and Negri's Challenge to Theology and Ethics," in *Evangelicals and Empires: Christian Alternatives to the Political Status Quo,* ed. Bruce Ellis Benson and Peter Goodwin Heltzel (Grand Rapids: Brazos, 2008), 201–17.

on Hardt and Negri, in their book *Empire*. While he insists that immanence cannot be simply affirmed over and against transcendence, he also
does not propose a "return to a fully fledged transcendence." Instead, he
argues as follows:

> The social terrain is structured, in my view, not as completely imma-
> nent or as the result of some transcendent structure, but through
> what we could call *failed transcendence*. Transcendence appears
> with the social as the presence of an absence. It is around a constitu-
> tive lack that the social is organized.[30]

Laclau's transcendence has its appearing as "the presence of an absence."
Note, this *is* a notion for Laclau of transcendence, albeit of a "failed"
transcendence. The dialectical relation to transcendence is necessary, otherwise Laclau's alternative political projects are unthinkable. Laclau must
refer to it, and does, to its failure. As to what this failure consists of, we
only need recall the structures of domination and the patterns of suffering worked by them in sovereign rule's reductions of life to "bare life."[31]
Nancy himself does not use the language of "failed transcendence," but it
is clear throughout his work that he assumes the failure, and so speaks of
the world of his concern as without God, without another world, or as he
says more eloquently in *The Muses*, he focuses on an art that is "smoke
without fire, vestige without God."[32] Yet—and here is the acute tension he
thinks within—Nancy introduces transimmanence in relation to necessary
treatments of transcendence.

   In a similar manner, "the theological" developed in this book is no
simple rejection of Theology, no mere opposite to it, in spite of my
critique of the ethos of references to a transcendent and the imperio-
colonial sense Theology often features. The transimmanence intrinsic to the theological of this book is not the transcendent so important
to Theology. Nor is it one more instance of the various "immanental
transcendences" that appear to be a radical affirmation of immanence.
Transimmanence is not transcendental immanence. What precisely it is,

---

30. Ernesto Laclau, *On Populist Reason* (New York: Verso, 2005), 244 (emphasis in the
original).
   31. For other instances of "failed transcendence" that Laclau has in mind, see ibid.,
239–43.
   32. Nancy, *The Muses*, 96.

and how it is differentiated from transcendental immanence, will emerge presently. Here, the basic point is only that transimmanence *is* thought as dialectical development of transcendence, albeit with a sense of the latter's failure.

In sum, we might highlight both transimmanence's continuity with transcendence and its refusal. As to its continuity with transcendence, we can note the prefix *trans-* (from the Latin *trans,* "across"). In other words, transimmanence is a crossing, but not the kind of crossing at work in transcendence, the latter usually entailing a going above, or outside, the world(s) of society and earth. Nancy preserves from the ethos of transcendence the "crossing over" but without the ascendance (*scandere,* climb). The refusal can be understood as a refusal of the alchemy of ascendance and sovereignty at work in the agonistic political, especially when symbols of the transcendent in Theology support symbolic violence. The ascendance at work in symbolic capital of human practice is what is refused. To understand what this "crossing over" is, which is not an ascendance, we need to continue with further reflection on our extract from Nancy.

The Transitive Character of Transimmanence

A second set of descriptions in the Nancy text highlights what can be termed the transitive character of transimmanence. This emerges from two key phrases that Nancy sets in juxtaposition, which are particularly complex in the English because of ambiguities of the genitive form of the phrase "transcendence *of* immanence." Recall, it is transimmanence that Nancy is seeking to clarify, but within a discussion of how art is transimmanental. His view of art we need not attend to at this point, but note here what more he says about transimmanence in the following two phrases: first, that it is "the transcendence of immanence as such . . . ," and second, "the transcendence of an immanence that does not go outside itself in transcending . . ."[33]

Once again he is utilizing the language of transcendence, even while distinguishing transimmanence from it. What emerge from these two phrases are two slightly different but related clarifications of transimmanence. First, as the first phrase suggests, it is to be distinguished from

---

33. Ibid., 35.

"immanence as such." Immanence as such would be pure immanence. Nancy is affirming that there is no simple affirmation of an absolute immanence over and against transcendence. This is to remind that the transimmanental exists in dialectical relation with the transcendent, and this is important to stress because it is easy to misread Nancy's avowed "atheism" and denials of all other worlds, and of God, as sheer, unmitigated pure immanence. As philosopher Simon Critchley rightly observes in passing, Nancy resists the "social fantasies of 'immanentism'," which would presume social affairs, and the having and making of worlds, are only matters of "fusion, unity, fullness and completion."[34] The first phrase ("transimmanence of immanence as such"), then, accents Nancy's claim that transimmanence is not an undifferentiated immanence posed against transcendence. Transimmanence is something other than and goes beyond "immanence as such."

The second phrase clarifies *how* transimmanence goes beyond. Here, the claim is that transimmanence belongs to a certain kind of transcendence that is also a certain kind of immanence, that is, "an immanence that does not go outside of itself in transcending." This way of putting it is important. Transimmanence refuses, resists, a going outside of itself. Nevertheless, in so refusing, there is still a transcending. To recall our earlier language, in transimmanence there is still a crossing, but a crossing that does not go outside, or "above," this world. Just what is crossed and how the crossing occurs is yet to be discussed; at this point we simply focus on its character as *crossing within*, this transitive quality that is and is not a "transcending." For further explication of this crossing, we must not linger here, and move quickly to his notion of ek-sisting. For in that notion Nancy clarifies further the kind of transitive move that marks transimmanence.

The "Ek-sisting" World of Transimmanence

Transimmanence features a "transitive" work that is "ek-sistant," not "ex-static"—a transitive move that is a being within, not a being or standing without. This contrast now brings into view another important feature, the ek-sisting feature of transimmanence. As stressed by the two previous

---

34. Simon Critchley, *Infinitely Demanding: Ethics of Commitment, Politics of Resistance* (New York: Verso, 2007), 118.

points, transimmanence is not a standing outside of world, but being within it. What more, however, does "ek-sisting" add to our understanding of the transitive move within the world?

Consider the two Greek prefixes, *ex-* and *ek-*, which are contrasted by Nancy in his terms *ex-stasis* and *ek-sistant*. To be sure, both of these prefixes can be translated in the English as meaning generally "out of"; therefore, it can be difficult to see significant difference between them. *Ek-*, in the Greek, however, has a different shade of meaning. It focuses less on a state or a place "outside of" some entity (e.g., world, self)—say, the regions of a town that lie outside of one's room—and more on "outside of" as a movement *toward* an envisioned outside. It is not an actual going outside of, say again, of one's room. It is a going to the "outside of," to the outer parts of, the room, whose edges are deemed "outside" because one does envision, project, an outside (a town, a larger space) beyond room. Here we meet again transimmanence's assumption of and dialectical relation to transcendence. This outer within is a liminal place in the room, because it is at the limit of room. It is a threshold site at which some outside is envisioned without moving outside. The emphasis is on movement toward that outside place that is within.

Ek- as having its original form, *eík*, is a point whence action or motion proceeds. Understood in this way, the being "out of," which is characteristic of transimmanence as *ek-sisting*, is a movement that need not entail moving "out of" world or self but, rather, could be a moving "into" the outer regions within—within some modality of self and world as both are yoked dynamically one to another in ever more complex matrices of world. And even within world or self, the movement of concern is not focused on the origin of the movement any more than on its endpoint. The emphasis falls on the sliding through, the passing through.[35] This movement is central to transimmanence as developed by Nancy throughout his writings. Ek-sisting then is the continual transiting through the complexities of world, finding edges, but also new routes to edges, new dimensions of depths within, tracing the textures and layerings through which movement explores unceasingly.

In *The Muses*, Nancy's description of transimmanence's movement takes many interesting turns. It is a passing, and passage, about "coming,

---

35. See the definition of "transimmanence" in B. C. Hutchens, *Jean-Luc Nancy and the Future of Philosophy* (Montreal: McGill/Queen's University Press, 2005), 168.

departure, succession, passing the limits, moving away, rhythm and syn-copated blackout of being."[36] The latter phrase, "syncopated blackout of being," may be especially puzzling. At this point I suggest it is for Nancy the calibrated, measured, coordinated experience of delirium, loss of place, which is often intrinsic to much passage in existence.[37] Transimmanence's passing and moving, thus, is not only some tranquil floating. It can also be a place of vertigo, often described as facing an "unknown," again, however, an unknown *within* world, self, society and history, the unknown within passings and passages of and through a singular plural world. Wright's "dark part" and "dread and fear" come to mind again. Not all passings are marked by the "blackout of being" ("whiteout" would be be a metaphor working just as well); there are also comings, departures, passing of limits in existence that are not so much fraught with unknowing but with "shocks of recognition," of knowing marked by various kinds of intensification—not just erasure and vertigo, but also surprise, wonder, joy, poignancy, anguish, melancholy, rage. All this belongs to the passing of being *ek-sistant*, as a distinctive quality or modality. All this is transimmanence.

In the passage of *The Muses* that reflects on existing, Nancy also makes clear that on his understanding, existence as *ek-sisting* means also a kind of passing that has a certain orientation to a whole. I have already hinted at this in stressing the movement within as toward edges, depths, and layers and motions among them all. These movements, for Nancy, do not make up a drive for the whole that relates all of existence within some "master narrative," some adequate totality or framework, certainly not a homogeneous one. Here Nancy comments again on the notion of "sense," which I already introduced, writing about "passage as the whole *taking place* of sense."[38] Sense is meaning and being as these always cir-culate in a world that is never not singular plural. Existing, then, and tran-simmanence as Nancy understands it, is *ek-sisting*, emerges as a kind of movement, a passing, "the passage as the *whole* taking place of sense,"[39] where "whole" refers to a full matrix of existing.

---

36. Nancy, *The Muses*, 99.

37. On "delirium" as an aspect of an authentic politics of solidarity, see my presenta-tion in the article "Subalternity and Advocacy as Kairos for Theology," in Joerg Rieger, ed., *Opting for the Margins: Postmodernity and Liberation in Christian Theology* (New York: Oxford University Press, 2003), 23–44.

38. Nancy, *The Muses*, 99.

39. Ibid. Italics added.

Now we can understand better why the way of ek-sisting that is transimmanence is often also discussed by Nancy and his commentators as a kind of "open immanence," as distinct from a "closed immanence." On a more comprehensive level of meaning, one might say that transimmanence is that kind of crossing, transiting, that moves from closed to open immanence. When immanence is "closed" there is usually presumed to be a transcendent One or world of transcendence, some "ground" of the whole which marks the closing, the boundary of what is thought to be immanent. In terms of Nancy's notion of weighted world, closed immanence is the bodies of world "concentrated," piled up, ordered, counted. As "open" transimmanence, without the ethos of transcendence being enforced and reinforced to close it off, transimmanence is the world's weight in extension, with intimacies and distances coordinated so that the multiple modes of the world's weighing are at work. Hutchens gives an elegant summary when he explains that open immanence is

> a totality of infinite relationships without exteriority. The world in its infinitely expressed but singular sense consists of a plurality of singular "ones." Each singular being is not merely an individual together with others in community. It is absolutely different on each occasion in which it is exposed to existence and sharing this exposure.[40]

What "takes place," as transimmanence, is that kind of passage that has the whole singular plurality of world in view, or at stake.

I say "at stake" because, even though the singular plurality of the world is for Nancy incapable of being removed, or totally effaced, the transimmanence of passage in the whole taking place of sense is also something under threat. This becomes especially clear in Nancy's later work. There, "globalization" as a world political, economic, and cultural process emerges in Nancy's discourse, as we noted first in chapter 1, as a kind of nemesis, a homogenizing totality, a globe or *glomus* that weighs down on the preferred singular plural world.[41] That world of transimmanence always needs to be invented, Nancy stresses in this work, with agents of its creation remaining immanent within the world, traversing its passings and passageways. In recalling the *glomus*, we might say that

---

40. Hutchens, *Jean-Luc Nancy and the Future of Philosophy*, 167.
41. Jean-Luc Nancy, *CWoG*, 67–71.

Nancy is again speaking of "weight of the world" as concentrated.[42] With *glomus*, the world's fragile but ineradicable, singular plurality suffers the weight of the West's totalizing process of globalization. Nevertheless, the world also has another complex mode of weighing, the weighing-in of those suffering imposed social suffering, suffering what Nancy calls the *immonde* or *im-mundus* (the "unworld" or "nonworld"). It is intolerable because in it—and this is a key feature of the *glomus*—"everything is weighed in advance,"[43] and is imposed, is burdensome weight, concentrated and destructive of world. Those who weigh-in on the *glomus* are always passing within it, and in so doing ever more intricately giving density, thickness, opacity to world, indeed, making world in re-creative ways by reforging and weaving its delicate extension of bodies. In this reforging and weaving, there is a weighing-in amid the weight of the world that is a creative, world-making force amid and rivaling the *glomus*.

Note here, that in the transiting through the whole of a singular plural world, amid the concentrating weight of glomus, transimmanence also displays a resisting or liberating quality. We do well, therefore, to recall the notion of freedom that Nancy proposes in *Corpus*: ". . . *mutual intimacy and distancing* where bodies, their masses, their singular and always indefinitely multipliable events have their absence of ground (and hence, identically, their rigorous equality)."[44] Claiming this "absence of ground," at least ground (*grund*) that is not also abyss (*abgrund*), is a way to resist closure, the invoking of a transcendent that would be either summit or anchor. It is an ek-sisting always (re)making the singular plurality of the whole that continually releases world from its shifting to *glomus*, its yielding to homogenizing concentration. Ek-sisting is the continual liberating of world's singular plurality. It is a remaking of its whole complexity amid the weight of concentration, by a passing that ceaselessly (re)creates mutual intimacy and distancing. This is liberating, (re)creative power.

How this transimmanental ek-sisting is practiced as the theological we will treat later. Here the concern is to highlight the character of transimmanence as a distinctive mode of existing, of passing that is an

---

42. Jean-Luc Nancy, *Corpus*, trans. Richard A. Rand (New York: Fordham University Press, 2008 [French 2007]), 77, 79.

43. Ibid., 95.

44. Ibid., 101. Italics added.

"ek-sisting." The theological, as an unfolding of transimmanental passage of sense in a world of singular plurality, concerns that which, in Hutchens's language, "passes along being without issuing from within it or from outside it; it slides through social relations without substantializing them. It makes them meaningful without giving them a (reducible) meaning."[45] In this way it is liberatory amid the agonistic political of all being.

What more particularly does this look like? What kind of discourse and practice might be proper to the theological, if this transimmanence is its focus and concern? What kind of discourse and practice is especially appropriate to transimmanence? It is here that we must turn to a final point of commentary on our extract from Nancy, one that deals with the notion of art and the arts.

Transimmanence as "Ex-positional" through Art and Arts

In the extract from *The Muses* Nancy says that "Art is [transimmanence's] ex-position." Transimmanence is ex-positional through art and arts. Here Nancy is playing off of two meanings of "exposition." First, there is exposition as a discursive practice of writing an essay or a speech, as, say, in Kant's philosophical expositions on experience and knowledge, or neo-Confucian scholar Chu Hsi's exposition on "the sage." Second, however, there is "exposition" as the positioning or putting "into place" (Old French, *poser*) of something or someone, setting out things, laying them out in some setting. In this latter sense there is an indication of being, being some place, being located, having world. Art ex-posits. It creates that in which it is entailed, a larger whole, a "being-in-the-world." As this latter construct suggests, there is a consonance between Nancy and Martin Heidegger, particularly the later Heidegger, for whom language has an eruptive, presence-making function for being-in-the-world.[46] This sets Nancy off as distinct from others according to several commentators, such as his contemporary, philosopher Alain Badiou, who makes room for arts

---

45. Ibid., 168.
46. Martin Heidegger, "The Origin of the Work of Art" (with the 1959 addendum), trans. Albert Hofstadter, in *Martin Heidegger: Basic Writings*, rev. and exp. ed., ed. David Farrell Krell (San Francisco: HarperSanFrancisco, 1993), 143–212, esp. 198–200.

but in ways that are much more suspicious of the value of the poetic and other aesthetic reflections.[47]

When discussing art's ex-positing, or ex-positioning function relative to transimmanence, Nancy stresses that "patency of the world" is what occurs. Here he seems to draw on the medical and phonetic uses of "patency" that refer to a state of being unblocked, being articulated with other dimensions such that free flow, passing and connecting, occurs. In other words, the ex-positioning work of art is one of clearing passageways, of moving deftly, creatively to create place(s) and space(s) of world. This is the patency of transimmanence, and it is given with art. Art, and especially the several arts in their multiplicity and plurality, not only mark and register transimmanence, they ex-posit it, they bring it into being. This notion of "exposition" is further clarified in the later work, *Corpus*. There, "the very being (what's called 'existing')," as an ex-positing, gives rise to an aesthetics of bodies in the world. Actually, "aesthetic body" is a tautology, suggests Nancy, so intrinsic is artful ex-position to existing bodies. "One on top of the other, inside the other, right at the other, thus exposed are all those aesthetics whose assembly—discrete, multiple, and swarming—is the body."[48] The ex-positing that is the work of art is the reforging of the world in extension, expressing both "intimacy and withdrawal" in the multiple-sensed bodies of the singular plural world.[49] Again, this is world weighing as extended, not as concentrated. The art of transimmanence is an exposing of the spacing of bodies, a "fixing of the eyes"—Nancy can also use others of the senses in the taking-in of art—wherein "vision does not penetrate, but glides along swerves and follows along departures. It is a touching that does not absorb but moves along lines and recesses, inscribing and exscribing the body."[50]

It will become clearer that this is not a simple revering of multiplicity and plurality, a "diversity" adhering generally in "being-in-the-world," as characterizing so much liberal discourse. Nor is it, as in some deconstructionist thought, an emphasis simply on an endless "play of meanings."

---

47. For example, see Kate Jenckes, "Thinking the Multiple: Alain Badiou and Jean-Luc Nancy," in *theory@buffalo* 9 (2004): 61–73. See also Alain Badiou, "Third Sketch of a Manifesto of Affirmationist Art," in Badiou, *Polemics,* trans. with an introduction by Steve Corcoran (New York: Verso, 2007), 142–48.

48. Nancy, *Corpus,* 35.

49. Ibid., 33, 35.

50. Ibid., 45.

No, the multiplicity and plurality of transimmanence's patency is the kind
that enables creativity—an ex-positing—that (re)creates, makes, releases
and liberates world amid *glomus.* There are discourses of difference and
multiplicity, especially in the liberal discourses that presuppose harmo-
nies of being and that neglect agonistic politics, which actually service
and reinforce the homogenizing and concentrated weight of the *glomus.*
Nancy's ex-posited, aesthetic bodies of world in extension are a positioning *against* the world as concentrated, but this being "against" emerges
from ex-positing a teemingly diverse singular plurality of world, not
simply the tracking of binary opposition. The aesthetic of ex-positing is
birthed precisely amid the friction between the world weighing as extension and the world weighing as concentration of imposed sufferings. This
site of friction is agonistic, but not a conflict of binaries, even if binaries and oppositions are one form of the world's singular plurality. The
labile tension between extension and concentration is one such "binary,"
except that it is never known or eruptive apart from its multiple ways of
being present, or ek-sisting.

Transimmanental Ex-position and Artful Force

Because this multiplicity entails a creative world-projecting and world-
making power, Nancy also introduces a notion of "force" in relation
to transimmanence. With this move, transimmanence's connection to
the agonistic political comes even more to the fore. Here force is carried in "separation, isolation, intensification, and metamorphosis."[51] All
of these modalities are crucial to sustaining and forging extension in
the weighted world. In these ways, "art forces a sense to touch itself,
to be this sense that it is."[52] Consider what a particular work of art does,
whether in music, painting, sculpture, poetry, song; more particularly
still, note Nancy's words about art's force, for creating the "body of
sense" that is world:

> Out of something that was part of a unity of signification and rep-
> resentation, it makes something else, which is not a detached part
> but the touch of another unity—which is no longer the unity of

51. Nancy, *The Muses, 22.*
52. Ibid., 21.

signification. It is a suspension of the latter; it touches on meaning's extremities.[53]

Touching on meaning's extremities is what Wright's poem "Between the World and Me," with both deconstructive and liberating effects regarding social death, constructs for subjects. It is not so much that the extremities intrinsic to a public lynching and burning are depicted in the poem. Instead, it "touches on meaning's extremities" with a force that suspends the sense that would say, "this is a poem about a horrible lynching," and creates a reader's visceral and transformative connection to that scene and its many layers. *That* is the force of art.

Art is transimmanence's way of marking and bringing/forcing into being worlds of passage, with all those comings, departures, successions, passings of limits, and the shifting rhythms of these passages that are often also accompanied by ecstasy, joy, wonder, anguish, rage, poignancy, delirium, and so on. The ex-positing of art, in these senses, is liberatory. Art works in the realm that is *not* "idea." It works as "motion, coming, passage, the going-on of coming-to-presence."[54] In these ways, the arts ex-posit, create the ex-position of the crossings that endlessly circulate in a singular plural world. Art forms and creates world though it's endless ex-positing of these crossings. Art is thus definitive of transimmanence's endless opening of existence to itself.

It is this ex-positing art, so crucial to the discourse of the theological, especially as it works amid the weight of *glomus*, that reforges the delicate liberatory structuring of world in extension amid the piled and concentrated, "weighed in advance," globalizing *immonde*. The theological is not a referencing of the symbols of transcendence that risks the violence of symbolic misrecognition that Bourdieu criticized, but a wrestling with the artful imaging of transimmanence.

What kind of force does this artful imaging have? In *The Muses*, Nancy has a tendency to privilege what he calls "vestige art" over "image-art," the latter connected with theologians' attempts to find the transcendent in a worldly image, while the vestige is about sensible traces, leaving marks of stepping and passing (*transire*, going across) and hence more the

---

53. Ibid. For more examples in Nancy of the "force" of art and the arts, see ibid., 19–20.
54. Ibid., 98.

expositing of transimmanence.⁵⁵ In his later work, however, particularly in *The Ground of the Image*, he turns to discussions of image,⁵⁶ interpreting images as also at work in transimmanence. Throughout the first two chapters of this work, for example, Nancy discusses the image's distinct role as having, again, "the force" of art, an "energy, pressure, and intensity," which also has that ex-positing function: it "crosses" distances, but not through establishing simple continuities. Rather, it enacts in the world (ex-posits) relation. This kind of relation that facilitates passage, Nancy terms a "rapport."⁵⁷ The image again has a tangibility, a sensateness in its ex-positing of world, or, in Nancy's language, as the world is created, "the ground rises to us in the image."⁵⁸ JanMohamed discerns this in Wright's poem, and he terms it the poem's power of "intransitive identification," which works readers' understanding of a predicament across intersubjective boundaries.⁵⁹

Some may object that the treatment above suggests that "force" is not the best term for how transimmanental imaging works, how it ex-posits. Perhaps the language of "intensifying"—or creating intensity—is better than force. Force has a connotation of being not just overwhelming but even violative of nature and human agency. That is clearly not Nancy's meaning, as we have already indicated by the way he links this force to creation of world. Nancy's notion of force is one by which singular plural being shows itself, and in ways that resist *glomus*, the homogenizing blockages of passing and passaging. His notion of force, undertaking this creative purpose, is intrinsic to the emergence of being singular plural, which is not always gradual and predicted, but often comes with the surprise and shock of re-cognition and re-construction of world. Force speaks to the sense of being compelled to new insight, a dimension of even the most sophisticated of argument. This kind of experience of force is crucial to understanding Nancy's meaning of art and its imaging as "sacred," an emphasis to which we now turn.

55. Ibid., 96, for the distinction between "image-art" and "vestige art."
56. Jean-Luc Nancy, *The Ground of the Image* [hereafter, *GI*], trans. Jeff Fort (New York: Fordham University Press, 2005), 140 n.13.
57. Ibid., 3.
58. Ibid., 13.
59. JanMohamed, *The Death-Bound Subject,* 29–30.

Transimmanence, Sacral Image, and Art-Force

Art, as having force, what I often in this book refer to as art-force, is crucial for understanding the notion of "seething presence." The absent, the dead, the unjustly slain, the living dead—these all seethe in the present through and because of their artful rendering. To be sure, it is not just artful form in itself that gives art a force. More importantly, art has force through its synergy with complexities of the psychic and social life, especially with the liminal realms of social death to which many are expelled. It is this being steeped in the agonistic political that prompts sufferers to reach for art. Art attains it force through a resonance with those liminal realms. This resonance enables the spectral seething quality to appear as "monstrous"; indeed, art-force is monstrous to those orders that concentrate the weight of the world against those who bear the world's imposed sufferings. With a monstrous affect and effect, the image has a catalyzing forcefulness so distinctive that Nancy uses the term *sacred* to describe it: "The image is always sacred."[60] This is not to reintroduce notions of transcendence and God, both of which, especially for Western minds, are intrinsically associated with the term *sacred*. It is a way of marking, setting apart (*sacer*, holy), highlighting the distinctive catalyzing dynamic and power that is worked by images of transimmanence. This is not a move outside of world, though Nancy does not hesitate to speak of "the outside of finitude" and "outside of world." But these are, again, outsides *within* finitude and world, where "outside" signifies a distinctive, often unnoticed, qualitative intensification, an openness in which fully differentiated singularities and pluralities interplay. "The 'outside' of the world has an openness that is 'within it'."[61]

How can we understand better this force of art? In especially *The Ground of the Image* and *The Creation of the World* or *Globalization* Nancy has developed a view of the images of transimmanence that develop this notion of force, even as violence and monstrosity, in ways that he suggests are world-forming and justice-making.

Consider the following imagery at work in two different poetic expressions, neither of which Nancy discusses but which I offer to illustrate his

---

60. Ibid., 1.
61. Nancy, *CWoG*, 52.

points about the image's force or violence. Popular U.S. musician and songwriter Bruce Springsteen writes:

> A dream of life comes to me
> like a catfish dancin' on the end of my line.[62]

An oft-quoted Zen *sutra* holds:

> Poetry is like
> a finger pointing to the moon.[63]

Because the images in these poetic expressions would not, I suspect, be heard by most as disturbing or abrasive, nor connoting violence, these expressions are perhaps especially helpful for illustrating what Nancy might mean by their force or violence. If there be such here, in expressions relatively pacific in nature, we may discern better the "force" at work, and find that catalyzing function which renders images "sacred," distinctively powerful.

The force is present in the way the images "throw in my face," suggests Nancy, "an intimacy that reaches me in the midst of intimacy."[64] In the Springsteen lyric, the intimacy thrown is a connection forged between a dream of life and a catfish; in the Zen sutra, between poetry and a finger pointing to the moon. At the same time, this intimacy of juxtaposed phrasings "reaches me in the midst of intimacy"—another intimacy, this one being my own dream of life or my own wonder or inquiry about poetry. All this is done by the poets' artful work, combining and recombining meanings and sounds. This also occurs across the whole range of images' uses, in other contexts of art's creativity—beyond the visual and poetic, also perhaps through "the tactile, olfactory or gustatory, kinesthetic and

---

62. Bruce Springsteen, "The Rising," on compact disc *The Rising* (New York: Columbia Records, 2002). I think I can make my point with the fishing image here, while bracketing the disturbing question, for now, of whether a hooked fish feels pain and whether fishing, or angling, is itself an act of violence, or, as the poet Byron wrote, "the cruelest, coldest and stupidest of pretended sports." For a taste of the debate, see http://www.animal-liberationfront.com/Practical/Fishing--Hunting/Fishing/fish%20feel%20pain.htm, accessed September 17, 2010.

63. *Lankavatara Sutra: A Mahayana Text,* trans. Moti Lal Pandit (Philadelphia: Coronet, 1999).

64. Nancy, *GI*, 4.

so on."[65] Whatever the art form, there often is in the force-full image a deploying of a synesthesia, of multiple sensing, which then creates a new sense of the singular plural world. Wright taps into this force in a way that is even clearer if one considers his entire poem, "Between the World and Me," not just the fragment that JanMohamed considers. There is the seeing (of a clearing in the woods where "the thing" happened), the smelling (of sooty ash and burnt flesh), the touching (of one's skin gripping tar), the tasting (of liquor from the lynchers' gin-flask, or of bloody teeth broken in the lynched man's throat), the hearing (the roar of lynchers' voices drowning out the cries of pain).[66] The synesthesia here—including, finally, a mind frozen, a pity grown cold—is what works the force, expressing not only Wright's sense of there being this "thing" between the world and him, but also a "thing" of which readers also feel the force, as horror, as violation, but also as transforming judgment on the past *and* present.

An entire world "comes out," writes Nancy. Return to the Springsteen lyric. Who has felt the distinctive, dancing pull and tug of a catfish on their fishing line who would not also be able to see and feel through this song's artful image the hand grip on a fishing pole, the taut but tentative stretch of line from one body on a riverbank to the pulling twists of another body, this a riverine one from the depths of water (unseen but known)? Maybe, too, one can see and feel a larger outdoor scene, with woods and breeze, a whole bioregion and narrative memory of journey to and from the river. Then, to have that riverbank world—centered on two bodies joined by taut pulling action—still further likened to a coming "dream of life" is to find oneself facing intimacies of envisioned self, others, and future, having a new world conjured, a new dream state in life for pursuing being and practice. When the Springsteen song ("The Rising") is sung, from which these lyrics can be read in still larger and in often various narratives, there is "a world we enter while remaining before it."[67] This remaining or standing "before it," to which Nancy refers, suggests that even while the image works our entry into a new insight— to be in-sight and in-sense anew—it does not dissolve the sense of being

---

65. Ibid.

66. Richard Wright, "Between the World and Me," in Ellen Wright and Michel Fabre, eds., *The Richard Wright Reader* (New York: Da Capo, 1997), 246–47.

67. Nancy, *GI,* 5.

before something/someone other. A difference remains characteristic of the artful image's world, even as we participate in it.

This world-making, intimacy-engaging image is the power and force of art. How, though, is it a violence? For Nancy, this quality emerges from the fact that disclosed truths generally also have a link to violence. In other words, although truth often comes through patient exploration and slowly nurtured discipline and awakening, it also comes with a certain "violent eruption." This is its "terrible ambiguity." Simple oppositions are "effaced," boundaries are "transgressed," previous claims and misguided opinions are countered. There is a dimension of destruction of other views in truth's emergent criticisms, as well as in its unfolding criticism of its own claims. We are referencing here an aspect of a truth event, though, I stress, not the entirety of that event. The entirety is not best characterized as destructive. In its entirety, it is a restoration of the whole in a recreated sense of a fully reticulated singular plural world, a resonance with being and nature, with world, amid destruction—not destruction in general, but destruction of *glomus*.[68] Even if one were to take a fully *maieutic* view of truth—truth disclosed through a midwifery, a working with the body and bodies—the agonistic, wrenching dimension cannot be fully removed.

Art's images, which make worlds, throwing intimacies together, and "in our faces," to recall Nancy's image, participate in the violence of a critical and necessary agonism. Our gentler spirits, perhaps our more academic gentilities, as well as our legitimate and desperate yearning for peace in an already too violent world, weighted by modes of social suffering especially, may protest against this agonistic, eruptive, seemingly harsh view of truth's and art's coming. To be sure, violence and destruction are not the only qualities of that coming. But one does not know the fullness of an image's power, surely not if exposed to the fullness of an image's work in giving presence to the singular plural world, without facing the ambiguity created by art's violence. Nancy is also clear in distinguishing truth's violence from that of the fist and its distinctive violating acts, and also from the violence of the physical blow.[69]

---

68. Ibid., 18.

69. "The violence of truth . . . is a violence that withdraws even as it erupts, and—because this irruption is itself a withdrawal—that opens and frees a space for the manifest presentation of the true" (ibid.). Regarding art, Nancy avers, "the violence of art differs from that of blows, not because art is semblance, but, on the contrary, because art touches

These differentiations of art and truth from destructive violence do not detract from the element or dimension of violence that resides in images. Is there really violence, we might ask, in the images I have considered, namely, the catfish and the pointing finger? Would it not be enough to affirm that they are "forceful and striking," without also indicating that they are "violent"? The use of the term *violence* remains warranted, I suggest, because there is more than just a forceful or striking move into our awareness. Violence captures the dimension of disorientation or even negation, which is intrinsic to an image's ability to illumine or inspire. Nancy signals this disorientation with his notion of images being "thrown," and thrown "in the face." The catfish pulling on the end of my line is not just a reference to a fishing experience I may have had. The process of likening a catfish's pull on a line to how "a dream of life comes to me" is an unexpected, perhaps disorienting juxtaposition. But through the disorientation, something new seeps in to create or recreate understanding of how the dream of life comes, and, indeed, how it comes in a way that life, finally, not destruction of life, is the value. But again, the whole process is not without the image's violent aspect.

Even more is this so with the Zen *sutra*. As many commentators have stressed, a hearer does not experience the image's insightfulness (here that of a metaphor) without knowing the *non*-identity of poetry and finger. When one hears "poetry *is* a finger pointing to the moon," one also hears the "is not": "poetry is [not] a finger pointing to the moon." This negation, that forced combination in the metaphorical construct, is crucial to a fusion that catalyzes new insight and that may create a world that, again, "we enter while still standing before it."

For those still concerned about claims concerning the violence that Nancy attributes to images of transimmanence, it needs to be noted that this is a legitimate concern. It is not merely some politically correct squeamishness, and should not be dismissed as that, since humanity amid the *glomus* already is steeped in both action and images of violence. Nevertheless, it needs to be underscored as a rejoinder to this warranted concern, that Nancy's "violence" *is* that of an image, and if it bears on practice with violent effect, this is registered in destruction of *glomus*. What kinds of image have this destructive effect, what kind of effectivity

---

the real—which is groundless and bottomless—while the blow is in itself and in the moment its own ground" (ibid.).

undoes *glomus*, is still to be clarified, but it cannot be until we turn to the particular movements and performances of the artful image in the latter chapters of this book. By way of anticipation, however, we can affirm that we are moving to an appropriation of transimmanental violent imagery that has its effectivity through nonviolent but militant movements and spectral practices. When these lance the boil of violence that the *glomus* is, subvert the concentrated weight of the world, violence and destruction often occur. The political movement in the United States for racial justice in the 1950s and 1960s, and in India against British colonialism, are both exemplary of this: imageries and performances of protest (in the Salt March and the March at Selma) were perceived as violent and occasioned violence, even while seeking to be effective through nonviolent movement. The effective image, which seeks to end the violence of *glomus*, cannot presume to be free of violent imagery even though it must, as its highest calling, pursue movements and practices of nonviolence.[70] Thus, its violent imagery also has something of the monstrous, the next theme that must be introduced here.

"The image is of the order of the monster," writes Nancy.[71] There are, of course, some shared etymological connections here that are important. The image's showing, or "self-showing," as "monstrative" or "monstrant,"[72] is linked to its character as also monstrous, as *monstrum*, a prodigious sign "which warns *moneo*."[73] More substantively, though, we might ask what more the monstrousness of the image adds that was not already signaled by pointing out its force, even violence. The response is that the violence of disorientation and negation of common meanings is carried out by an "excess" and "extravagance" of power. The image that disorients or negates in bringing insight does so with a sense of eventfulness, of erupting, and these are noteworthy against a backdrop of a previously undisturbed, uninterrupted surface, as it were. However variegated the surface, as singular and plural it may be, the image irrupts through that

70. Gandhi's own, often neglected comment on the limits to nonviolent practice warrant recall: "He who cannot protect himself or his nearest and dearest or their honor by non-violently facing death, may and ought to do so by violently dealing with the oppressor. He who can do neither of the two is a burden." Gandhi, in Thomas Merton, ed., *Gandhi on Non-Violence: Selected Writings of Mahatma Gandhi* (New York: New Directions, 1965), 36.

71. Nancy, *GI*, 22.

72. Ibid., 21.

73. Ibid., 22.

surface, often unexpectedly, as excess, as a reworking of the familiar. There is a sense of a previous holding back that might have continued, but now is no more. An excess of power has come forth, as a catfish tug from riverine depths awakens a coming dream of life, or as a finger pointing to the moon now unleashes new views, perhaps new experiences, through poetry. In this excess at work in the image's emergence, there is what Nancy terms "the duplicity of the monster." Consider his conceptually difficult language about its self-showing performance:

> The image cannot but have the duplicity of the monster: that which presents presence can just as well hold it back, immobile and dense, obstructed and stuffed into the ground of its unity, as it can project presence ahead of itself, a presence always too singular to be mere self-identical.[74]

With more literary flair, Nancy writes, "The image is the prodigious force-sign of an improbable presence irrupting from the heart of a restlessness on which nothing can be built."[75] The world created and re-created, amid and against the agony of its concentrated weighing, comes as a kind of monstrosity. This monstrousness will be a needed property of the image especially if it is to be a specter to *glomus,* especially if it is to be adequate to the task of making world in "brutal collision" with the forces of globalization that would unmake the world.

Transimmanental World-Making

The world-forming images of transimmanence are a prodigious force needed in relation to the operations that Nancy groups under the term *globalization.* It is not to be confused with the French term *mondialisation.* While the French and English terms are often used interchangeably, Nancy seizes on a slight difference of meaning between them. *Mondialisation* connotes a "more concrete tonality"[76] in his transimmanental vision and practice of world-forming—the process of ever inventing the sense of world in its singular plurality. World is made amid and against the threats

74. Ibid., 25.
75. Ibid., 23.
76. Ibid., 27.

and structures of "globalization," which is a more homogenizing process (culturally, politically, economically) that usually generates patterns of exclusion and unjust suffering.[77] Indeed, he sets up the contrast in a way that poses transimmanental world-making as a challenge (a "divine threat"[78]) to globalization. In so doing, we can here understand the theological in relation to Nancy's transimmanence but, more importantly, in agonistic relation to the world weighted as globalization. This weighting of the world creates an excess of suffering marked by the inequalities inhering in its global division of labor and power.[79] Globalization is another exercise of sovereignty, again complexly structured, as anthropologist Aihwa Ong emphasizes, as a "graduated sovereignty," in which governments give power to corporations to control citizens in zones that intersect financial capital and global production in different ways. In this graduated control, sovereignty still exercises a disciplinary role, especially over labor, continuing "to exploit incarceral modes of labor control."[80]

Transimmanence, the dynamic passaging that always keeps open the singular plural world amid globalization, confronts *glomus* in ways as multiple as the manifold domains of shared life and in that life's ever widening and numerous contexts. Nancy's transimmanental world-making, thus, is creative in ways that (re)make complexity in a striking number of various forms of sharing. Just how various these can be is noted in Nancy's *Compearance* (1992). There, he names the forms of sharing that constitute the "we" in and through which sense circulates, transimmanentally,

> Economic dependencies, the transformation of classes, of statutes, of generations, of families; the differences of the sexes, of cultures, of languages; the networks and disruptions of communication; the interaction of scientific and technical interactions; organ transplants and genetic and viral recombinations, contagions, pollution, ecological entanglements, the world system of geographers, the measuring of eight billion "human beings," the interbreeding of plastic and musical

77. Enrique Dussel, *Ética de la liberación: en la edad de la globalización y de la exclusión* (Madrid: Editorial Trotta, 1998); and Marjorie Kelly, *The Divine Right of Capital: Dethroning the Corporate Aristocracy* (San Francisco: Berrett-Koehler, 2003).

78. Nancy, *GI*, 22.

79. James H. Mittelman, *The Globalization Syndrome: Transformation and Resistance* (Princeton: Princeton University Press, 2000), 41–54, 90.

80. Aihwa Ong, *Neoliberalism as Exception: Mutations in Citizenship and Sovereignty* (Durham: Duke University Press, 2006), 78.

designs; the tectonic slippage of public space, or cities, states, asso-
ciations, sporting fields, spectacles and demonstrations, the blurring
of war and truces . . .[81]

Such a diversity of forms (classes, musical designs, etc.) and of dynamic
relations and events (dependency, transformation, disruption, war, entanglement, tectonic slippages, etc.), such a "we," shows that the matrix
of the singular plural world is far more complex than can be handled
by discourses on "self-other," "subject-object," "subject-subject," or even
intersubjectivity. The "we" that signals the forms of sharing of the world
is far more complex, entailing practices, institutions, and forces of relation. In short, the singular plural world pervades the whole complexity of
being and practice, or power and symbol, examined in the earlier chapter
on the agonistic political.

In his book *The Creation of the World* or *Globalization*, Nancy discusses the complex panoply of "the we," of the singular plural world, as
"the political" (*le politique*, again, as distinct from the realm of "politics,"
la politique) in which the whole life of the world is "at stake." Note again
how with the political we have an antagonism, emergent here as part of
the world's labile tension, its agonism. The political emerges as a "limit
concept," again highlighting senses in which reflection and practice seem
driven to their limits, pressed to ask questions with urgency, a sense of
high stakes being involved. Nancy's continuous interrogation of globalization highlights the urgency.

In contrast to the way world-forming activity, with its transimmanental imaging and passaging, keeps the world open, endlessly circulating
sense and highlighting the world's singular plurality, globalization cuts
short this process. The "we" cannot thrive. The multiple unfolding of the
singular plural is subordinated to another kind of networking, a totalizing
one that works not with the "more concrete tonality" of world-forming,
but with an "indistinct integrality."[82] This is not to say that there are no
distinctions or differentiations in the cultures and dynamics of globalization. There are differences—geographical, cultural, also economic and
personal—but these are put to servicing a privileged "difference" that

---

81. Jean-Luc Nancy, "*La Comparution/The Compearance*," trans. Tracy B. Strong, *Political Theory* 20, no. 3 (August 1992): 371–98, at 375. Cited from Hutchens, *Jean-Luc Nancy
and the Future of Philosophy*, 49–50.
    82. Nancy, *CWoG*, 27.

creates a privileged "same"—of class, of race (the "fundamental pillar of modernizing globalization"[83]), of language (primarily, English), of nations and emergent power organizations that serve them (largely G-7 nation-states who compete but also maintain their distance from others, from long-colonized nations and regions). To recall Nancy's language in *Corpus*, in the world of globalization this is not so much the world weighing as extension through intimacies and withdrawals, but a concentration, a "non-world (*im-mundus*)" which is intolerable, working on "the presupposition that everything is weighed in advance."[84]

The privileged difference and privileged sectors make up "the political" of globalization that is a "megapolitical, metropolitan, or co-rational" network, which Nancy discusses as always in agonistic strife with a network of resisting peoples, groups, and organizations worldwide.[85] The network of the *glomus* "happens to us," he writes, "sweeps over us by the name of globalization; namely, the exponential growth of the globalist (dare we say *glomicity* of the) market—of the circulation of everything in the form of a commodity . . ."[86] This is no mere demonization of the large-scale, of the network *per se*, or of the impressive inventiveness of contemporary cultures of communications and transportation technology. Nancy features few if any Luddite resistances toward these new technical accomplishments; in fact, his thought can also be read as a celebration of them, since he lauds the necessary and valuable "denaturation" of life that human technological being in the world has entailed.[87] This denaturing makes the very problematizing of nature, and human relation to it, possible. To acknowledge this, however, is not to endorse the present "eco-technological enframing" that is globalization today, which spurs and is caught up in the "vanishing of possibilities of forms of life and/or of common ground" (a *singular plural* "common ground," of course).[88] Nancy thus makes no sweeping depreciation of technology's gifts. Instead, the focus of his concern is "the political" that

---

83. David Theo Goldberg, *The Threat of Race: Reflections on Racial Neoliberalism* (London: Wiley Blackwell, 2009), 329–30. In the same volume, see especially, "Neoliberalizing Race," 331–39.

84. Nancy, *Corpus*, 95.

85. Nancy, *CWoG*, 35.

86. Ibid., 37.

87. Ibid., 86–87.

88. Ibid., 95.

frames, constitutes, and animates the ecotechnology of globalization. The agonistic political that reigns today, expressed in today's structures of sovereignty, is one of "agglomeration." With this, the concern is "with senses of conglomeration, of a piling up," in particular, "with a sense of accumulation that, on the one hand, *concentrates* (in a few neighborhoods, in a few houses, sometimes in a few protected mini-cities) the well-being that used to be more urban and more civil, while, on the other hand, also proliferates what bears the quite simple and unmerciful name, misery."[89]

The clustering of these inequalities and technological power and economic reason's ability to work them for the benefit of a relative few, privileged classes, enables the West's powers to assume new forms as empire. Nancy leaves the notion of "empire" unspecific, sometimes naming U.S. hegemony as empire, since it is the dominant controller and purveyor of global military force. At other times, empire is for Nancy the West's matrix of nations, the G-7, which still leads the agenda of economy and international world trade politics. Although new and creative challenges are being offered by the economies and new regionalist strategies of Venezuela, China, India, and Brazil, the G-7 nations are still the present powers that draw special vigor from legacies of colonizing empires and are able to maintain a sovereignty of the West.[90]

There are, of course, the arguments to be made about centuries of change that have brought welcome transformation in humanity's conditions, even for its poor.[91] It is, however, the differentiations of inequality and various disparities in the concentrated political structures of globalization that have grown comparatively greater[92] and create an onerous misery. Thus, growing immoderation marks the "unworld," "the *glomus*," as "land of exile" and "vale of tears."[93] Indeed, in reaching to describe

89. Ibid., 33. Italics added.

90. Walter D. Mignolo, *Local Histories/Global Designs: Coloniality, Subaltern Knowledges, and Border Thinking* (Princeton: Princeton University Press, 2000), 277–80.

91. Eric Hobsbawm, *At the Edge of the New Century* (New York: New Press, 2001), 157–59.

92. On documenting this disparity, primarily in the United States, see Edward N. Wolff, *Top Heavy: The Increasing Inequality of Wealth in America and What Can Be Done about It* (New York: New Press, 2002), 29–30. On increasing global inequities of income and health care, see medical anthropologist Paul Farmer, *Pathologies of Power: Health, Human Rights, and the New War on the Poor* (Berkeley: University of California Press, 2004), 102–3.

93. Nancy, *CWoG*, 42.

the *immonde* that is *glomus,* Nancy writes of its appearance as "unprecedented, geopolitical, and ecological catastrophe," characterizing globalization also as "the suppression of all world-forming of the world."[94]

In *The Creation of the World* or *Globalization,* Nancy writes with a
sense of poignancy about a time in post–9/11 global politics when the
prevailing discourse of rulers becomes that of two figures of monotheism. In the contrasts between the tactics of the United States and those
of an Islamist fanaticism, there is a clash, as Nancy writes, between, on
the one hand, a God whose name "is inscribed on the dollar," and, on
the other, the God in whose name one declares a "holy war."[95] However
different from one another, they both inscribe their obeisance to Hegel's
undifferentiated infinite, the "bad infinite." In contrast, what is needed is
respect, a surfacing of desire, for what Nancy terms an "actual infinite," a
world-forming dynamic that inscribes an infinite justice.[96] By infinite justice, Nancy means recognizing and doing justice to the singular, holding
it as valuable. But this also means a doing justice to and valuing of the
plural—the full panoply of "the we"—in the ways the many singularities
are always creating a touching/nontouching fullness of relation. "Justice
is thus the return to each existent its due according to its unique creation,
singular in its coexistence with all other creations. The two measures are
not separate: the singular property exists according to the singular line
that joins it to the other properties. What distinguishes it is also what connects 'with' and 'together.' "[97]

This all is something of the grand philosopher's dream, Nancy knows.
For as he says, "This infinite justice is visible nowhere. On the contrary,
an unbearable injustice is unleashed everywhere: the earth trembles, the
viruses infect, men are criminals, liars, and executioners."[98] One only has
to recall the extent of torture's rise within the repertoire of "civilized"
twenty-first-century state powers to grasp the point.[99] In short, a globalizing "concentration" seems to overwhelm the world's more delicate
"extension."

---

94. Ibid., 50.
95. Ibid., 39.
96. On the "actual infinite," see ibid., 46.
97. Ibid., 110–11.
98. Ibid., 111.
99. Darius Rejali, *Torture and Democracy* (Princeton: Princeton University Press,
2007).

Part of the conceptual import of Nancy's language and theory is that he does not merely counter his "infinite justice"—the desirable actual infinite—to the infinite injustice of the world. He knows that they are bound up with one another, the just and the unjust, the world's weight shifting often from extension to concentration, just as are conjoined the theological with Theology, transimmanence with transcendence. Thus, he acknowledges that "justice cannot be removed from the mire or fog of injustice, any more than it can be projected as a supreme conversion of injustice." Or again: "The infinite, as it were, appears and disappears, divides itself and coexists: it is the movement, the agitation of the general diversity of the world, which make the world (and which 'unmake' it as well)."[100] Nevertheless, he does not allow this complexity to mask, or prevent emphasizing, a profound recognition of the lines that generate conflict within the complexity. He retains a sense of opposition of the special difference between the singular plural world itself, and globalization's *immonde* and growing injustice. In fact, he writes, "it is intrinsic to infinite justice that it *must collide brutally* with injustice."[101] The tautness and tenseness of the concentrated weight of the agonistic political is again evident.

With this mention of the agonistic political as a brutal collision we are called not so much to war (holy or unholy), as waged by the champions of monotheism and transcendent sovereignties, but to a world-making by way of the image, that figuring force which Nancy describes as always "sacred," as coming with a distinctive violence, a prodigious sign-force, belonging to "the order of the monster." This sign-force is the inventive power of world forming amid the *glomus* today. As a transimmanental power, it and its infinite justice "[do] not come from the outside (what outside?) to hover above the world, to repair or accomplish it. [They are] given with the world, in it and as the very law of its givenness."[102]

We might ask: "given *with* the world and *in* it—where?" And "given," *how*? The response of this book is that it is a discourse, "the theological" that gives a more formal shape to the effort of world-making amid globalization. It is a newly congealing discourse that traces transimmanental world-making in distinctive practices, spectral practices, working amid

---

100. Nancy, *CWoG*, 111–12.
101. Ibid., 112. Italics added.
102. Ibid. Italics added.

the ruins of "failed transcendence" at a variety of disciplinary and public sites, engaging the imperio-colonial sense of Theology, but unsettling it, haunting it, dissolving its power.

Conclusion: Transimmanence and the Theological

At the conclusion of this chapter, we are in a position to say more clearly what "the theological" is, what are the features of its discourse. If, as I have argued throughout, the theological is a discourse that is carried by and traces transimmanence in agonistic politics, how more particularly does this treatment of transimmanence enable us to describe the theological? Four features are now evident.

First, *the theological is a discourse that has as its primary subject-matter (the subjects and topics that matter most to it) the change of terrain that is "beyond transcendence and immanence."* It assumes the failures of the logics and practices of the transcendent, thus moving beyond it, yet the theological does not posit pure immanence as antidote, knowing that a more discerning move is necessary, namely, a tracing, lifting up, and journeying through the terrain of transimmanence. This is the change of terrain. Engaging the transimmanental terrain not only takes us beyond transcendence by dialectically working amid, through, and then breaking with its failings; it also goes beyond "immanence as such." This going beyond immanence, however, is not a going "outside of" immanence, but "into" it—in a distinctive way. That distinctive way requires our recalling the other features of the theological.

Second, as we have noted from the beginning, *the theological is marked by its exploring the terrain of transimmanence from those sites of disciplined inquiry that are not typically worked by guild Theology.* In the Western academy, then, the theological works more typically from trans-disciplinary and cross-disciplinary sites. The theological as a discourse can be found at work in multiple disciplines: comparative literature, philosophy, American studies, history, critical geography, political and critical legal theory, psychology, and in various program units of educational institutions, especially those that foreground the histories and subaltern knowledges of the often hidden, excluded, and repressed perspectives of those who have borne the concentrated weight of the Western world, laden with ethnocentrism and racism, colonialism and imperialism. Such program units would include the various "centers"—of Asian American, U.S. Hispanic and Latino/a, African American, as well as those that focus key problems in the concentrated and weighted world: poverty, environmental and ecological catastrophe, injustice suffered by women, immigrating families in the United States, and gendered, sexual, racial othering everywhere.

In addition to being transdisciplinary and cross-disciplinary in Western academe, the theological also works at disciplinary sites that are intercultural and countercolonial. As "intercultural" the theological that traces transimmanence is borne usually by those who are at least bilingual and bicultural, who think across worlds congealing language, family custom, gendered and sexed identities, economic modes, organized political power, and racial/ethnic heritage in distinctive ways that make up the polycultural and pluricontextual world.[103] These give the texture and complexity to the singular plural world of which Nancy so often speaks. The theological concern with transimmanence, however, if it is to trace the complex extension of these world contexts against the often virulent "concentration" of the world's weight in the modern/colonial world system, must also be countercolonial. It is insufficiently intercultural to think only across the cultural differences of, say, British and U.S. cultures, or German and French ones. For the theological, reflection also works across what Mignolo terms "the colonial difference," the difference between colonized and colonizer—a difference always racially marked and sexually charged, and still often featuring a functional division between the world South and the global North, or a "functioning core" of developed nations versus "nonintegrating gap" made up of more neglected, usually exploitable, peoples and nations.[104] The theological works out of, reflects from and upon, these divides as a wound of thought. This may require

---

103. On the intercultural, see Choe Hyondok, "Introduction to Intercultural Philosophy: Its Concept and History," in her *In Quest of Intercultural Philosophy: Communication and Solidarity in the Era of Globalization* (Gwangju, Korea: Chonnam National University, 2006); and Raúl Fornet-Betancourt, *Interculturalidad y globalización neoliberal* (San Jose, Costa Rica: DEI, 2000).

104. Mignolo, *Local Histories/Global Designs*, ix–x, 197. On both race and sex in colonialism and imperialism, see Anne McClintock, *Imperial Leather: Race, Gender, and Sexuality in the Colonial Contest* (New York: Routledge, 1995). On the "functioning core" versus "nonintegrating gap" division, see Thomas P. M. Barnett, *The Pentagon's New Map: War and Peace in the Twenty-First Century* (New York: Putnam's, 2004).

the "anticolonial" moves of a Frantz Fanon, the "decolonial" readings and practices of a Gloria Anzaldúa and Laura Pérez, or the postcolonial moves of an Edward Said, Homi Bhabha, or Gayatri Chakravorty Spivak. Indeed, in these intercultural and countercolonial discourses theologians have been at work, often within guild Theology. In doing so, however, they often exist at Theology's margins, and their interests and theoretical resources seem increasingly found in the more cross-disciplinary sites that better serve their intercultural and countercolonial aims and projects, whether working in a U.S. or more international field of reference.[105]

Third, *the theological's tracings focus on the transitive qualities of the world.* The theological is concerned with the inventive passing and passages that preserve and create the openness of the singular plural world, an openness *insofar as it is also* a freeing, a liberating of world from the *immonde* and immiseration of our times. It is the running of meaning, the creative transit through a singular plural world amid the indistinct and homogenizing integration of the *glomus*. As transitive, a kind of running and running on of meaning, entailing openness to that "wandering labor of sense" (Rancière), its character is not a "crossing" (*trans-*) that moves above or outside world, but into the modes of the world's weighing. It traces and addresses, particularly, the shifting of the world's weight from extension to the concentrations of imposed social suffering at work in immiserating poverty, mass incarceration, stubbornly pervasive racism, and the powerful constructs of gendering and sexualizing. Its transitive concern also focuses on the organizing of social and political movements, in which practices are forged and congeal as counterweight to concentrated power, as catalyst for reforging world, for reconstructing world's delicate extension.

---

105. For a sample of theologians at work in these ways, see María Pilar Aquino, "Feminist Intercultural Theology," in María Pilar Aquino and María José Rosada-Nunes, *Feminist Intercultural Theology: Latina Explorations for a Just World* (Maryknoll, N.Y.: Orbis, 2007), 9–28; Wonhee Anne Joh, *Heart of the Cross: A Postcolonial Theology* (Louisville: Westminster John Knox, 2007); Victor Anderson, *Creative Exchange: A Constructive Theology of African American Religious Experience* (Minneapolis: Fortress Press, 2008); Peter C. Phan, *Christianity with an Asian Face: Asian-American Theology in the Making* (Maryknoll, N.Y.: Orbis, 2003); Naim Stifan Ateek, *Justice and Only Justice: A Palestinian Theology of Liberation* (Maryknoll, N.Y.: Orbis, 1989); J. Kameron Carter, *Race: A Theological Account* (New York: Oxford University Press, 2008); Laurel Schneider, *Beyond Monotheism: A Theology of Multiplicity* (New York: Routledge, 2008); and David A. Sánchez, *From Patmos to the Barrio: Subverting Imperial Myths* (Minneapolis: Fortress Press, 2008).

Fourth, *the theological comes to its fullest expression in the prodigious force of artful signs, a symbolic force that engages the agonistic politics produced by practices of symbolic capital, but in ways that open the world, seek to liberate it from its concentrated and onerous weight.* To accent this point, we may return to the case of Richard Wright's narrative and poetic art forms, with which we opened this chapter. His art emerges, recall, from the liminal world of social death that resulted from concentrated racialized and sexualized practices of the Jim Crow era. Wright's art has its force as an intentionally crafted schema for dealing with the transimmanental worlds where the agonism of political being is strongly marked. Wright himself was conscious of this, both of his crafting of schema, and of his doing so from the highly charged liminal space that transimmanence is. To clarify this, I call attention, first, to the following passage that treats of his creative mode of working amid his own estrangement. From that liminal space of estrangement and vision, he developed his main character, Bigger Thomas, in his well-known novel *Native Son*. Within that space, Wright was

> more than ever resolved toward the task of creating with words *a scheme of images and symbols* whose direction could enlist the sympathies, loyalties and yearnings of the millions of Bigger Thomases in every land and race . . .[106]

The theological is concerned with this "scheme of images and symbols." This scheme can take various forms and be given by different genres of art; in Wright's work, it is a highly elaborate narrative and poetic art form that enables a jousting with social death, in pursuit of that "symbolic death" which yet can have emancipative effect. Here again is Nancy's prodigious, at times monstrous, art form. Note that Wright is aware of the space from which he works; in fact, he generalizes it beyond the plight of black men in the United States to realms where the "loyalties and yearning of the millions of Bigger Thomases in every land and race" can be found. For all of them, the solaces of the transcendent may be gone, "metaphysical meanings have vanished." He adds, too, "God no longer existed as a daily focal point of men's [sic] lives; a world in which men

---

106. Richard Wright, "How 'Bigger' was Born," in *Richard Wright: Early Works* (New York: Library of America, 1991 [1940]), 865. Italics added.

could no longer retain their faith in an ultimate hereafter."[107] Again Wright observes, and accepts, his contemporaries' denial of the transcendent. He does not try to prop it back up, or put it back in place. Instead, his art form's symbolic force is wielded in relation to transimmanental space, and he eloquently summarizes his own description of this space. This is evident in a second passage that I quote at length here from "How 'Bigger' was Born," since it foregrounds so effectively the transimmanental space of the agonistic political that is the special concern of the theological.

> There seems to hover somewhere in that dark part of all our lives, in some more than in others, an objectless, timeless, spaceless element of primal fear and dread, stemming, perhaps, from our birth . . . , a fear and dread, which exercises an impelling influence upon our lives all out of proportion to its obscurity. And, accompanying this *first fear*, is, for the want of a better name, a reflex urge toward ecstasy, complete submission and trust. The springs of religion are here, and also the origins of rebellion.[108]

Wright goes on to suggest that the main character, Bigger, not only had no religion or helpful frame, he also had no scheme. It is precisely this which is provided in the "scheme of images and symbols" in Wright's often harrowing but path-making art-force. And it is this which is the discourse of the theological.

Wright's work is only one such example of this art-force. Scholars of the theological have available to them a wide array of genres of art that might be deployed to similar effect, providing a "scheme of images and symbols" that enable our tracing and reflecting on how those suffering social death, the world's concentrated weight, its imposed social suffering, still create world, forge liberatory space. Readers will have their own art forms to propose; and while there are too many to name, I list here just a few that I have used over the years, personally or in the classroom: Leslie Marmon Silko's *Ceremony* and *Almanac of the Dead,* Joy Kogawa's *Obasan* and *Itsuka,* Toni Morrison's *A Mercy* and *Beloved,* Ngũgĩ Wa Thiong'o's *Matigari,* Jean Genet's *Our Lady of the Flowers,* William Gibson's *Neuromancer,* Ha Jin's *War Trash,* Graciela Limon's *Erased Faces,*

---

107. Ibid., 865–66.
108. Ibid. 871–72 (italics in the original).

Jessica Hagedorn's *Dogeaters*, Ana Castillo's *So Far from God*, Paula Gunn Allen's *The Woman Who Owned the Shadows*, Lawrence Thornton's *Ghost Woman*, V. J. Naipaul's *A Bend in the River*, James Baldwin's *Going to Meet the Man*, Alice Walker's *Meridian*.

Collections of poetry work this power, too; exemplary are Martín Espada's *Poetry Like Bread*, Peter Dale Scott's *Minding the Darkness*, Kim Chi Ha's *Cry of the People and Other Poems*, Otto René Castillo's *Tomorrow Triumphant*, Victoria Chang and Marilyn Chin's *Asian-American Poetry: The Next Generation*, Aimé Césaire's *The Collected Poetry*, César Vallejo's *The Complete Poetry*, and June Jordan's *Kissing God Good-bye*.

These works and more tap the power of art, in story and other genres, working from that liminal space of transimmanence. The story in literature is especially powerful. "Going into a narrative," reminds Margaret Atwood, "is a dark road." Moreover, "It is a desire to make the risky trip to the Underworld, and to bring something or someone back from the dead." When brought back in the story or the art, the dead often, though not always, "want the blood of the living, or at least they want that blood put at risk on behalf of their own cause."[109] The art-full story is crucial to the prodigious force wielded by those facing and living social death. With the struggle and deaths of indigenous peoples weighing heavily upon her, Silko reminds, "You don't have anything if you don't have the stories."[110]

The great storytellers can weigh-in with their art in their music, too, challenging the concentrated weight of the world, notably Bob Marley and Bruce Springsteen, also Michael Franti, Common, and the hip-hop Persian-Filipino duo Blue Scholars, and the storied articulation of agonistic woundedness and overcoming in the *p'ansori* singers of Korea,[111] the laments and resilience of the blues, the mournful song-tales of Portuguese *fado* music, or the *duende* sensibilities of flamenco.[112] The above artists and many others of many times can write, sing, dance, and be joined by

---

109. Margaret Atwood, *Negotiating with the Dead: A Writer on Writing* (New York: Anchor, 2002), 156, 166, 176.

110. Leslie Marmon Silko, *Ceremony,* deluxe ed. with a new preface by the author (New York: Penguin, 2006 [1977]), 2.

111. Chan Park, *Voices from the Straw Mat: Toward an Ethnography of Korean Story Singing* (Honolulu: University of Hawaii Press, 2003).

112. Frederico García Lorca and Christopher Maurer, *In Search of Duende* (New York: New Directions, 1978).

others who paint, sculpt, or embroider the stories that yield artful forms of symbolic force to rival symbolic capital's modes of domination.

Some may well ask, So is the theological here proposed but a new name for reflection on the arts and its powers? It is that, but if only that there would be little gained in this book's foregrounding and theorizing the theological. What I am proposing is that it is a formalizable discourse that, yes, reflects on the power of art forms, but especially of the popular art form that relates in a unity the discourses of each of the four traits treated in this conclusion. This means, to recall the other traits, that the theological is a distinctive discourse that not only deploys prodigious art forms, but does so by discerning and working the change of terrain that is beyond transcendence and immanence, the realm of transimmanence. It is also a polysited discourse, evident not only beyond the guild discourses of Theology and throughout the disciplines of the Western academe, but especially in those of intercultural and countercolonial reflection. Third, when it traces the arts it does so as a transitive process of creating world, that wandering labor of sense that not only wanders but in so doing also liberates amid the concentrated miseries of *immonde*, with all its dread, its fear, its agony. This is the theological.

Chapter Four

THE WEIGHT OF
TRANSIMMANENCE

The Guantánamo poems are full of longing; they sound the incarcerated body as it makes its appeal. Its breathing is impeded, and yet it continues to breathe. The poems communicate another sense of solidarity, of interconnected lives that carry on each others' words, suffer each others' tears, and form networks that pose an incendiary risk not only to national security, but to the form of global sovereignty championed by the US.[1]—Judith Butler

The poems penned by the prisoners of Guantánamo carry not just the weight of suffering, but also their own more positive, transformative weight—the weight of transimmanence, the subject of this chapter. These poems and their artistic force are not the only such carriers of this weight—we have already met this force in the literary narratives of Richard Wright, for example—but the poems, mentioned by Butler above, inaugurate this chapter in a distinctive way. They prompt us to take up more explicitly the question of the strange weight of transimmanence as a "weighing-in," by

---

1. Judith Butler, *Frames of War: When Is Life Grievable?* (New York: Verso, 2009), 61–62.

which the "seething presence" of the dead, to recall Avery Gordon's language again, haunts the present from that terrain beyond transcendence and immanence. From that terrain, their ghostly presence is also spectral, that is, laden with threat and promise. But what is the threat, and what the promise? And how do either body forth in the present? By responding to these questions I develop further the notion of the theological.

This chapter responds to such questions, first, in an opening section that interprets the prodigious art forms, and others like them, as carried by *practices*. With the turning to art forms that have force, which can (re)make world under conditions of *glomus*, there also emerges the need to examine practices as the carriers of that force, to engage the agonistic political and its forces. Sufferers of imposed social suffering use the force of art, weigh-in with it, not just as art, but as *practice*. In a second section, I stress the importance of the symbolic art-force of transimmanence because the transcendent, with its sovereign powers that concentrate weight against the weak and poor, itself makes use of an aesthetic regime, and thus the symbolic art-force of transimmanence is needed to deflect and undermine its power. Moreover, since both Richard Wright's and the Guantánamo poets' art emerge from sites of torture, and because the torture room is so stark a site of the practice of sovereignty, this second section also turns to torture to illustrate the destructive consequences of sovereign power's way of using its aesthetic regime. The chapter's third section considers one more time how it is that the prodigious art form has its weight, how it is effective, even at times working an incendiary, liberatory impact. A concluding section turns again to the theological, summarizing it this time as spectral practice.

Consider the Guantánamo poems. They are communications from men gathered in cages at the U.S. detention center at Guantánamo Bay, Cuba, founded in 2002. On that site, they are denied the protections of due process mandated by both U.S. and international laws, exposed to a whole gamut of torture techniques developed over decades of experimentation by the United States.[2] The U.S. detention center there, and the

---

2. One of the earliest studies was by constitutional-rights attorney Michael Ratner and investigative journalist Ellen Ray, *Guantánamo: What the World Should Know* (White River Junction, Vt.: Chelsea Green, 2004). See also historian Alfred W. McCoy, *A Question of Torture: CIA Interrogation, from the Cold War to the War on Terror* (New York: Metropolitan Books, 2006), 179–87, 195–98. James Yee, a chaplain working at Guantánamo who was later relieved of his post and was himself tortured, reported his findings in *For God and Country: Faith and Patriotism Under Fire* (Washington, D.C.: Public Affairs, 2005).

secret interrogation site within it, "Camp No"—a nickname for the site because its existence was always to be denied[3]—are part of an archipelago of U.S. secret holding centers, so-called black sites that dot the globe, where U.S. authorities use a variety of Justice Department-sanctioned torture techniques.[4] Dozens of Guantánamo confinees have attempted suicide by hanging and "by hoarding and then overdosing on medicine, or by slashing their wrists."[5] The U.S. media-drenched public knows almost nothing of this present travail, or of the mothers and fathers of these prisoners, who have given in the past tenderness to their now confined children, and who hoped at least a little for them, probably much. The media rarely grants these prisoners the status of storied lives. Instead, we are given names that conjure the fears of a U.S. public: Salah Ahmed Al-Salami, Mani Shaman Al-Utaybi, and Yasser Talal Al-Zahrani, to name first the notable three who reportedly hung themselves in 2006 but whose deaths now are being investigated as possible homicides at the hands of U.S. interrogators.[6] For much of the U.S. public the names signify the feared and dreaded "other," usually terrorist "other." It is a natural reflex for an American public that since its founding has built its national sensibility and state power by the construction, demonization, and then exploitation of "others," working the deaths and stolen lands of indigenous peoples, the enslavement of African bodies, and from its inception a war-making opposition to "the Orient" ("Far East" and "Middle East)[7]—in short, deploying a set of binaries that set a white, virtuous sovereignty of national project against swarthy, darker, nonwhite cultural, sexual, and religious "others." Ronald Takaki's *Iron Cages* remains a detailed and persuasive testimony to the role of these binaries in the U.S. nation's development.[8]

3. Scott Horton, "The Guantánamo 'Suicides,'" *Harper's Magazine* 320, no. 1918 (March 2010): 27–37, at 29.

4. Jane Meyer, *The Dark Side: The Inside Story of How the War on Terror Turned into a War on American Ideals* (New York: Doubleday, 2008).

5. Marc Falkoff, ed., *Poems from Guantánamo: The Detainees Speak* (Iowa City: University of Iowa Press, 2007), 4.

6. Horton, The Guantánamo 'Suicides,'" 27.

7. Robert J. Allison, *The Crescent Obscured: The United States and the Muslim World, 1776–1815* (New York: Oxford University Press, 1995), xiv–xv, 59.

8. Ronald Takaki, *Iron Cages: Race and Culture in 19th-Century America.* Revised edition (New York: Oxford University Press, 2000).

The Theological and the Practice of Weighing-In

The Guantánamo poems register the weight of transimmanence. They set before us yet again the prodigious art forms of the theological, but with this section, as in the entire chapter, I stress that the power of the art to weigh-in with force lies in its being wielded as practice. It is at this point that our political ontology of practices, which constitutes the agonistic political, returns to become important. It is practices, in synergistic interplay with powerful art forms of "spectral humans," that haunt the national order steeped in its racialized, religious, and nationalist binaries. In so doing the confined and tortured also refurbish their dignity, bear witness to their plight, and dream release and justice. Simply the poem titles convey much: "O Prison Darkness," "Homeward Bound," "Death Poem," "Humiliated in the Shackles," "They Cannot Help," "Hunger Strike Poem," "I Write My Hidden Longing," "Ode to the Sea," and "Even if the Pain." About the weighty power that holds him, styled as a modern-day pharaoh, one poet articulates the haunting specter he and his fellow prisoners embody: "The whirlpool of our tears/Is moving fast towards him/No one can endure the power of this force."[9] As Wright's relic of a grisly lynching and burning, the "stony skull," becomes a face ". . . staring in yellow surprise at the sun," so the Guantánamo poet's caged and battered body and psyche is a body breathing, expressing what Ariel Dorfman wrote when first feeling the poems' impact, "the simple, almost primeval, arithmetic of breathing in and breathing out."[10]

This again is Richard Wright's "power of the skull." To illustrate this prodigious art-force, I have perhaps relied too much on the gifted art of the published and dramatic writer Richard Wright. I have done so, however, not to foreground that kind of productivity as the only site of the theological, of this prodigious art-force. By no means. I am thinking, too, of the scrawls of the confined on their walls; of that tray hurled by the prisoner I recalled and discussed in chapter 1 of this book. Was it not an artful gesture, a skilled defiance of concentration, for that tray to be angled through the air just right to hurl past and through the bars of confinement? I think especially, however, of the scores of those abandoned

---

9. Ustad Badruzzaman Badr, "Lion's Cage," in Falkoff, ed., *Poems from Guantánamo*, 28.

10. Ariel Dorfman, "Where the Buried Flame Burns," in ibid., 71.

not only in the mass incarceration of U.S. prisons, but also in the communities and institutions, "zones of abandonment," that anthropologist João Biehl portrays movingly in his book *Vita*. That work is his ethnography of the life of Catarina, a young woman increasingly paralyzed and said to be mad, living out the rest of her days in one of the spaces of abandonment that one finds throughout Brazil's large cities—and indeed, globally. Hers is a form of life deemed as "no longer worth living," to be set aside from the living. Biehl reminds rightly, however, that we miss something when we too easily render this "bare life" (Agamben), because among the abandoned, as he writes, "language and desire continue."[11] Biehl counters with another term, "ex-human," embraced "most hesitantly," he admits. It is born of Catarina's own self-references as "ex-wife," having an "ex-family," but used by Biehl to name the orders of things, people, and systems that render her an "ex-," which thereby cross her off the lists of those still deemed "human." Catarina's language and desire persist, and to this she bears a powerful witness in what she refers to as her "dictionary," a collection of personal reflections, given in lists of phrases, often stanza-like poetry. These are something like "raw poems," observes Biehl, which exhibit her constant effort "to address the unspeakable of the ordinary" and to lift up also her compatriots in abandonment who are "counterparts to the null, the place of leftover into which she has been cast."[12] With her raw poems—and here there is continuity with Wright's raw poem "Between the World and Me"—her "dictionary" filled over twenty-one notebooks, testifying to a strange life in her body, refusing erasure amid abandonment. "Her seemingly disaggregated words," Biehl writes, "were in many ways an extension of the abject figure she had become in family life, in medicine, in Brazil. All her efforts to constitute herself as daughter, sister, woman, worker, lover, wife, mother, patient, and citizen were deemed worthless." Yet, there is the sounding of her incarcerated/abandoned body:

I want to leave and never again be treated by the state
By the women of this city
By Jandir Luchesi
Death sentence

---

11. João Biehl, *Vita: Life in a Zone of Abandonment* (Berkeley: University of California Press, 2005), 318. Used by permission of University of California Press.
12. Ibid., 318–19.

Here I am being expelled
I don't have my body for business
I am not a slave
I do what I can do

I prefer death a thousand times
Than to endure leftovers

Trenches
Locked in captivity
People go hungry
They want us to be a bag of misery
And say that Catrina is a whore
Sacrilege
Skull
Burying place
Miracle Hole Mystery
Catieki[13]

There is both art-force and life-force in this raw poem from a zone of abandonment. It rises amid the *glomicity* (Nancy) of globalization—and it is world-making. It is the mode of the sufferer's weighing-in against concentrated weight. There remains in Catarina's raw words the "I prefer" against the "They want" and the "They say." The one with this speech, this resiliency of voice—with these poems raw with life—defies her family, her neighbors, and the neoliberal labyrinths of practitioners who had declared her "ex-human." Along with the defiance, though, there is again the sheer persistence of her life-power, her desire, her work.

It remains to underscore and repeat, that however dramatic the individual performance of Catarina's "raw poems," of Wright's highly crafted poem of the staring skull and his entire literary oeuvre, or of the Guantánamo poets, their weighing-in is a *practice*. The prodigious art-force that is the fullest expression of the theological is not only an individual creative performance, as necessary and impressive and as cunning and

---

13. Catarina, "The Dictionary," from Book XII, in ibid., 338–39. "Catieki" is one of the powerful names she gives to herself in her duress, along with other forms like "Catkina," "Catakina," and "Catkine." On these name changes see also João Biehl and Peter Cooke, "Deleuze and the Anthropology of Becoming," in *Current Anthropology* 51, no. 3 (June 2010): 317–51.

brilliant a display of individual resilience though it may be. As a practice of weighing-in, the creators of these art-full forms take on their force through the ways humans organize actions with and through them. Practice, as we noted through the social-site ontology of chapter 2, entails some constraint and enablement in action, an asymmetrical power of the social (vis-à-vis individuals). Especially if we recall Schatzki's theory of human practices as complex linking phenomena—involving a feel for the game, rules, teleo-affective structure, and general understanding—we will know that the individual's resilient art-force has its force *as linked* in practical activity, to other persons, structures, and practices. This is forthrightly named in this chapter's epigraph by Judith Butler. If the Guantánamo poems continue to breathe, she writes, it is because they communicate a "sense of solidarity," an "interconnection between lives," and most importantly, because they "form networks." It is this linking and linked practical activity that gives the art forms their force, making them a risk to even U.S. projects in global sovereignty.[14]

Bourdieu's social theory of practical logic is crucial, too. From his perspective, we recall that the prodigious art forms have their force as part of a somatized sociality, a social life that is inscribed in a socialized body, always facing domination worked by the exercise of symbolic capital playing across the many social fields. Now that we have surfaced the transimmanental working of schemas of images and symbols, which are not merely the schemas of domination worked by negative symbolic capital, we can preserve the powerful emphasis that Bourdieu, along with Schatzki, gives to practical activity as locus of the artful forms of symbolic force.

Such practical activity is the matrix of this prodigious art-force, of the "scheme of images and symbols" (Wright). It is what makes the art prodigious. The importance of networking in practices is evidenced by reflection on the pathways of practice the art forms have had to travel. For the Guantánamo poems to "form networks" the release of their poetry had to be fought for. Their coming to light was a product of lawyers, activists,

---

14. "The military . . . confiscated nearly all twenty-five thousand lines of poetry composed by Shaikh Abdurraheem Muslim Dost, returning to him only a handful upon his release . . . the Pentagon refuses to allow most of the detainees' poems to be made public, arguing that poetry 'presents a special risk' to national security because of its 'content and format.'" Falkoff, ed., *Poems from Guantánamo*, 4.

publishers struggling to resituate them, re-site them outside the camps and compounds of detention. U.S. activists have performed the poems, dressing themselves in the orange garb of detainees and reciting them at new sites, "voicing" the poets' words for audiences throughout the world. Wright's poetry and oeuvre, too, are dependent upon the practices of publishers, of teachers and Web masters who disseminate his powerful poetry and novels, as well as upon the brilliant writing activity of literary critics like Abdul R. JanMohamed, and his archaeological excavation of Wright's "death-bound subject." Moreover, Catarina's raw poems are, as anthropologist Biehl acknowledges, arranged in stanzas by him so as to be published in a university press book for Beihl to comment upon still further before audiences organized to hear him on campuses and in bookstores. Biehl admits to being present, an actor in Catarina's world, and so points, I believe, to the *inter*subjective practical matrix of her powerful art form. She, as others, can become a haunting, seething presence, in part because of his working "through juxtaposed fields and particular conditions in which lives are—concurrently, as it were—shaped and foreclosed."[15] In connection with Catarina comes the disclosure that her "human ruin is in fact symbiotic with several social processes: her migrant family's industrious adherence to new demands of progress and eventual fragmentation, the automatism of medical practices, the increasing pharmaceuticalization of affective breakdowns, and the difficult political truth of Vita as a death script."[16] All this, as Biehl shows eloquently, is a result of the neoliberal regime of globalization.[17] The theological is *a practice* of weighing-in, involving a plurality of subjects who carry the art form, enabling it to become spectral—potent and portentous for countering the concentrated weight of the world.

---

15. Biehl, *Vita*, 20.

16. Ibid., 18.

17. I use the term "neoliberal regime" to name the disciplinary and exploitative apparatus of globalization, which also includes a new information technology (IT) as a set of techniques and technical culture that is not always in itself exploitative, however much the neoliberal regime always controls IT culture. *Neoliberalismo* is much discussed in Latin American settings (e.g., Rosalía López Paníagua, *Pobreza y neoliberalismo en México: formas de acceso de la vivienda y alternativas política social* [México, D.F.: Universidad Nacional Autonoma, 2004]). For a profound study from a U.S. publisher, see Aiwha Ong, *Neoliberalism as Exception: Mutations in Citizenship and Sovereignty* (Durham: Duke University Press, 2006).

Aesthetic Regime, Sovereignty, Torture

To understand more fully the significance of practices of the prodigious art form, which constitutes the weight of transimmanence, it is important to emphasize that art's force is already at work in the concentration of weight that disseminates oppression and imposed social suffering. It is intrinsic to the power of the sovereign state to wield an aesthetic. The agonistic political, as I have already emphasized, has at the heart of its practices a teleoaffective structure, which binds affective assumptions about beauty and desire to the *telos* of actions (Schatzki), and the practices of the agonistic political also are created and sustained by an "economy of symbols" that works domination across diverse fields of social life (Bourdieu). Now that we have corrected the ways both Schatzki and Bourdieu underplay the symbolic, often neglecting the powers of the artful image, we can reemphasize art's importance by noting how it engages the aesthetic dimension of sovereignty's power.

Jacque Rancière's notion of the "aesthetic regime" enables discernment of how the arts help effect practices of sovereignty, and how the aesthetic regime might also be contested. I will illustrate sovereignty's dependence on an aesthetic regime by reference to the practice of contemporary torture. This will be appropriate here, given that the prodigious art forms we have considered emanate from sites of torture: Wright's from the lynching and burning rituals of the U.S. past, the Guantánamo poets' from the torture detention units of the U.S. present, even Catarina's from Vita, a Brazilian city's zone of abandonment.

Aesthetic Regime

What is an aesthetic regime? As I use it here, it is neither the mere ornamentations of state, nor the beauty or impressiveness of its dramatic practices. Rancière takes a different approach. He links the notion of aesthetics not just to the Greek form, *aesthesis* (sense), but especially to *aesthetos* (sensible). The major subject matter of "aesthetics," then, is not just sensing, but that which makes something sensible, able to be sensed in the ways it is formed in social life. The focus falls on a "distribution of the sensible" (*partage du sensible*), a dividing of worlds that "reveals who can have a share in what is common to the community, based upon what they do and on the time and space in which this activity is performed."[18] This is what makes aesthetics so crucial to the political. In distributing perception, a division is often worked, such that organized affect gives value and significance to some over others. Especially, because of its function in distributing the sensible, aesthetics is at "the core of politics."[19] In that core, the aesthetics participates and helps in constructing a sovereign state's regime. It is thus crucial to the concentration of the world's weight as sovereignty. Across many works, and especially in his *Disagreement,* Rancière criticizes Western modernity and its view of politics, especially when it is not attentive to this distribution of the sensible at work in the political order.[20] Modernity, as we have already stressed with the aid of Gayatri Chakravorty Spivak's analysis, not only fails often to advert to the politics of its aesthetics, but also fails to note how axiomatic to its colonialism and imperialism are its foreclosures of certain subjects. An aesthetic regime, the way it divides the sensible, the visible, the sayable— indeed, the grievable (Butler)—is crucial in effecting the foreclosure of certain subjects whom Spivak traced when uncovering the axiomatics of European colonialism and imperialism.

For Rancière, "politics" in the sense worthy of its name, as he argues in *Disagreement,* will think and work across all the parts of society, especially "the part with no part." When the truly "political" thinker, in Rancière's sense, thinks and works with "the part with no part," the modern order is unsettled. It is crucial to Rancière's thinking, too, that the social orders that would exclude "the part with no part" often deploy a police function to maintain the order consonant with its aesthetic regime. Rancière throughout declares his intent "to reserve the term *politics* for an extremely determined activity *antagonistic to* policing: whatever [activity] breaks with the tangible configuration whereby parties and parts or lack of them are defined by a presupposition that, by definition, has no place in that configuration—that of the part of those who have no part. . . ." Rancière continues, "Political activity is *whatever shifts a body from the place assigned to it* or changes a place's destination. *It makes visible what had no business being seen, and makes heard a discourse where once*

18. Jacques Rancière, *The Politics of Aesthetics: The Distribution of the Sensible,* trans. Gabriel Rockhill (New York: Continuum, 2004), 12.

19. Ibid., 13.

20. Jacques Rancière, *Disagreement: Politics and Philosophy,* trans. Julie Rose (Minneapolis: University of Minnesota Press, 1999 [1995]), 58–59.

there was only place for noise; it makes understood as discourse what was once only heard as noise. . . . Spectacular or otherwise, political activity is always a mode of expression that undoes the perceptible divisions of the police order . . ."[21] The political, on this view, contests foreclosure. To recall the theoretical point I introduced into Nancy's notion of weight, the political seeks, works for, and creates the shift of bodies from concentration to world-making extension.

It is the special role of the prodigious art-force of transimmanence to contest the ways the aesthetic regime of state power polices the foreclosures, refusing to shift its weight from concentration to extension. Through the police function, guided and buttressed by its aesthetic regime, the modern state even seeks "political control over dying, the dead, and the representation of the dead," as Claudio Lomnitz remarks about the Mexican state. Nevertheless, Lomnitz quickly adds: "the dead always exceed or fall short of their [the agents of the state] manipulative intentions."[22]

It is precisely the role of the prodigious art-force of transimmanental practice to "exceed" and "fall short" of state manipulations, especially as the state seeks representation of, and hence control over, death and dying. If the nucleus of sovereignty, as we have noted, is the power of exception, a declaration that includes the excluded but only in realms of intended "bare life" (Agamben), of "trembling flesh" and "meat" (JanMohamed), or of "ex-humanness" (Biehl), it is precisely these declarations of the exception that are refused by transimmanental practice's artful form. The "part that has no part," I suggest, by demanding its part, which must be some remaking of the whole, is involved in what I would call a "repartitioning" of the sensible world through its own art-force, and so displays and effects its presence in practices of that sort. One recalls the long pilgrimages of indigenous peoples of 1992, snaking across the landscapes of South, Central, and North America, marking the five hundred years of colonization in the Americas, with their marches, dances, art images, and signs, insisting, "*¡No nos aniquilaron!*/They did not annihilate us!" This is not only to assert, "We are still here!" It is also to say that the political order built on an attempt to annihilate them is an illegitimate one. These and more such forceful practices of sign-force will often deploy the

---

21. Ibid., 30. Italics added.

22. Claudio Lomnitz, *Death and the Idea of Mexico* (New York: Zone Books, 2005), 483.

"violent" and "in-the-face" kind of imagery that Nancy discerned, as "the prodigious force-sign of an improbable presence irrupting."[23] I suggest that the power of the skull in Wright's poetry, the poetry of the Guantánamo prisoners, and of Catarina's "raw poems"—and many more such exemplary wieldings of art-force—do precisely this, especially as practice gives them a teleo-affective structure and power, pointing them toward centers of state power, contending with the onerous concentrations of the weight of the world.

We must now test such claims about art-force in transimmanental practice, though, by reference to one of *the* most onerous of state manipulations and controls over death and dying, namely, torture. It, too, depends upon and expresses the aesthetic regime of sovereignty. Can the sufferers of the weight of the world—the direct sufferers and those of us who dare to know of them—effect a challenge to the torture state? How might spectral practice of art-force exceed these manipulations of the tortured body and the tortured body politic it would produce? I turn to torture, first, as it depends on an aesthetics, noting especially its practice as a site of sovereignty, before ending this chapter by pointing out ways that "spectral humans" forge a spectral practice that, indeed, does take on the torture state.

Torture

The practice of torture in modernity and the contemporary period exhibits not only the structure of state sovereignty but also its dependence upon an aesthetic regime. Torture endures, holds good, in part because of an important aesthetic regime that, especially in the case of the United States, serves also economic, political, and cultural interests. Torture depends on the aesthetic regime's distribution of the sensible. It needs the divisions, boundaries, and set of inclusions and exclusions that an aesthetic regime provides to state powers seeking to maintain and reassert sovereign power.

Torture's dependence upon an aesthetic regime as this kind of distribution of the sensible is evident in three key aspects of torture practice: its practical understanding/*habitus,* its teleo-affective structure, and its crucial

---

23. Jean-Luc Nancy, *The Ground of the Image,* trans. Jeff Fort (New York: Fordham University Press, 2005 [2003]), 23.

general understanding or "structure of feeling." In the "practical understanding" or *habitus*, torturers, according to Darius Rejali in *Torture and
Democracy*, learn though craft apprenticeship not only the techniques of
torture, but also a "feel for the game."[24] This "feel" develops as they are
nurtured by ideologies that divide the world into those who belong to the
realm of the human and those who do not, because they are enemies of
the state, "dirty," terrorists, immigrants, "ex-human," hopeless street children—all deemed failures at meeting various social status expectations.
Being schooled in such a division among peoples and groups is part of a
disciplined *aesthesis* required by the practice of torture.[25]

In the "teleo-affective structure" of torture practice, too, *aesthesis* is
just as important. Here, recall, a practice nurtures a link between goal-
oriented activities and an affective group bonding through moods and
emotions. This bonding, especially, is dependent upon a division of the
sensible. This division not only demarcates between the torturer and tortured, but also sets the stage at the torture site for a sense of theatricality
and spectacle that is often intrinsic to exercises of atrocity. This sustains
what analysts of torture such as Franz Graziano, Elaine Scarry, and Jacobo
Timmerman, himself a survivor, have often noted at the sites of torture:
the perpetrators' sense of performance and theatricality.[26] Torturers use
masks, aliases (stage names), and nurture fantasies that turn sites of torture into what they can even describe, disturbingly, as having an "institutional beauty."[27] The *aesthesis* is necessary to the forging of the teleology
of a group of torturers with their sense of affective attachment to the
process. Indeed, they are constituted as a group by that *aesthesis*.

Then, finally, the dimension of practice called "general understanding" (Schatzki) or "structure of feeling" (Raymond Williams) is also operative in the practice of torture. Torture practice in this dimension is highly
dependent upon an aesthetic regime as carried in the romanticized rheto-
ric of nationalism and affective belonging to homeland, especially. This

---

24. Darius Rejali, *Torture and Democracy* (Princeton: Princeton University Press, 2007),
421.

25. On the importance of this division among "humans" in relation to torture, see also
Franz Graziano, *Divine Violence: Spectacle, Psychosexuality, and Radical Christianity in
the Argentine "Dirty War"* (Boulder: Westview, 1992), 93–96.

26. On the "strategic theatrics of atrocity," see ibid., 61–106; Elaine Scarry, *The Body in
Pain: The Making and Unmaking of the World* (New York: Oxford University Press, 1985),
37; and Jacobo Timmerman, cited in Graziano, *Divine Violence*, 94.

27. Graziano, *Divine Violence*, 94–95.

conveys to agents and supporters of torture a reinforcement of their bifur-
cated view of world, usually of one's own nation against others. There
is with this bifurcation also a distribution of values that celebrates one's
own national project as distinct from those of most others. Such general
understanding, or "structure of feeling," pervades the practice, unifies it,
and gives it an often nearly irresistible force for eliciting citizen consent
or toleration. In the case of the United States especially, loyalty to nation,
and threats real and perceived to it, to "the homeland's security," attend
almost all debates, and often forestall criticism of the use of "harsh interrogation" and torture of suspects in U.S. detention. The powers coursing through U.S. publics, past and present, which historians discuss as
"American exceptionalism,"[28] require a continuing aesthetic division and
a framing for citizens, regarding which collectivities in the international
community are laudatory and worth protecting and which are not.

The aesthetic regime, operating in the practice of torture in these
ways, clearly indicates that the torture room cannot be seen as an exceptional site of barbaric extremity, isolated from the wider matrix of social
and civil life. Its intersubjectivity as historical and social practice links the
torture cell to groups and often to nation and state power. As a practice
it is human organizing that continually links actions so that torture cell
and other sites are bundled together. Torture practice is, as Rejali emphasizes, a *bricolage* that takes place with historical traditions and present
social interests.[29] All this lends further credence to criticisms of the exceptionalist views of torture that see it only as the occasional aberration of
"rogue" states. Making this point most recently is Jasbir Puar, in her book
Terrorist Assemblages, who argues that torture is a "fundamental modality of citizen production," part of the practical logic of the U.S. nation-
state's "war on terror."[30] In this claim, argued throughout her book, she
is building on scholars such as Rejali and Talal Asad, who also have criticized the "exceptionalist" view of torture. There are significant differences
between Rejali and Asad, and between both of them and Puar, especially
because Puar so well shows how the constructions of gender, sexuality, and nation are all intertwined in the practice and public imaging of

---

28. See William V. Spanos, *American Exceptionalism in the Age of Globalization: The
Specter of Vietnam* (Albany: State University of New York Press, 2008), 187–242.

29. Rejali, *Torture and Democracy,* 421.

30. Jasbir K. Puar, *Terrorist Assemblages: Homonationalism in Queer Times* (Durham:
Duke University Press, 2007), 100.

torture.[31] All are in agreement, however, that the practice of torture is so linked into broader matrices of social life that one can speak of "modern democratic torture," that is, torture as intrinsic to the exercise of the sovereignty defended by modern "democratic" powers. Asad concludes in one analysis, "The use of torture by liberal-democratic states relates to their attempt to control populations of those who are not citizens."[32] Rejali deploys a "civic discipline model" to explain this prevalence of torture in modernity. He sees it rooted in Athenian democratic tradition that used torture as a way to mark the boundary between slave and citizen through scarring, in traditions emanating from U.S. slavery and forced labor practices, and also in the use of torture techniques by U.S. police and prison institutions.[33] Rejali's summary and discerning words about how torture is used in modern life today are important to quote at length:

> Whether one can go here or there without fear of being beaten, whether one can travel in one's car without being pulled over or electrified, these are experiences constitutive of citizenship. Citizenship, after all, is not merely holding a passport, but understanding what treatment is due to one in daily life. . . . Some people expect torture, while others would be shocked to know it was "happening here." These different life experiences amount to, in some cases, insurmountable barriers between groups in democracies. In these cases, torture is not merely following pre-established legal understandings of who is or is not a citizen, falling solely on foreigners. It is conferring identities, shaping a finely graded civic order. *It reminds lesser citizens who they are and where they belong. . . . [We] live in a world in which torture is returning to a role it had in ancient Greece, inducing civic discipline and shaping civic order in liberal democracies.*[34]

---

31. Ibid., 79–113. See also Brian Keith Axel, *The Nation's Tortured Body: Violence, Representation, and the Formation of a Sikh 'Diaspora'* (Durham: Duke University Press, 2001).

32. Talal Asad, "On Torture, or Cruel, Inhuman, and Degrading Treatment," in *Social Suffering,* ed. Arthur Kleinman, Veen Das, and Margaret Lock (Berkeley: University of California Press, 1997), 296.

33. Rejali, *Torture and Democracy,* 22, 41, 56–57. See also Bonnie Kerness, "America's abuse of prisoners didn't begin in Iraq," *Newark Star Ledger,* May 18, 2004, available at http://redeem-her.org/index_files/Page658.htm, accessed September 20, 2010.

34. Rejali, *Torture and Democracy,* 58, 59. Italics added.

In the allegedly flexible and nondisciplinary control of labor power today, where we have what Aiwah Ong terms a "graduated sovereignty" that gives corporations indirect power over the political conditions of citizens, for maintenance of that indirect power, the civic discipline of torture, a more direct control over a human body is resorted to. This is especially so when nations charged with defending the interests of transnational capital—as is the United States with its primary hegemony over use of militarized force—are felt to be facing severe challenge and crisis, as the United States did after the September 11, 2001, attacks on its mainland.[35] The United States, however, has a long history of the use of torture, pre-dating those attacks, to safeguard what it considers its sovereign interests,[36] throughout the global South, especially throughout Latin America.

Torture victims themselves often bear witness to the ways torture's application procures such sovereignty. Sovereignty, in almost any way it is defined, is the pervading ethos at the site of torture. In one of the more brilliant, if harrowing, reflections by a victim on his torture, Jean Améry reflects on sovereignty. Améry probes the meanings of his torture by the Gestapo on the way to his confinement in the concentration camps. In his *At the Mind's Limits*, he keeps his personal narrative of torture brief, but offers it with such vividness and poignancy that another concentration-camp survivor, Primo Levi, observed, "these are pages that one reads with almost physical pain . . ."[37]

After a brief account of his own torture, Améry stresses that, through torture, the torturer realizes "his own total sovereignty." He manifests an attempt to "nullify the world by negating his fellow man [sic]." Keeping the tortured at the edge of life and death—until death comes, if it is allowed—"the torturer and murderer realizes his own destructive being, without having to lose himself in it entirely, like his martyred victim." Améry, with a deft and discerning turn of phrase, renders the sovereign power of the torturer in this way:

---

35. See Mayer, *The Dark Side,* for an account of the rise of official approval of torture techniques after September 11, 2001.

36. In addition to Alfred W. McCoy, *A Question of Torture,* cited above, see Jennifer K. Harbury, *Truth, Torture, and the American Way: The History and Consequences of U.S. Involvement in Torture* (Boston: Beacon, 2005).

37. Primo Levi, back-cover book endorsement for Jean Améry, *At the Mind's Limits: Contemplations by a Survivor of Auschwitz and Its Realities* (Bloomington: Indiana University Press, 1998).

He has control of the other's scream of pain and death; he is master over flesh and spirit, life and death. In this way, torture becomes the total inversion of the social world, in which we can live only if we grant our fellow man life, ease his suffering, and bridle the desire of our ego to expand. But in the world of torture man exists only by ruining the other person who stands before him. A slight pressure by the tool-wielding hand is enough to turn the other—along with his head, in which are perhaps stored Kant and Hegel, and all nine symphonies, and *The World as Will and Representation*—into a shrilly squealing piglet at slaughter.[38]

What is particularly poignant and at the same time so persuasive about the linkage between sovereignty, on the one hand, and torture's destructive reduction of human being to flesh, on the other—a reduction on which Améry reflects throughout the book[39]—is his admission that even amid his torture sessions, he possessed an almost instinctive admiration of this sovereignty. Although Améry named his torture an "orgy of unchecked self-expansion" on the part of the torturers, he adds this:

I also have not forgotten that there were moments when I felt a kind of wretched admiration for the agonizing sovereignty they exercised over me. For is not the one who can reduce a person so entirely to a body and a whimpering prey of death a god or, at least, a demigod?[40]

Améry also terms this "wretched admiration" a mode of amazement. "Amazed, the tortured person experienced that in this world there can be the other as absolute sovereign, and sovereignty revealed itself as the power to inflict suffering and to destroy."[41] Yet, the destructive effects, the permanence of physical, psychic, and social scars—especially the psychic and social ones—empty out torture of any positive content worthy of "admiration" and "amazement." Torture leaves one wretched, always tortured, whatever might also be the degree of survival and recovery of humanity afterward. The final paragraph Améry pens in his chapter on torture has been affirmed by scores of those victimized by torture:

---

38. Améry, *At the Mind's Limits*, 35.
39. Ibid., 22, 33.
40. Ibid., 36.
41. Ibid., 39.

Whoever has succumbed to torture can no longer feel at home in the world. The shame of destruction cannot be erased. Trust in the world, which already collapsed in part at the first blow, but in the end, under torture, fully, will not be regained. That one's fellow man was experienced as the anti-man remains in the tortured person as accumulated horror. It blocks the view into a world in which the principle of hope rules. One who was martyred is a defenseless prisoner of fear. It is *fear* that henceforth reigns over him. Fear—and also what is called resentments. They remain, and have scarcely a chance to concentrate into a seething, purifying thirst for revenge.[42]

We note here, especially, torture's destruction of a capacity for interdependence, its destroying the communal as a condition of living, and especially of citizens' efforts to create empowerment and community. It is a direct attack on the "we," upon the intimate spacing and weighing of extension. Recalling Rejali's "civic discipline model" of torture, or the long history of Western colonizing powers' use of terror to control enslaved and colonized populations, we can discern how important to sovereign power is a technique like torture that weakens both the tortured person *and* the communities from which they come. Western sovereign states have long harbored, and still do harbor, strong ideological interests in—indeed, a material dependency upon—the practice of torture and the terror it can unleash in communities. In the context of the threatened national sovereignties of Western powers in the early twenty-first century, victims selected for torture will continue to be from traditionally colonized populations, especially dissenting ones the world over—in the United States, for example, from Muslim traditions, black communities, racialized immigrant groups, dissenting movements, or the criminalized poor.

In Christianized political orders, such as in the United States or in Christian countries throughout Latin America, sovereignty's interest in torture can also invoke, on the side of the torturer, its discourse of the transcendent and God. One particularly gruesome site of this invocation can be found in the discourse of the torture centers during the Argentine "Dirty

---

42. Ibid., 40. This description also is apt for the experience of Maher Arar, an innocent Canadian citizen who suffered rendition by U.S. authorities to Syria, where he was confined and tortured for two months. On his experience and the aftermath, see Mayer, *The Dark Side,* 134.

War" of the 1970s/1980s. The political junta of that period was steeped in a strongly traditional, transcendentalized mode of Christian ethos, and so the language of a punitive transcendent God could be invoked to protect a threatened "Christian order" from the threats of subversives. One torturer, "El Tejano," the nickname of a U.S.-trained and educated torturer, confiscated a razor blade that one torture victim tried to use to kill herself during torture. As he took it he said, "You're not going to be able to die, little girl, until we want you to. We are God here."[43] Graziano reports that such claims were frequently reported throughout Argentine torture centers, and often referred not only to the Christian God, but also to the Gods of Olympus. Whatever the god, the transcendent invocation was what mattered, conveying a "transcendental authority" to the sovereign agents of the state and its para-state, in government and in the torture cell.[44] In the more Christianized discourses, victims could also be declared surrogates, sacrifices for the common good of "civil" order. Leaders of the junta were known to acknowledge their use of torture, even when it was ongoing in rooms beneath their site of consultation with dignitaries from other countries. One junta leader inserted himself into a Christian passion narrative, making a gesture of washing his hands, then smiling and saying, "You remember what happened with Pontius Pilate." About such deployments of Christian crucifixion narrative, Graziano summarizes, "Each *desaparecido* [a person disappeared and usually into a torture center] was always bearing about in the body the dying of the Lord Jesus, that the life also of Jesus might be made manifest in the body."[45] One Argentine novelist dramatized the logic at work by having a torturer preface his application of torture with the words, "We are going to make you Christ."[46]

This mixing of transcendent God with a will to torture should not be seen only as a propensity of some other nation or culture, here, the Argentine "other." In the first place, many of the Argentine torturers were

---

43. The tortured person was Graciela Geuna. Her testimony is archived by the Center for Legal and Social Studies (CELS), cited in Marguerite Feitlowitz, *A Lexicon of Terror: Argentina and the Legacies of Torture* (New York: Oxford University Press, 1998), 10 and 260 n.24. The real name of the torturer is given as Sergeant Elpidio Rosario Tejeda.

44. Graziano, *Divine Violence,* 203.

45. Ibid., 207, citing 2 Corinthians 4:10 from the New Testament.

46. Ibid., 205.

the product of a U.S. training enterprise.[47] Of equal concern is the fact that
U.S. Christian cultures themselves are replete with religious symbolics of
torturous violence. The novels that are historically some of the best sell-
ing among adults in the United States, particularly among Christians, are
those of the "Left Behind" series, about Jesus' return after the saved have
been raptured above earth, with portraits of the conquering lord wading
in blood, delighting in the suffering of the wicked.[48] That the novels were
especially popular with the Christian Right, which had unique access to
the highest of U.S. national powers when the regime of George W. Bush
sanctioned torture in a direct and extensive manner,[49] signals the mutual
reinforcement that can exist between an ethos that references a sovereign
God, on the one hand, and one that can accommodate torture and muti-
lation of perceived enemies, on the other. Again, this is not a new event,
this co-belonging of transcendence and torture. In European colonizers' theater of social control over colonized populations, terror and torture were staples of governance. Historians Peter Linebaugh and Marcus
Rediker document how extensively applied such tactics were.[50] Historian
of the Caribbean, Vincent Brown, shows how such torture functioned
as the colonizers' "courting of the supernatural," an attempt at crafting
"ritual execution to lend to worldly authority a sacred, even supernatural, dimension. . . . Dead bodies, dismembered and disfigured as they
were, would be symbols of the power and dominion of slave masters."[51]
Nevertheless, as Brown also notes, what colonizers reaped was not just
secured dominion and terror among their subordinates; they also reaped
resistance and revolt. In the words I have deployed in this text, colonizers, like the powerful often everywhere, underestimated the prodigious
art-force of those weighing-in with a spectral, transimmanental practice.
They could weigh-in even from under the weight of torture.

---

47. Feitlowitz, *A Lexicon of Terror,* 10–11.

48. For analysis of the "Left Behind" series, see James W. Jones, *Blood That Cries Out
from the Earth: The Psychology of Religious Terrorism* (New York: Oxford University Press,
2008), 88–114.

49. McCoy, *A Question of Torture,* 108–50.

50. Peter Linebaugh and Marcus Rediker, *The Many-Headed Hydra: Sailors, Slaves,
Commoners, and the Hidden History of the Revolutionary Atlantic* (Boston: Beacon, 2000),
51–57.

51. Vincent Brown, *The Reaper's Garden: Death and Power in the World of Atlantic
Slavery* (Cambridge: Harvard University Press, 2007), 135–36.

"Spectral Humans": Their Incendiary, Artful Imagery

Further reflection on the spectral character of persons suffering exclusion and oppression is necessary to understand the being that can conjure and mobilize resistance to the aesthetic regime of sovereignty buttressed by practices of terror and torture. Butler conjoins spectrality with human being with her term "spectral humans," which she uses in a published conversation with Spivak to reference the slaves, children, and disenfranchised persons who make possible the reproduction of the Greek city-state and its political life.

> These spectral humans, deprived of ontological weight and failing the tests of social intelligibility required for minimal recognition include those whose age, gender, race, nationality, and labor status not only disqualify them for citizenship but actively "qualify" them for statelessness.[52]

Portraying such humans as "deprived of ontological weight" may seem a different usage of "weight" than we find in Nancy, but even in his work the crushing described as concentration effects also a certain weightlessness for some in the wound that bodies without extension suffer. Being thus crushed in the world's concentrated weight, they can be left without power, with a kind of weightless being, deemed not to matter in the order of things. Spectral humans are often left in the shadows when the political virtues of the Greek polis are discussed or championed, as they often are in the discourses of the West. Butler, however, insists on politically theorizing the polis with these excluded ones in mind. She refuses to foreclose them, and so her theorization etches antagonism between them and the polis into her political analysis. Politics, the political, comes into being with thinking within and across this agonistic polis. The political again is foregrounded, in Rancière's language, as a fundamental disagreement that is built into its structure as a wrong constituted by the gulf existing between the sphere of leaders and citizens deliberating in the polis, and the sphere of those excluded, placed outside, consigned to be "the part who has no part."

---

52. Judith Butler, in Butler and Gayatri Chakravorty Spivak, *Who Sings the Nation-State? Language, Politics, Belonging* (London: Seagull, 2007), 15.

To designate them "spectral humans," however, is a more positive rendering. It does not replace descriptors connoting suffering or negativity—"part that has no part," excluded, oppressed, bearing the weight of suffering, and so on—but it makes intrinsic to the carrying of that negativity a collective agency. As "spectral," these humans pose threat and promise, "an incendiary risk" as Butler writes regarding Guantánamo detainees' poems. In reflecting on spectral humans further she helps to explain the conditions that defy the reductions to "bare life" (Agamben) and to "mere meat" (JanMohamed). And so Butler is on record as giving a warning— one needed often by some segments of Western liberalism too ready to lament the reductions of peoples to "bare life," offering them little hope, overlooking their creativity, foreclosing their resilient emergence from the shadows to which they are consigned. Agamben risks a certain sense of fatality, more than JanMohamed, since the latter's excavation of symbolic death also limns liberatory possibilities. If we reduce analysis of dispossession and destitution to only the two notions of sovereignty and bare life, Butler writes, "we deprive ourselves of the lexicon we need to understand the other networks of power to which it belongs, or how power is recast in that place or even saturated in that place."[53]

A dimension of this saturated place is the haunting power of the dispossessed, their art-force as reenvisioning (aesthetically repartitioning the sensible), thus remaking world. In their seeming utter deprivation of being, they find and know "a remainder of 'life'—suspended and spectral—that limns and haunts every normative instance of life."[54] Saturation is thus not unlike Nancy's concentration, in this respect, in which there resides as vitalizing force, a "haunting presence . . . anonymous and exponential," giving rise to a creating of "world."[55] About the practices and productions of sovereign powers that would deprive humans of their lives, of their "ontological weight,"[56] Butler writes at one point, those sovereign powers are limited. "Production is partial and is, indeed, perpetually haunted by its ontologically uncertain double."[57] What she has in mind by this uncertain double is the image, a "figural form" that resides

53. Ibid., 42–43.
54. Ibid., 7.
55. Jean-Luc Nancy, *Corpus*, trans. Richard Rand (New York: Fordham University Press, 2008), 78, 70.
56. Butler, *Who Sings the Nation-State*, 15.
57. Ibid.

in the dominant public imagination even as the spectral human's being is marked for erasure.

The visibility and invisibility of torture subjects within the aegis of U.S. state power are exemplary of this process. They are said by some not to exist at all. "The United States does not torture," declares many a U.S. politician. If incidents of torture *are* acknowledged, then public reports and representations usually construct those sufferers as "other," unrecognizable as humans, unworthy of grief, outside the pale of "humanity." Yet certain figural forms remain, and not just the ideal abstract possibility of torture victims. There are also the depictions of today's tortured and confined, the photos of Abu-Ghraib, which for all their own ways of furthering the dehumanization of the Arab/Muslim/terrorist "other," nevertheless keep the tortured as figured in our midst.[58] Then, too, the monitoring regimes of human rights organizations, and the performances of activists who *do* grieve their torture and so parade and demonstrate their solidarity by wearing in public the orange prison garb of Guantánamo prisoners—these also keep before the public "figural forms" that are the "ontologically uncertain double" of those marked for deprivation of any ontological weight. Images of the tortured persist in the imaginary of a U.S. public, even when it wants to forget and deny the weight borne by the tortured.

> Indeed, every normative instance is shadowed by its own failure, and very often that failure assumes a figural form. The figure lays claim to no certain ontological status, and though it can be apprehended as "living," it is not always recognized as a life. . . . It falls outside the frame furnished by the norm, but only as a relentless double whose ontology cannot be secured, but whose living status is open to apprehension.[59]

I suggest that the relentless aspect of the double is especially exhibited in the Guantánamo poems cited in this chapter's Butler epigraph. The spectral, haunting double, the figural form, which persists and is immanent in public life in spite of erasures and framings that deny it ontological weight, can coalesce for resistance and transformation, being

---

58. Puar, *Terrorist Assemblages,* 79–113 ("Abu-Ghraib and U.S. Sexual Exceptionalism").
59. Ibid., 7–8.

reworked in a spectral practice of artful imaging. And so the tortured and incarcerated body sounds itself, figures its presence to and through networks of resistance and transformation amid state power—and all this, especially through the poetic form and artful imaging that we have met not only in the Guantánamo poets, but in Richard Wright's oeuvre and Catarina's dictionary.

If one needs another example of spectral humans' power, consider the Vietnam War, not only a time of warfare, but also of programmatic application of torture by the United States (especially through its Phoenix program).[60] "Spectral humans" of that conflict weighed-in, with distinctive practices, to force retreat of an overwhelming enemy, the U.S. military. The U.S. imperial project arrayed against the Vietnamese and its military power was forged earlier on the anvil of occupation, mass bombings, massacres, and partition in post–World War II Korea[61]—and played out also throughout the world by the United States in Greece, Iran, Guatemala, Cuba, Nicaragua, Panama, and elsewhere.[62] The Vietnam War, amid all the horror of loss of life and destruction of environment, stands nevertheless as a witness which generates some hope that when imperial form commits to the pursuit of sovereignty through what William Spanos terms "the violent practice of genocidal power,"[63] it can be defeated. The line the U.S. drew in Vietnam was to be the U.S. "southern wall" against communism, with its line already slashed, agonizingly, across Korea and its people as its northern wall.[64] The southern wall, however, would not stand.

The "Vietnamese other" achieved its repulsion of U.S. forces from its lands by refusing to resist the U.S. military apparatus with a frontal assault. In Vietnam, resisters chose what Spanos terms a "strategy of absence (of invisibility and silence) in the face of a massive and formidable military force that, whatever its exceptionalist claims, was utterly and pervasively

60. McCoy, *A Question of Torture*, 64–71.

61. On the importance of U.S. actions in the Korean occupation and war, for constructing U.S. imperial policy globally, see Bruce Cumings, *The Korean War: A History* (New York: Modern Library, 2010), 205–22.

62. Bruce Cumings, "Decoupled from History: North Korea in the 'Axis of Evil,'" in Bruce Cumings, Ervand Abrahamian, Moshe Ma'oz, *Inventing the Axis of Evil: The Truth about North Korea, Iran, and Syria* (New York: New Press, 2004), 22.

63. William V. Spanos, *America's Shadow: An Anatomy of Empire* (Minneapolis: University of Minnesota Press, 2000), 165.

64. Frances Fitzgerald, *Fire in the Lake: The Vietnamese and the Americans in Vietnam* (Boston: Little, Brown, 1972), 67.

inscribed in a European cultural narrative of presence."[65] The Vietnamese forces deployed a "figural form," we might say, an uncertain ontological double that haunted its subordinated status and so spectrally engaged a greater power. Crucial to the U.S. and European exercises of sovereign power, as Spanos shows throughout his book *America's Shadow*, was a tendency to see power only in direct oppositions of force and, in particular, in massively organized and frontally assaulting force.

> The strategy of the Vietnamese Other . . . was analogous to that of the Eastern martial arts (most notably those deriving from the Tao), which, grounded on a comportment toward being that acknowledges the harmonious belongingness of being and nothing, privileges a passivity that allows the aggressor to defeat himself. Based on the predictability of the American reaction, this "feminine" Vietnamese strategy of resistance fragmented and disarticulated a totalized military structure . . .[66]

Crucial to this strategy was also a certain portentous sign making and imaging. This, too, was evident in the Vietnamese resistance. Even though they refused to deploy the binary forms of power the American military trusted in, they conjured their "seething presence" through agitprop of multitudinous forms, depicting the U.S. military as an "enemy" requiring the force of focused and disciplined Vietnamese wrath, and even hatred.[67]

The result was not only the United States withdrawing in defeat from Vietnam—after a deadly toll had been exacted in U.S. and even more in Vietnamese lives—but also a haunting of the U.S. cultural and political landscape ever since, as the nation and many of its citizens still struggle between "repression" of the Vietnamese failure but then the "return" of it in desperate new forays into military adventuring—all to shake "the Vietnam syndrome." Nothing was easy about this forcing of the U.S. troops from Vietnam's lands. There is no romance to any war, no easy victories, no unambiguous order left in the wake of U.S. retreat. The Vietnamese "other," however, still testifies to the power of the oblique way, of

---

65. Spanos, *America's Shadow*, 150.

66. Ibid.

67. Fitzgerald, *Fire in the Lake*, 168–75. The effectivity of what Fitzgerald documents is also discussed at greater length in Spanos's analysis of the post–Vietnam War novels in the United States that dramatize the way the Vietnamese became unsettling and subversive powers to U.S. forces. See Spanos, *America's Shadow*, 57–186.

spectral humans' figural form, its mode of weighing-in upon the world of the powerful that would impose its concentrated weight, its destruction of world, its distortion of singular plural world, its erection of global sovereignty.

The effectivity in the weight of the dead and dying may be seen by practitioners of dominating power as that of the lightweight, but its figural form is actually a transformative power of overcoming. It is a counterweight through the way of transimmanence. It is neither transcendent, deploying some "higher power" that is "above and beyond" life and history, nor simply an immanence, a detranscendentalized materialism that is opposed to those projected transcendent powers. Vietnam's struggle against colonizing and imperial ways was not unprecedented. As Vincent Brown argues, ritual figurations of the dead and dying have ritually been mobilized by the colonized, the enslaved, and the victims of war. Think not only of Korea and Vietnam, but also of Haiti, Jamaica, and more—sites from which the figural form of the excluded and slain emerge, as spectral humans, to haunt and subvert sovereign colonizing power. This force of the past is a resource still. A lengthy passage from Brown secures the point:

> The heirs of slavery in the United States continued to create alliances and antagonism from the carnage of the Civil War and the Jim Crow lynching pogroms that produced the "strange fruit" immortalized by Abel Meeropol and Billie Holiday. Victims of racial terror haunted and animated the civil rights movement. . . . As the dead circulate with accelerating speed and near-boundless reach in today's electronic media, who can tell what kinds of social formations, political movements, and practices of remembrance will result from the global AIDS pandemic and the twenty-first-century wars of terror, in which mass killing, martyrdom, and the rhetoric of perpetual hostility dominate the cultural landscape?[68]

Conclusion: Spectral Practice and the Theological

At the end of the previous chapter I summarized the discourse of the theological in relation to transimmanence, foregrounding the theological as a discourse (a) exploring a "changed terrain" beyond transcendence

---

68. Brown, *The Reaper's Garden*, 257.

and immanence, (b) developing a transdisciplinary discourse that abides especially in intercultural and countercolonial perspectives and thematics, (c) being transitive in its coursing through the liminal passageways that liberate singular plural being, and especially (d) wielding the symbolic force of art-full form.[69]

At the end of this chapter on the weight of transimmanence, the key point is that the theological is discourse in which all these features interplay, *as practice.* The theological in this way effects a power by which those bearing the concentrated weight of the world "weigh-in" through practices to effect liberatory change, to create world amid *immonde.* Here, in this chapter, we have displayed that practice of weighing-in, first, by reference to the poems of Guantánamo detainees, then revisiting the powerful poetry and fiction of Richard Wright, and hearing also the voice of one deemed "ex-human," Catarina, from a zone of social abandonment. In all these cases—whether confined by a U.S. imperial power in a detention-center cage, lynched in the era of Jim Crow, or abandoned to zones of ex-humanness—their reduction is resisted, not final. There is a remainder of life and it takes the form of life "suspended and spectral," to recall Butler's language again. The spectrality that remains, I emphasize, is not only the arresting art-force. The theological is that art-force borne by practices. The synergy of prodigious art-force *with* practice makes it spectral.

One of the important consequences of acknowledging the practical character of the theological is that we note how intrinsic to the spectral power are the connections between primary sufferers of the world's concentrated weight and those whose suffering is more tangential to it, or seemingly removed from it. As spectrality in practice, the theological is an intersubjective event, a co-working, a movement of collectivity in the national and international *socius*, which involves, essentially, the agencies of direct sufferers *and* those who network with them. As this chapter also stressed, the spectral practice often has to position and re-site its powerful art forms in an engagement with an aesthetic regime that state powers often deploy to buttress their sovereignty. This clash of artful forces occurs at many sites, but the site that this chapter has foregrounded, and which we will focus on more directly in the next chapter, is that of the torture room. This torture room, like Foucault's prison cell,

---

69. See above, chap. 3, "Conclusion: Transimmanence and the Theological," 152–58.

is the culmination of an entire parapenal state of institutions and powerful nations, and often, too, has written on its walls some form of the theoscopic divine, reminding that "God sees you."[70] In fact, as we have seen, rituals of torture and terror often deploy a metaphysic, involving a discourse about a transcendent figure above the world, wherein torturers actually cite "God" as sovereign guarantor of their actions in an ordered world wherein victims find their place in a kind of theogonic play. If, to counter all this, the tortured are to become a spectral, countering power to a sovereign torture-state, then the figural form of the tortured needs to be held up, disseminated, always re-sited and displayed, in practices forged by many communities, religious and secular.

The "figural form" of spectral practice is especially significant for highlighting, at the close of this chapter, another feature of the theological. The theological has both a discursive and an extradiscursive aspect. These aspects are intricately bound up with one another, however much we have had to distinguish them, as I already have, in this work. The theological, in its discursive aspect, traces and reflects upon spectral practice, as something going on in the wider field of social practices, beyond academic sites of reflection. By attending to, and giving recognition to, the many spectral practices, the theological is discursively figuring that practice in its intellectual work. But the theological can also be a kind of spectral practice itself, as when *within the academy* voices and perspectives of the long excluded and oppressed come to voice and, perhaps, to empowering presence, occupying faculty positions, altering curricula, or changing the modes of pedagogy. Thus, we can say that the theological is a figural form both reflecting on spectral practice (discursively) and also, at times constituting itself as spectral practice (becoming extra-discursive, a practice in its own right). In both cases, the occluded, those parts with no part, weigh-in with a world-creating practice.

Perhaps for the theologian, especially those still working in the ethos of guild Theology, as does this writer, the most intense fusion of the discursive and extradiscursive aspects of the theological occurs when the representatives of long-excluded and repressed communities bring their subordinated knowledges into the guild, a bringing that always requires practices to effect it. This emergence of "subordinated knowledges"

---

70. Michel Foucault, *Discipline and Punish: The Birth of the Prison* (New York: Pantheon, 1977 [French 1975]), 294.

(Foucault) within guild Theology, though, is only one site at which the fusing of discursive and extradiscursive aspects of the theological can occur. Wherever reflection upon spectral practice becomes also a struggle of spectral humans themselves, there will be this fusion of the discursive and extradiscursive aspects. In these cases, the theological is, as Foucault would write, a "discursive practice."[71] In short, the theological, as thought, is no more something apart from practices of the socialized body than is any thought. The theological as spectral practice is a particularly vivid and transformative site of thought and bodies "touching each other, the touch of their breaking down, and into, each other."[72]

In order to show one more time the power of the theological, as "figural form" entailed in spectral practice, the next and final chapter enters into greater analysis of a single case of contemporary struggle to resist reduction to bare life and ex-humanness. I will stay with the challenge posed by the suffering at the site of torture, but engage in a closer reading of a struggle to survive and resist, as portrayed in the autobiographical account by Sister Dianna Ortiz, a U.S. citizen working in Guatemala and subject to torture there. By so doing, the spectral practice of transimmanence, which is the theological, will emerge as still better understood, perhaps, by the radical practices survivors deploy in struggle for humanness and life.

---

71. Michel Foucault, *The Archaeology of Knowledge & the Discourse on Language*, trans. A. M. Sheridan Smith (New York: Harper & Row, 1972 [French 1969]), 46–49.
72. Nancy, *Corpus,* 37.

Chapter Five

TRANSIMMANENCE
AND RADICAL
PRACTICES

As a political phenomenon, then, colonial necromancy forces us to turn our attention to strategies for manipulating cultural practices in a world where the dead were an active social presence, and where domination, dissent, and the threat of incredible violence plagued every interaction.[1]—Vincent Brown

My fingers closed around the cross Raúl had given me, the dolphin from Mary, and the piece of bone that had formed part of Victor's body. Touching it reminded me of his mother. And then I thought of Rosa and Miguel, of obligations I hadn't fulfilled, and of the damage silence can do. And I started to read.[2]—Sister Dianna Ortiz

Yes, Sister Dianna Ortiz started to read. She began to read a statement at a press conference in Guatemala City. As she recounts in her eloquent and searing testimonial, *The Blindfold's Eyes: My Story from Torture to*

---

1. Vincent Brown, *The Reaper's Garden: Death and Power in the World of Atlantic Slavery* (Cambridge: Harvard University Press, 2008), 151–52.

2. Sister Dianna Ortiz, with Patricia Davis, *The Blindfold's Eyes: My Journey from Torture to Truth* (Maryknoll, N.Y.: Orbis, 2007), 213.

Truth, she had returned in 1993 to the city in which she was tortured in November of 1989. The torture had come after a year of work with a rural community in Guatemala, while she served as a member of the Ursuline Catholic order. In the months leading up to her abduction and torture by U.S.-backed Guatemalan authorities, Ortiz had received numerous death threats, her community work deemed a threat in the militarized ethos of Guatemala, long considered a "blue-chip investment" for U.S.-based corporate interests.[3]

Guatemala and "The Peoples of the Sea"

Guatemala. Is it in Central America, as the cartography of most mapmakers places it, or might it be part of the Caribbean, given the mobile cultures and flows of that nation's southeastern shore? To be sure, Guatemala's mountainous terrain where Ortiz worked anticipates the more landed and northerly ranges of Mexico's mountains, its isthmus, the coasts ringing the Gulf of Mexico. Not only, however, does Guatemala have its cultures of the Caribbean, its agonistic politics of past and present are also those of what Antonio Benítez-Rojo named the "Caribbean archipelago." Pedro de Alvarado, the conqueror and governor of Guatemala had traveled with Hernan Cortes along a colonizing path from Hispaniola and Cuba across the Caribbean and into Yucatan, Mexico, before moving on later to Guatemala. This colonial route may be taken as one signal that the history of Guatemala and the Caribbean are bound together historically, economically, and often culturally, too.[4] Benítez-Rojo suggests the Caribbean

---

3. Piero Gleijeses, *Shattered Hope: The Guatemalan Revolution and the United States, 1944–1954* (Princeton: Princeton University Press, 1991); and Alfonso Bauer Paiz, *Como opera el capital yanqui en Centroamérica: El caso Guatemala* (Mexico City: Ed. Ibero Mexicana, 1956).

4. It is important to note that Spanish repression on the mainland often lacked the intensity of plantation repression in the islands, though they were bound in one "world system." See Antonio Benítez-Rojo on Guatemala in his *The Repeating Island: The Caribbean and the Postmodern Perspective*, 2d ed. (Durham: Duke University Press, 1996), 59–60. In spite of this difference, on the persistent interplay, see Frederick Douglass Opie, *Black Labor Migration in Caribbean Guatemala, 1882–1923* (Gainesville: University Press of Florida, 2009). For ways the national music, the marimba tradition, powerfully binds Guatemala and the Caribbean, see Sergio Navarrete Pellicer, *Maya Achi Marimba Music in Guatemala* (Philadelphia: Temple University Press, 2005).

might be better rendered "meta-archipelago," which "has the virtue of having neither a boundary nor a center," flowing

> outward past the limits of its own sea with a vengeance, and its *ultima Thule* [outermost limits] may be found on the outskirts of Bombay, near the low and murmuring shores of Gambia, in a Cantonese tavern of circa 1850, at a Balinese temple, in an old Bristol pub, in a commercial warehouse in Bordeaux at the time of Colbert, in a windmill beside the Zuider Zee, at a café in a barrio of Manhattan, in the existential *saudade* of an old Portuguese lyric.[5]

Benítez-Rojo's Caribbean, however, is not impressive simply by an expanse that takes in these geographic and cultural scenes, but more by its production, its fusion of indigenous, European, African, and Asian peoples' bodies and histories into a kind of machine. Along with the machine, however, there is also an eruption of peoples' collectively embodied spirit of survival, contestation, and sustained revolt. Although not all these dynamics are present in Guatemala, the machinery of capital and coloniality surely has been. As a machine, the Caribbean produced the Atlantic's "navel of capitalism." The Caribbean, Benítez-Rojo writes, had "the blood of Africa" poured into it, as indigenous peoples were decimated in their numbers, with Asians pulled in for labor from the Philippines, China, and India, all this lubricated with institutionalized racism, missionizing religion, and plantation culture, making the engines of capital and colonialism whir.

Yet the productivity of the Caribbean is, as Benítez-Rojo stresses with equal force, an eruption of peoples' sustained revolt, an artful, spectral practice, a necromancy in which the dead circulate to undermine the religious and often political authority of conquerors.[6] The sheer concentration of singularities in this center of capital releases also the specter of its dissolution. If capital is a prime site of the weighted world's onerous, concentrated power, as we noted in Nancy's theorization,[7] and if

---

5. Benítez-Rojo, *The Repeating Island*, 4.

6. Brown, *The Reaper's Garden*, 255–61. On Haiti see Benítez-Rojo, *The Repeating Island*, 160–66. See also Peter Linebaugh and Marcus Rediker, *The Many-Headed Hydra: Sailors, Slaves, Commoners, and the Hidden History of the Revolutionary Atlantic* (Boston: Beacon, 2000), 22–27.

7. Jean-Luc Nancy, *Corpus,* trans. Richard Rand (New York: Fordham University Press, 2008), 109, 111.

it is from the wounds of that concentration that a haunting emerges, as he also argues, then it should come as no surprise that the Caribbean concentration of hybridized peoples and the violence suffered should spawn also a most spectral practice. By the Caribbean's collective and subversive practice, I refer to what Benítez-Rojo terms a polyrhythmic cultural art and tradition. This should not be reduced, as in popular stereotypes, to the syncopations of a salsa or a samba, but more expansively to a whole "cultural discourse of the Peoples of the Sea" (African, Asian, Amerindian)[8] which seeks, he argues, "to neutralize violence and to refer society to the transhistorical codes of Nature."[9] The "Caribbean rhythm is in fact a metarhythm" "which can be arrived at through any system of signs, whether it be dance, music, language, text, or body language, etc."[10] They work diversely to counter the colonizing rhythms of Europe and its servicing agents, offering up a contrapuntal ensemble of practices for resistance to the concentrated weights of capital and coloniality, the latter working as "whiter rhythms," he suggests, which are more binary, marching and territorializing. The polyform and polyrhythmic discourse give historical reference and concreteness, a collective embodied site, to Nancy's more abstract and cryptic accounts of how capital's concentration can be undone. Creativity and extension in a just, singular plural world, he writes, is "a mingling of sea and sun, spacing as the resistance and revolt of created bodies." This is what works, for Nancy, "the liberation of bodies, the reopening of a space where capital concentrates and overinvests in time that's more and more constricted, more intense, more strident. A body *made in time*."[11] It is this that the cultural rhythms of the people of the sea resist. It is this liberation they create. Different as America's indigenous may be from Africa in its art forms and culture, or both from Asia, there arises in the Carribean archipelago—and its far-flung and elusive meta-archipelago—a shared coalitional interest. Historically, the maroon communities of Jamaica, Mexico, and elsewhere (including Guatemala at points) bore witness to this overlap. "The copper, black, and yellow rhythms, if quite different from one another, have something in common: they belong to the Peoples of the Sea."[12]

---

8. Benítez-Rojo, *The Repeating Island*, 16–17.
9. Ibid., 17.
10. Ibid., 18.
11. Nancy, *Corpus*, 111.
12. Benítez-Rojo, *The Repeating Island*, 26.

Returning now to Dianna Ortiz, so many elements of her witness and struggle to survive torture show signs of the scarring of capital in the Caribbean archipelago. Viewing her experience in this way can be a way to grasp better the deeper significance of her story and struggle as resistance to the U.S. militarized culture of capital, as well. Moreover, the U.S. power that backed the Guatemalan military is one with the military interventionism in the Caribbean that has been a pattern the United States has long maintained (recall Haiti, the Dominican Republic, Puerto Rico, Jamaica, Cuba). Recognizing this is a way to emphasize what Ortiz herself reiterates, that her experience of sovereignty in the torture cell was to come full up against the sovereignty of Western colonial powers, in the form of a U.S.-backed military power in Guatemala. Even more importantly, she learned strategies of survival and practices of resistance from a colonial necromancy of the Peoples of the Sea, one shared with many of the mainland indigenous from the hybridized cultures of the Caribbean.[13] From a woman of the Maya, for example, and from several indigenous traditional elements, Ortiz would experience a haunting of her own Catholic faith, of her life, which not only occasioned her own survival beyond torture, but also became spectral to the powers arrayed against her. The prodigious art of the peoples thrown together by the coloniality of power in the Americas, then, set new rhythms playing in her life—often polyform in character and defying cognitive synthesis—which enabled her practice to be spectral, with threat and promise amid sovereign powers that still hold sway. This is the theological at work again in spectral practice, contending with the imperio-colonial senses of Theology, and yet dwelling, as we shall see, in a kind of grotesque embrace with the very powers, religious and political, that concentrate violation.

Before turning directly to discussion of Ortiz's spectral practice, it should be mentioned that the United States, too, Ortiz's country of citizenship, can be seen as part of the Caribbean archipelago. This is implied by the specific sites named already in the above quote from Benítez-Rojo. This gives still greater import to my focus on spectral practices in the story of this U.S. citizen in her struggle for justice in the United States and the Americas. If the story of the United States were not so internally framed between two coasts, and told from the usual standpoint of a

---

13. On the fusion in Guatemala of African, Spanish, and indigenous cultures and musics, see Navarrete Pellicer, *Maya Achi Marimba Music in Guatemala,* 120–23.

westward advancing and founding Anglo-Protestant group of East Coast
white settlers, we might render the U.S. story a Caribbean story, furthering historians' recent reframing of U.S. history as an Atlantic story.[14] To
do so would focus better the shared violation and oppression borne by
African, Asian, Amerindian, and others (including Europeans) who suffer
together the concentrated weight of capital and colonialism. The devasta-
tion of Native Americans and their lands for use by the United States is
a continuance of the decimations begun by Columbus in the Caribbean,
on the island of Hispaniola.[15] The African slaves whose labor was crucial
to jump-starting the industrial growth of the United States were often
unloaded through the Caribbean, and U.S. slave resistance often tapped
into a synergy between U.S. and Caribbean contexts.[16] Asians—their con-
tinent of origin always having been on the minds of Westerners obsessed
with "the Orient" even when headed for "the Occident"[17]—were also
pulled into the Caribbean (as elsewhere into the Americas), especially
Filipinos, Chinese, and Indians.[18] With "Coolie Ships" often modeled after
African slave ships and their oceanic transport and servitude often no
less onerous than that of Africans in the Caribbean, their bonded labor
was also crucial to the Caribbean machinery of American colonization.[19]
Numbers of those Asians would find places in the United States: Filipinos, as the oldest Asian community in the bayous of Louisiana (1760s);
Indo-Guyanese northward to New York; and many Chinese westward to
join the thousands entering directly from China, to become indispens-
able to California's economic, cultural, and political founding, and to the

14. For one example of a turn to "the Atlantic paradigm" in history, see Bianca Premo,
"On Currents and Comparisons: Gender and the Atlantic 'Turn' in Spanish America," *History Compass* 8, no. 3 (2010): 223–37.

15. David E. Stannard, *American Holocaust: The Conquest of the New World* (New York:
Oxford University Press, 1993), 57–148.

16. Daniel E. Walker, *Slavery and Cultural Resistance in Havana and New Orleans*
(Minneapolis: University of Minnesota Press, 2004).

17. Walter D. Mignolo, *Local Histories/Global Designs: Coloniality, Subaltern Knowledges, and Border Thinking* (Princeton: Princeton University Press, 2000), 57–62.

18. Floro L. Mercene, *Manila Men in the New World: Filipino Migration to Mexico and
the Americas from the Sixteenth Century* (Honolulu: University of Hawaii Press, 2007); Wal-
ton Look-Lai and Tan Chee-Beng, eds., *The Chinese in Latin America and the Caribbean*
(Leiden: Brill, 2010); Dilip K. Basu, *The Rise and Growth of Colonial Port Cities in Asia*
(Lanham, Md.: Rowman & Littlefield, 1986).

19. Lisa Yun, *The Coolie Speaks: Chinese Indentured Laborers and African Slaves in
Cuba* (Philadelphia: Temple University Press, 2008), 14–27.

construction of the U.S. transcontinental railroad that hastened the entire nation's growth.[20]

Again, all these together are an emblem not just of capital's and coloniality's concentration of weight, intense as the suffering was for Asian, Amerindian, or African. These Peoples of the Seas brought to the United States, too, a collective formation of bodies that set a pace for transformation. Chinese Americans, amid harsh labor conditions, exclusion, and discrimination laid a groundwork for civil rights struggle, especially when reaching out to Mexican American and African American workers to contest the hatred and dispossession that threatened from white labor and capital together, and especially in their battles in the courts for civil rights protections.[21] African Americans are well known for the freedom struggle they have bequeathed the nation from the beginning. Indigenous North Americans had lives and land extracted from them, but some of their cultural traditions of governance provided options for consideration and debate among those crafting founding documents for the U.S. government.[22]

As a U.S. citizen, working with indigenous peoples of Guatemala, often dominated by U.S. interests, Ortiz and her story, then, can appropriately be read as a struggle with U.S. forms of national sovereignty. Yet, as we shall see, the traditions of resistance by "Peoples of the Sea" were also available to her, playing a role in bringing her forward through torture— toward, not healing, but practices that begin to dissolve the sovereign states and orders of things that institutionalize so vicious and concentrated a mode of violence. As Ortiz seeks to survive her own experience of the long tradition of U.S. torture, for example, she learns something of what Vincent Brown terms a "colonial necromancy," wherein strategies for manipulating cultural practices have long acknowledged that "the dead

---

20. Iris Chang, *The Chinese in America: A Narrative History* (New York: Penguin, 2003), 53–64.

21. Charles J. McClain, *In Search of Equality: The Chinese Struggle against Discrimination in Nineteenth-Century America* (Berkeley: University of California Press, 1996).

22. One sign of the interchange of ideas in late eighteenth-century formation of the United States is the word *caucus*, still a staple of U.S. political party and governance vernacular, the word from the Algonquian *cau-cau-as'u* ("advisor"). See Judy Pearsall, ed, "Caucus," in *The Concise Oxford English Dictionary,* 10th ed., rev. (New York: Oxford University Press, 2002), 224. Just how extensive the influence of indigenous governance was on the early form of U.S. government is still often debated. See Samuel B. Payne, "The Iroquois League, Articles of Confederation and the Constitution," in *The William and Mary Quarterly,* vol. 3, no. 3 (July 1996): 605–29.

were an active social presence . . . where domination, dissent, and the threat of incredible violence plagued every interaction."[23] What form does this necromancy take in the story and struggle of Sister Dianna Ortiz?

The Blindfold's Eyes as Art-Force and Spectral Practice

In 1993 at that press conference in Guatemala City, four years after her torture in the city's *Politecnica* building, a school for military training, Ortiz was still only slowly gaining her power to narrate her ordeal. The statement she read at the Guatemala City press conference focused on the torture victim's "revictimization and the after-effects of torture."[24] As a survivor of torture, she herself had experienced that revictimization along with a series of flashbacks, nightmares, flights from her body, shame, disgust, broken relationships, fear, rage—all of which had followed her through attempts after torture to reconnect with family and her Catholic order. Her journey of survival included a "second confinement" in a mental hospital in the United States. Friends, activists, and a Catholic Worker support house nurtured her along the way. Such community contacts have been crucial to her waging the practice of struggle for survival.

She has shared narratives of her torture with U.S. audiences. At a 2006 conference in Princeton, for example, she told it briefly and soberly, with a crisp clarity, even if, still in a trembling breath, that moved profoundly her conference listeners.

> I have told you that I was burned with cigarettes [111 burns]. I was gang raped. I was also lowered into an open pit filled with human bodies—bodies of children, women, and men—some decapitated, some caked with blood, some dead, some alive. Beyond this, I was forced to participate in the torture of another human being. I was also subjected to other forms of torture that I will not describe here. Worse than the physical torture, was hearing the screams of the others being tortured. Can you hear the screams? I can.[25]

---

23. Brown, *The Reaper's Garden*, 151–52; on the dead's circulation today, see 257–58.

24. Ortiz, *The Blindfold's Eyes*, 215–16.

25. Dianna Ortiz, "A Survivor's View of Torture," in George Hunsinger, ed., *Torture Is a Moral Issue: Christians, Jews, Muslims, and People of Conscience Speak Out* (Grand Rapids: Eerdmans, 2008), 23. Read and presented by Ortiz at Princeton Theological Seminary, January 2006.

For years afterward, Ortiz carried a razor blade, giving her solace that she could end her life. When she mentions in her accounts of torture her being "forced to participate in the torture of another human being," she is referring to having had her own hands trapped and pressed by torturers around a machete and then forcibly manipulated to stab another already beaten and tortured woman repeatedly. "The blood is splattering everywhere," she recounts in her memoir, "My cries are lost in the cries of the Woman."[26] To signify just how powerful a specter this particular event was for her, and how haunted she remained by this person she was forced to attack, she capitalizes her reference to this female form, as "the Woman," and refers to her in that manner throughout *The Blindfold's Eyes*.

Her U.S. audience would have to wrestle with a special sense of accountability and obligation, since Ortiz also explained at the conference:

> When I was being tortured by members of the Guatemalan security forces, they referred to their boss, Alejandro. I met Alejandro in that clandestine prison. He spoke perfect American English. His Spanish was spoken with a North American accent. He spoke of a friend at the American embassy and, referring to the death threats I had received, he said, "We tried to warn you."[27]

I do not know what kind of personal vision and faith sustained her at that 2006 conference, or at more recent presentations she has given in New York City, Chicago, and at many other public venues. But at that 1993 press conference, her strength for bearing witness to what had happened to her in Guatemala and for working to expose her torturers was sustained by a special vision and imagery. These are signaled by the epigraph above, in which she closes her fingers around not only a cross, but also a small dolphin figurine and a "piece of bone."[28] She would draw strength from her touching of these, and she would need it; for she read the statement not only to discuss torture victims' revictimization, but also to say at the press conference to her torturers and to the officials backing them, both Guatemalan and U.S.-American, "'I'm back and I'm strong. You're not going to beat me. You failed.' I had to insist on that, even though it was hard to hold my head up, to find space in my throat for

---

26. Ortiz, *The Blindfold's Eyes*, 72–73.
27. Ibid., 22.
28. Ibid., 215.

words." She managed to complete the hard labor of the press conference statement that she read, as she recalls, by "remembering the dolphin arching above the water."[29]

What are we to make of this imagery? In this chapter, I will trace this poetic exercise of spectral imagery in practice, which is evident throughout Ortiz's rich narrative about her struggle to forge a practice of survival. I seek not just to foreground a moving personal narrative, though it is unquestionably that, and has been hailed by many readers as such. More particularly, here, I seek to read *The Blindfold's Eyes* as a poetic and narrative art form, a text that is itself a case of spectral imaging in practice, as much as is the artful and inventive religio-political vision that Ortiz forged in her own life struggle before writing the book. Both the images at work in her life, and also those that are held up in the book's narrative, are exemplary of the artful imaging of "spectral humans." In Judith Butler's words, those on the underside of imposed social suffering refuse that subordination, and "communicate another mode of solidarity, of interconnected lives that carry on each others' works, suffer each others' tears, and form networks that pose an incendiary risk not only to national security, but to the form of global sovereignty championed by the US."[30] Ortiz's spectral practice is perhaps a "neocolonial necromancy," to gloss Victor Brown's discussion of "colonial necromancy,"[31] one that allows the dead to circulate, and to do so with a power to subvert the concentrations of neocoloniality[32] in our presently weighted world.

Alice Zachmann, founder and director of the Guatemalan Human Rights Commission, has pointed out that amid the debates and disclosures concerning U.S. torture policy in the first decades of the twenty-first century, insufficient attention has been paid to the experience of the survivors.[33] That there are survivors is often mentioned, but just what their experience is in the wake of torture, and what they have now to offer to the world—all this is rarely made accessible to the broader public. This chapter is one

---

29. Ibid., 216.

30. Judith Butler, *Frames of War: When Is Life Grievable?* (London: Verso, 2009), 61–62.

31. Brown, *The Reaper's Garden*, 151–52.

32. On "neocoloniality" and "neocolonialism," see Robert J. C. Young, *Postcolonialism: An Historical Introduction* (Malden, Mass.: Blackwell, 2001), 44–56.

33. See Alice Zachmann, in *Breaking the Silence: Torture Survivors Speak Out*, DVD (Washington, D.C.: TASSC International, 2008).

attempt to do that, and it is done with the assumption that survivors might disclose not just truths about their struggle, but also about how the world's weight might be shouldered, how spectral practice might work.

Accordingly, this chapter devotes a section to each of four dimensions of a practice of survival and resistance that are discernible in *The Blindfold's Eyes*: somatic performance of the wounded body, anamnestic solidarity, revitalizing naturalism and "the Otherworld," and grotesque transcendentalism. These constitute the key dimensions of a spectral practice, of the theological. These dimensions enable the practices to be "radical" in the sense of facilitating revivifying struggle, shifting the weight of the world back toward the delicate fragility of extension, amid and in spite of the onerous weight of concentration. I stress that these are my own distillation from Ortiz's narrative. I make no claim that each of these dimensions can be transferred over to express how survival and resistance take place amid other forms of imposed social suffering, be these racism, the indefinite detention of immigrants and U.S. mass incarceration, domestic abuse and battery, harassment and exclusion of immigrant groups, and so on. I do suggest, however, that these four dimensions will find some place as invigorating resource in any coalescing movements that seek to forge survival and resistance amid structural injustice today. The experiences and approaches at work in the practice of torture survival and resistance can be instructive for all interested in liberatory change. Given that torture victims suffer what can hardly be doubted as anything other than "imposed social suffering," and given the near-overwhelming obstacles they face in forging survival and resistance after the near-total inscription of sovereignty onto their bodies, their strategies for survival are especially noteworthy.

Somatic Performance of Wounded Bodies

Bodily performance and action are intrinsic to the way the survivor and her spectral imaging weighs on the present. It is the body, and bodies together, that "stage words." Especially wounded bodies, perhaps, must be staged in order to have the force they need. Indeed, in a sense words are always "staged." They are events, performed by the play of breath, tongue, and teeth. A literary, text-oriented culture can forget that. In survival, resistance, and any future flourishing, the embodied word becomes all the more important. This is at times painfully clear in the case of torture survival, which reduces, or seeks to reduce, the tortured to pure broken flesh, to broken body. Any rising of the tortured, any surviving, will require some recuperation of the body, of the *soma* in the psycho-somatic trauma that torture is. The "figural form" that haunts power, even after so decimating an act as torture, is a phantom that through performance becomes seen and shared. As Avery Gordon notes, following Nicolas Abraham, "shared . . . phantoms find a way to be established as social practices along the lines of *staged words*."[34]

This first dimension of survival and resistant practice is evident in Ortiz's story, in what we can distinguish as "reactive" and as "proactive" bodily actions, somatic performances. Some seem unrelated to staging words, or to words at all. Yet as acts of the body they will become crucial to the words that are later staged in practices. The more "reactive" movements are those of the victim to the shower water, for cleansing, to the steam of water to attempt some purging, some reawakening of the body to create another, perhaps a countering affect or effect. There are numerous points in Ortiz's narrative where she makes resort to the company of water, immediately after the torture, at other times of stress and flashbacks. "The water is cleansing me," she writes in one of many such passages, "it is pushing me back into existence, back into myself. My blood throbs. I draw my head under the surface and listen to the faint beat of the water. I gulp the air when I let myself up."[35] As these words hint, there is not only revivification, but some danger. The water cuts off air needed for life, to which one returns. It was amid a watery place, a bathroom and shower, that she made a suicide attempt, from which her friends brought her back.[36] But in the main, the water is a site of cleansing, and finally, by book's end, it is a place of solace, even play, of splashing. In fact, a dolphin figure from the sea visits her in dreams and visions that come along the way of survival,[37] a figure whose representation of nature's healing powers will be noted further below.

This more positive valence of water blends with other more "proactive" elements of somatic performance. These are often ritual enactments, borrowed especially from women friends with access to indigenous

---

34. Avery F. Gordon, *Ghostly Matters: Haunting and the Sociological Imagination* (Minneapolis: University of Minnesota Press, 1997), 183.

35. Ortiz, *The Blindfold's Eyes*, 56.

36. Ibid.

37. Ibid., 193, 196, 201, 202.

spiritualities. Although those spiritualities have often been recolonized and appropriated by "New Age" spiritualities of Western communities, there is nevertheless a cultural heritage of "staging words" in the remembrance of the dead and dying, against the powers that work repression. Such remembrance is a significant legacy maintained by representatives of indigenous nations and peoples. Ortiz reports and details how she opened herself to those living indigenous traditions, in part because an indigenous woman was the first person she encountered after her escape from the torturers in 1989, who at some risk extended aid to her.[38] Thus, for Ortiz, somatic performance includes such rites of communal religiosity as burning sage, lighting candles, tapping on the drums, forming circle gatherings of supportive women and activists who arrange their bodies in these ways to mediate a shared collective strength.[39] It is in the midst of such gatherings that Ortiz experiences her visions and stories of strengthening, her travel to an "Otherworld" where mythic creatures hold her up, where the dead and dying of the pit and especially "the Woman" encounter her with sayings and encouragements. All this happens amid and in relation to the proactive work of somatic and collective performance.[40]

Some of the most effective ways of the "proactive" mode of somatic performance are the bodily movements and presences entailed by her later quest for justice and by her activism against the torture state. This is exemplified in several kinds of action: by her return, a veritable pilgrimage, to Guatemala City; by placing herself in front of audiences to address press conferences; by her testimonies at legislative hearings; by placing herself before the cameras of *60 Minutes* and other media venues; or by her conduct of hunger strikes. Such a hunger strike is a deprivation of the body, but more importantly, it is a re-presentation of her body in some public space where attention is drawn to the concerns and claims she seeks to foreground. Included here, too, are the carrying out of nonviolent direct action and civil disobedience, which also have been used by other antitorture activists, such as those in the Sebastian Acevedo Movement against Torture in Chile who would hang banners on clandestine torture centers bearing the words, "A Man Is Being Tortured Here!"[41]

---

38. Ibid., 193–95.

39. Ibid., 175, 199–202.

40. Ibid., 175.

41. See William T. Cavanaugh, *Torture and the Eucharist* (Malden, Mass.: Blackwell, 1998), 273–77.

These proactive social and political actions are all somatic performances, and conducting them was both psychically and physically taxing to her, driving her back often to the protection and compensation of the rites of water, cleansing and candles and sage. There was often a close interaction between the somatic performance at a press conference, like the one commented on at the beginning of this chapter, and the body's need for and remembrance of a "safe room" of bodily respite "where our sage and all our talismans were."[42]

This dimension of somatic performance may seem too banal a point to register here. After all, nearly all human action is mediated by bodily movement and performance. And yet it bears special mention here because torture's reduction to broken flesh so brutalizes the body, so breaks its sustaining power of connections to other bodies, that every subsequent performance of the body that is constructive—whether "reactive" or "proactive"—is crucial to developing strength for survival and resistance. What is more, at present the sovereign states that most deploy and disseminate torture, particularly the United States, are those in which the dominant Western spiritualities often symbolize and treat the body as but part of "matter," opposed to spirit. And thus, the body is foreclosed often as site of value. The torture survivor thus is in double need of the practice that valorizes and strengthens the body, and that can deploy the body in resistance. The double need lies in the fact that, first, the body has been directly attacked and brutalized under the power of the torturer's drive for "absolute sovereignty," and second, that she labors often in cultural milieus where the body is all too often juxtaposed to culture or spirit as the negative is to the positive. Somatic performance, and cultivation of the power and value of the body, is crucial to the ability to weigh-in with respect to systems of imposed social suffering.

In other modes of imposed social suffering—whether of racism, sexual violence and homophobia, or economic exploitation—it is also the sufferers' body that is put under duress. Hence, any recovery, survival, *and* resistance will require intentional mobilization of wounded bodies' somatic performance. The theological and its transimmanental way will arise from the agonistic political with a performance of bodies. With bodies the dead and dying weigh-in upon the sovereign structures of the present.

---

42. Ortiz, *The Blindfold's Eyes*, 215.

Anamnestic Solidarity

With this second dimension, we move from the reality of the body, in the survivor/resister's somatic performance, to what some will be tempted to see as a perhaps more nebulous realm, in which there is a haunting of the present by the dead and dying. In the narrative of Ortiz, however, even the most sober of realists are hard pressed to discount her sense of the interplay of the dead with the living in her present. This dimension of practices of the theological—anamnestic solidarity as a remembrance of the dead constitutes an effect of the dead in the present that re-members, re-constitutes, living communities. This is a way to render more particularly the seething presence integral to spectral practice.

Ortiz herself does not seem to question the reality of the voices of the dead. At first she regarded them, she writes, more as "rebukes." When appearing in her flashbacks, dreams and memories—whether from the others in the pit or from the Woman—the voices of the dead and dying in her consciousness were received by Ortiz as warnings: "Don't go on into the future. We weren't able to live. Why should you?" Later Ortiz undergoes a change in understanding: "But maybe the memories, dreams, and flashbacks were the only means those souls had of telling me they were with me."[43]

In this observation we have the first of several tones struck in what is the polytonal experience of "anamnestic solidarity." I deploy an audible and musical image here, because the coexistence of solidarity—this mutual being-with of the dead and the living—is in Ortiz's account so full of remembered sounds, such as moans, screams, other vocalizations. "Can you hear their screams? I can," she challenges her audiences.[44] The first tone or aspect of anamnestic solidarity is this being-with, this sense that the other dead and victims are with the survivor. The key mediator of this relation, this "solidarity," is memory, and hence it is an anamnestic solidarity.

Again I caution, this is no recourse to memory, such that one is dealing only with shadows from an imagined past that might be dismissed as "unreal," hardly reliable for someone who wants "the truth" of matters. Memory, especially when dealing with human trauma, and in nearly all

---

43. Ibid., 192.
44. Ortiz, "A Survivor's View of Torture," 23.

human experience, is a reality-shaping power, mediating past and present, conscious and unconscious life, the personal and the social, even if critical analysis always needs to be applied to memory, to sort out the complex relations between memory and history.[45] As Paul Ricoeur argues amid some of his most astute philosophical work, there is an "epistemic, *veridical* dimension of memory," and it comes to the fore particularly when it is united with the practical dimension in which memory is exercised.[46]

We might qualify the notion of solidarity, this being-with, by way of a reminder from activist and anthropologist Diane Nelson, who has come to prefer speaking of "fluidarity" for this experience. Solidarity, often so glibly invoked by revolutionary and activist communities, and as a mode of being in relation with others, does not always adequately convey the complexity of such a relation. The relation is fluid, changing, always in need of redefining, constituted also by the parties who coexist, challenging one another, challenging even the presumptions to "solidarity." Commenting on attempts by her and others to strike relations of solidarity and to build rapport for her research between 1985 and 1998, Nelson writes: "Fluidarity is a practice and theory of identity-in-formation, aware of its own investments, the pleasures of intervention, and the erotics of relational subject-making. It is historically specific and knows that it is very hard to give up solid bodies, clear-cut enemies and friends, but that this may be the most responsible way to approach the current conjuncture in Guatemala."[47] Note here, again, the importance of the body in the collective relation. With the anamnestic presence of the dead to Ortiz, there is every sign of this fluidarity, as Ortiz herself searches across her struggle for ever better understanding of this "being-with." In fact, Ortiz only rarely invokes the easy language of solidarity, using instead a variety of affirmations that the dead and dying are "with" her. Over and over, Ortiz speaks of these voices of the dead with her and in her, and of the need to open herself to them.

---

45. On memory and remembrance, see the still-valuable text, Edward S. Casey, *Remembering: A Phenomenological Study* (Bloomington: Indiana University Press, 1987).

46. Paul Ricoeur, *Memory, History, Forgetting* (Chicago: University of Chicago Press, 2004), 54–55. On the problematic of memory's "truthful status," see also 4, 7, 12–13, 21, 88, 285, 386.

47. Diane Nelson, *Finger in the Wound: Body Politics in Quincentennial Guatemala* (Berkeley: University of California Press, 1999), 37.

The Woman had found another way to speak to me, and I felt her presence more strongly, as if she were not only beside me but within me, vying for space with the torturers. The spirits of the people tossed into the pit I believe came back with me, too. By returning to Guatemala I had opened myself up to those spirits and allowed them to find refuge in me. I understood, now, that I was not a voice *for* the voiceless, but a voice *with* them.[48]

So, if we continue to speak of this anamnestic solidarity, as I will, I do so with this caveat about the fluid quality of this copresence, its shifting and challenging mode of mutual coexisting.

A second tone of this anamnestic solidarity/fluidarity is sounded almost simultaneously to the first, but it warrants specific and distinctive comment. It is the affirmation by Ortiz, and by others with whom she works collectively, that the dwelling within of the dead and tortured is no mere coexistence. It occurs, more importantly, as a strengthening in the present. The notion of healing after torture suggests often that the victim can reach a state of not being tortured. That is the lie. Once tortured, always tortured, as Améry and others have argued. Ortiz definitely ratifies it. But she does point to a strengthening that can occur over the time of survival, which comes by means of this anamnestic solidarity, this changing and dynamic copresence of the dead with her. As she worded it in one of her public addresses: "We believe the spirits of our tortured sisters and brothers who have gone before us dwell within us, giving us the strength to hold firm to our convictions of justice for all people and to bear witness to the heinous atrocities committed by oppressive governments like Guatemala's."[49] Here the dynamism of the copresence is understood as strengthening *and,* perhaps more importantly, a strengthening for the purpose of surviving and living for action toward justice for the unjustly suffering and slain. It is a strengthening for a power to weigh-in ever more effectively on the sovereign structures that prevent justice and that continue to reinforce the weights of transcendence.

The somatic performances mentioned in the previous section—the press conferences, the testimonies, the vigils, and so on—are ways to manifest this strength gained from anamnestic solidarity. And the somatic

---

48. Ortiz, *The Blindfold's Eyes*, 192.
49. Ibid., 191.

performances of a more ritual character, the ceremonial remembrances with sage, water, recounted stories, are ways to mobilize the memory, honor the "re-memories" (a kind of "social unconscious")[50] that convey the strength of the dead's dynamic copresence with the living. It is the strengthening for a work of justice, on behalf of and alongside the suffering and unjustly slain, that distinguishes this anamnestic solidarity from "remembrance of family ancestors." Though the remembrance may have some similar traits, the tone and goal is different. It is what Avery Gordon discussed as a "seething presence" of the dead, churning in the memories of the living, which mobilizes one for a present practice of resistance and justice. This is what often marks a difference between anamnestic solidarity and remembrance of departed family members.[51]

A third tone at work in anamnestic solidarity is the propensity of the copresent dead, in the "social unconscious" of the living, to galvanize new social networks in the world of the living. Thus, anamestic solidarity is not merely that of individual activists who possess and nurture their individual memories of the past. To the contrary, there are unique constellations in the present—gatherings, cell meetings, circles, networks— which are modes of sociality and collective signs of the strengthening presence of the dead among the living. There are two primary examples of this in *The Blindfold's Eyes*.

First, there is Ortiz's encounter of a Guatemalan journalist during her first visit to Guatemala after her torture. That first pilgrimage back did not go well, with neither U.S. nor Guatemalan officials, nor the media in either country, being open to her story and charges. At a press conference during this early trip, in spite of denials and refusals to take seriously her words, a journalist slipped her a note that read, "*Sea fuerte*" ("Be strong"). Ortiz writes, "I was sure that the Woman was speaking through him."[52] That note had an inspiring and encouraging impact. The tortured Woman, already copresent in Ortiz's present consciousness, was now linked into other agents in the social world of Ortiz's present. The journalist achieved a copresence with Ortiz, joining her in the sociality of resistance and strengthening that is part of the practice of torture survival.

---

50. Again, the term "re-memory" is Toni Morrison's in *Beloved* (New York: Knopf, 1987), 35, elaborated by Gordon, *Ghostly Matters*, 165–69, and 212 n.12.

51. On this difference, see Gordon, *Ghostly Matters*, 3–27.

52. Ortiz, *The Blindfold's Eyes*, 161.

A still more significant witness to this third tone of anamnestic solidarity is the circle of women among whom Ortiz regularly finds strength.
There is an interplay between the copresence with the dead in Ortiz's
memory, and the copresence she has with the circle of women in her
present. In fact, they mutually implicate and mobilize one another. At one
point in her book, for example, she envisions the circle around her. There
is not only "Mimi" and "Darleen" and others from the present struggle for
strength and resistance, but in the circle, too, is "my Woman Friend," and
she describes her own hands in that circle as locked with the Woman's,
just as they had been in the basement torture room of the *Politecnica*.
She then also views the other women of the circle in terms of her remembrance of the Woman who has joined the circle, such that the community
of the living is now depicted as full of women with "black and blue marks
on their bodies and their skin was rent and hung from open gashes. Dry
blood was caked on their thighs and lips."[53] The enabling community is
now a single, if variegated, cowounded unit, mobilized now for communal witness and effort. Differences, even conflicts, will remain among
some in the group. It is this community of anamnestic solidarity, however,
which blurs boundaries of past and present, and so becomes a context
for so many other events narrated in her book. In sensing this new sociality, she hears and constructs various stories of healing for her, discovers
certain new perspectives on her body, her vocation, her beliefs. It is in
this context, too, that the circle of women is also portrayed as enabling
Ortiz's journeying to what she calls "the Otherworld." In this Otherworld
it is evident that she is weaving a new mythos into her received Catholic spirituality. The imagery she creates equips her with a strength. This
strength, in turn, enables a spectral resistance that keeps her organizing
amid and against citadels of the torture state.[54] She makes references to
these newly woven, and communally nurtured, imagined worlds as she
navigates the corridors of power in the legislative halls of Congress, in
visits at the White House, in vigils outside the White House, at public
and media events at various sites. Altogether they contribute to Ortiz's
sense that she has "a team of people" with her to support her, and that
she is, as she writes, "not a passive, helpless victim, alone, abandoned,

---

53. Ibid., 200.
54. For this and other examples, see the chapter "Into the Otherworld," in ibid.
193–216.

and betrayed, but a forceful person with a community of people fighting beside me."[55]

In sum, anamnestic solidarity—or "fluidarity"—is made up of the sounding of three tones in the sensibility of survivors/resisters: first, the dead are copresent to and with the living; second, they strengthen those who bear the memories of the dead; and third, they become part of the creation of a social network of past and present that motivates and mobilizes the bodies of the living for survival and resistance to sovereign structures today. All three forge and raise action to the point of spectral practice.

Revitalizing Naturalism and the "Otherworld"

Enter the dolphin and the bone. If we delve still more deeply into the reforged and imagined world of the surviving and resisting Ortiz, as presented in *The Blindfold's Eyes*, we must reckon with what I term a "revitalizing naturalism." By this I mean that there is in her account a turning to nature, a reinterpretation of the natural world that is experienced as revitalizing for Ortiz's person and work. This certainly sits uncomfortably in relation to what most articulators of Catholic and Protestant guild theology would find "orthodox" or appropriate. The main traditions of Christian belief have usually marked off their belief structure, more or less emphatically, from a vitalistic interpretation of earth's and nature's powers, certainly from any elaborate and routine veneration of the figures of nature.

The artful moves at work in Ortiz's narrative constitute an imaginative version of the transimmanental way, a move into a configuration of nature and world. Ortiz's journey is into what she and her circle term "the Otherworld," but it is not a journey outside of nature or above it, to a supernatural plane. The configuration she enters might be appropriately termed its depths, given the way she presents her story of tunnel entries into this Otherworld. It ends up being a place replete with watery places, and it is in such regions of nature that she finds "her animal"—the animal, she is told, that "accompanies you on life's journeys, the animal that gives you power."[56] The circles of sociality at work in anamnestic solidarity

55. Ibid., 175.
56. Ibid., 194.

involve this reference to the animal realm of natural process. It is done as part of a personal and collective search for strength amid agonistic struggle. It is a naturalist faith. In one moment of special strengthening Ortiz writes of nature more broadly: "The warmth, the fields, the light— nature itself was a healing source."[57]

The dolphin is a particularly interesting figure in her imagery, since it becomes "her animal." A dolphin is hardly the fearsome, "monstrous" figure/image one would expect to constitute a specter. Yet it plays a key role in Ortiz's practice of survival, and this enables her to move as specter to the torture state. It is monstrous, perhaps, by reason of its powerful effect, that is, creating a resister like Ortiz and her colleagues who take on the sovereign state in the corridors of Congress, the White House, as well as in public parks and as activists at work at a variety of official and bureaucratic sites. As already mentioned, at various points she closes her fingers around the silver dolphin figure that she wore around her neck to inspire her in moments of threat and fear. Its metal could be warm in the palm, and it "let warmth travel through me."[58] The dolphin has many meanings as Ortiz relates her stories. Overall, the dolphin is a force of nature that mobilizes Ortiz's own capacity to deal with fear. Sometimes this is fear of the dark. At other times it is a fear of the abyss that being tortured opened up in her life, represented by the ocean, which the dolphin navigates so easily. At other times, the fear is of the lingering presence-to-mind of the torturers. The fear may also erupt when speaking to an audience or at a press conference, which can seem filled with the presence of her torturers since many sorts of officials can manifest the ethos of the torture state. At those times, as in one instance, she finds solace in "remembering the dolphin arching above the water."[59] The dolphin, in yet another dreamed scenario, takes her to the bottom of the ocean and shows her that at the depths of the earth and sea, "There was nothing scary there. There was nothing but peace."[60] Moreover, the dolphin splashes her, and in another narrated scene, enables her to glimpse the importance of playing. She resents at first the invitation to play. Later, though, she recounts how she came to see that when survivors guard their capacity to play and to

---

57. Ibid., 444.
58. Ibid., 212.
59. Ibid., 216.
60. Ibid., 196.

delight in creation, they may offer up the most radical act of defiance to the torturer who aimed to destroy all such delight as well as her capacity to dissent to power and to relate to others.[61] Play and protest are both intrinsic to transimmanence's weighing-in upon the world.

Perhaps the most important role of the dolphin in her narrated story is to turn her—to carry her, as it were—to the circle of women. The trust in nature here is consonant with the growing trust in the circle of sociality that nurtures anamnestic solidarity. The dolphin is said to exclaim at one point that she—and the dolphin is rendered throughout as "she"—is a part of the "we," the collective and encircling team of supporters who provide Ortiz strength and link her to the dead through "Otherworld."[62]

This variegated turn to nature is part of a faith shift that she herself highlights toward the end of the book. Ortiz recounts how her strengthening of person and activist orientation involved a kind of faith:

> And I was starting to have a kind of faith. I had started to believe in the goodness of nature. Squirrels, for example, no longer seemed evil to me. Nature was no longer suspect, a potential vehicle for the Devil—or the torturers—to work through. I was also starting to have faith in myself.[63]

This faith in herself is mentioned in the same breath with her respect for *not* forgiving the torturer, José, who actually asked her forgiveness at one point in her process of torture.[64] In the same vein, she tells of painting her fingernails "to exert my will and have my hands reflect it."[65] The conversation with the dolphin thus is transposed into a conversation and dwelling amid the circle of women, the community of the wounded who yet gave her strength for self and for relation. And in a crucial story of her book, where the powers of the dolphin and of the women's circle are linked, the women's circle is abundant with the power of connection that yields a "sense of solidarity" which the torturers could not break. "We were too strong for them," she exults. "The Woman," who was also in the

---

61. On play and enjoyment as defiance, see ibid., 199, 210.

62. Ibid., 199.

63. Ibid., 344.

64. Ibid., and on José's request for forgiveness during the torture, see page 10 in the same source.

65. Ibid., 223.

circle, now took Ortiz's hand and "a smile spread over her face," after she had said to Ortiz, "You did what any of us would have done under those circumstances. You fought and you're still fighting. You're fighting for all of us."[66]

The dolphin figure, however, is not the only piece of venerated nature at work in the narrative. Around her neck is also a piece of bone. This part of the natural world carries a more sobering, if still strengthening, set of meanings and memories. The bone was given to her outside a human rights office in Guatemala, pressed into her palm by a woman wearing traditional indigenous clothing. She had lost her son to Guatemalan violence, and had waited to thank Ortiz for what she was doing in seeking to expose the torturers. She explained the piece of bone that Ortiz was later to wear around her neck with the dolphin: "My son, Victor, they took him. He was lost for a long time, but we found his remains. The only thing that was left to me were some pieces of his bones."[67] This seeming piece of vertebra, as she thought it must be, was also a comforting, if gruesome, part of the natural world, receiving a veneration. "It sounds corny, maybe even sick—part of someone's body who was probably tortured to death brought me peace. But it was true. A peace or energy— maybe simple gratitude—was flowing through me."[68]

Thus, the dolphin, mediating a sense of newfound strength in the wake of her torture, was joined by this bone, a sign indicating that at least one more person from among the tortured was not forgotten. These two venerated items joined the more traditional cross around her neck. But this latter traditional symbol was naturalized, as it were, carved for and given to her by another victim of torture, Raúl. It did not mean something salvific. As Ortiz clarifies at one point, "Since November 1989, I have never seen a cross as anything other than an instrument of torture. So, I wore it as a symbol of the torture Raúl and other Guatemalans had suffered."[69]

To contemplate the diverse meanings carried in these amulets worn around Ortiz's neck—the dolphin, the bone, the cross—is to discern the complexity of a naturalist faith. It is no mere worship of nature as such.

---

66. Ibid., 200.
67. Ibid., 213.
68. Ibid.
69. Ibid., 201.

It is no embrace of nature as nonliving matter, to be opposed to spirit or culture, as so much of the Western religious imagination does.[70] On the contrary, the natural world is alive, a source of revivification. If Ortiz is a participant in the practice of survival and resistance that poses a specter to the torture state, to the imposed social suffering that is the weight of the world, she weighs-in with an imaging that is transimmanental, deftly navigating the powers of nature for revivification. The dolphin and bone are specters in her neocolonial necromancy, they circulate the dead—for life.

A Grotesque Transcendentalism

I have stressed throughout that the way of transimmanence is no mere counter-ethos to that of transcendence, and that a dialectical interplay is at work in thinking transcendence and transimmanence. The way of tran-simmanence works amid "failed transcendence," to recall Ernesto Laclau's formulation.[71] It passes, transits into spaces of the singular plural world, taking note of the ruins of transcendence. When those laboring on the undersides of imposed suffering weigh-in to interrupt the ethos and prac-tices of sovereignty with the force of their art in spectral practice, they do not eschew all the ways and tools of transcendence, however much they seek to rupture that sovereign order. Similarly, in Ortiz's narrative, we can see a mode of weighing-in, which at times creatively and strategically selects its engagements with the cultures and symbols of transcendence. The way of transimmanence includes, then—and we can see it as our fourth dimension of Ortiz's practice of surviving and resisting torture— what I will term a "grotesque transcendentalism."

In selecting the term *grotesque* for this dimension I make use of one of its meanings, "being strikingly incongruous and inappropriate." Here the incongruity is between an aesthetic politics of emancipation from the world's concentrated weight, on the one hand, and the use of key symbols from those citadels of concentrated, sovereign power, on the other. The

---

70. Barbara Tedlock, *Time and the Highland Maya,* rev. ed. (Albuquerque: University of New Mexico Press, 1992), 3–11. Tedlock traces what she terms the analytic dichotomiza-tion of spirit/matter in the Western religious perspectives, as distinct from the more dialecti-cal relation of the two in Mayan indigenous perspective.

71. Ernesto Laclau, *On Populist Reason* (London: Verso, 2005), 244.

engagement with the ethos of transcendence, which is evident in Ortiz's transimmanental weighing-in may also exhibit aspects of another meaning of "the grotesque," namely, "being comically or repulsively ugly or distorted." Ortiz's presence at various events and gatherings—described above as ghostly, or even hurtful, as she herself relates—could be experienced as odd, discomforting, interruptive, a sign of life's imposed suffering and ugliness. There can be something grotesque in such a one whose survival makes her spectral to the living.[72]

Ortiz is herself prone to use the word *grotesque*. She invokes it to characterize the overall strangeness of her surviving as well as her mode of surviving. In her Princeton address, for example, she spoke of her "grotesque resurrection," suggesting that after many unanswered prayers for relief and release in the torture cell, now "by some cruel irony the now-dead God still existed to force upon me a grotesque resurrection and return to unwanted life."[73] As we know from her narrative in *The Blindfold's Eyes*, she works through to a point of greater strength in which aspects of life are "wanted," "savored," "welcomed," however much the "bad times" and "bad days" persist.[74] "On my bad days I still say I should have died back in that prison, . . . I still wish I had died."[75] But the razor blade has been put away, buried under a tree—a cause for rejoicing, now, as Ortiz reports, by even the people in the pit and the Woman.[76]

How, in closing, can we understand Ortiz's struggle and the light it might shed on the grotesque transcendentalism of its transimmanental way? From the perspective of the spectral imaging in practice we have already surveyed, we can observe that her grotesque transcendentalism is made up of three moves.

The Critique of Transcendentalizing Religion

First, there is a critique of transcendentalizing religion, particularly of Christianity. This is particularly evident in the way she criticizes and changes her understanding of "God." She leaves behind, she writes, "the

---

72. On these different meanings of "grotesque," see Pearsall, ed., *Concise Oxford English Dictionary*, 627.

73. Ortiz, "A Survivor's View of Torture," 24.

74. Ortiz, *The Blindfold's Eyes*, 475.

75. Ibid., 475.

76. Ibid., 477.

God the sisters invoked, the God who was aware of the fall of every sparrow."[77] The God who controls and governs from outside, who is the sovereign of the world—which we have met before as grounding and reinforcing the "divine right" of earthly kings and sovereignties of state— this God is subject to critique, even put aside. Even when she makes a kind of peace with the figure of God, saying, in fact, "I have forgiven God for not working some dramatic miracle," this does not create any affirmation of "healing." It does not replace or prevent the persisting wish that she had died.[78] This apparent contradiction, a kind of impasse and uncertainty about what to do about the God concept, is partially resolved by the ways she reworks the God concept.

As transition to my discussion of that reworking, however, I must note first one other important feature of her criticism of key notions of Christianity. Given the torture that she suffered, and the readiness of torturers to see their victim's suffering as a theogonic drama (and one of her torturers, too, whispered in her ear after one of his more grisly acts, "Your God is dead"), her reflections on the cross and suffering are cru- cial. In most Christian understandings, the cross is a life-giving occasion of death that mediates, and so creates, "reconciliation" between a sov- ereign and transcendent figure, God, on the one side, and the world of humanity, fallen and broken, on the other. In her more naturalist faith, as we already noted, the cross is limited to being a wooden cross-piece for torture, to be understood on the level of the tools of the torture rooms of the *Politecnica* and of every torture cell anywhere. It is not salvific. It is a site of torture and, as I read Ortiz, her practice of survival never invokes the cross as itself life giving. A torture event—whether a crucifixion, rape, applications of electric shock, a lethal injection, a hanging, a burning and lynching ritual, being rendered "ex-human" into some zone of abandon- ment—these are not life giving. Being subjected to torture—as was Jesus of Christian traditions, Dianna Ortiz, Emmett Till, Vincent Chin, the many unnamed indigenous dead, or anyone else—is not construed as salvific or redemptive. It is significant that there is almost no explicit Christology in *The Blindfold's Eyes*, certainly not one that places the cross at the cen- ter of salvation. There is little discourse about Jesus in Ortiz's narrative, save the barest of references. The cross is grotesquely reworked by her

---

77. Ibid., 222.
78. Both statements occur on the same page in ibid., 475.

naturalist faith, exposed as the torture tool it was. (She wears the cross on the cover of her book and, tellingly, it is not gold or silver; instead, it and its cord are a deep red in color.)

Reworking the "God" Concept

In this second move, there is further reworking of the God concept and of other key notions of the transcendent in the Christian religion she had known. "God" is understood anew, strikingly found for her in that which "united all our voices, as one voice, calling for justice and truth—calling for an end to torture." God becomes a unitive power found in the anamnestic solidarity between the living and the dead, and pointed toward a liberating spectrality for the unjustly tortured and slain. This, she seems to say, is a "God" that she can sing to, and she attends a Mass where it is sung, held at one culminating point of her struggle to expose agents and abettors of her torture. In that song, she sees God as a light, "greater than grieving, more than death . . . a nameless voice . . . which the world will hear, deep in the night, when the river will rise."[79] Her retaining the notion of "God" at all can be seen as grotesque, too, an engagement with this traditional figure of the sovereign "One." And yet she makes the grotesque move, taking in that symbol, while reworking it in light of the naturalistic faith, explicating it with the sensible images of light, voice, and river.

The aspect of the grotesque may reside in the simple fact that she dares at all, through her journey, to continue invoking the name "God." Ortiz's persistence is an incongruous move, given what she perceived as God's silence, even callousness, in the most harrowing hours of her torture. It is also incongruous, given the way the notion of God is so often used to reinforce the notion of sovereignty and a hegemonic masculinism, which anchor the cultures of state sovereignty that disseminate the trauma of torture (and rape as torture) to constrain nationalist and citizen loyalties. And yet, she deploys the grotesque, even embraces it.

Her reworking of "God" occurs in conjunction with the final song she reports was sung at the group worshiping with the Assisi community, "The River Will Rise." About that event, she writes, "Assisi community members still talk about that Mass and singing that song and the moment

---

79. Ibid., 391.

of communion we had—whether it was the words or the melody, no one knows." What she distilled from the song concerning the notion of God must be quoted at length:

> The song defines God as our light, greater than grieving, more than our death, and says we can hear a nameless voice, crying within our hearts. And God is that nameless voice, and God is the name of the nameless voice, the name that no one calls alone, which the world will hear, deep in the night, when the river will rise. Peace will flow like a river and the river will rise.[80]

There is here a continuation of the revivifying naturalism, as God is referenced in conjunction with light ("our light") and whose nameless voice is heard in the depth of night, that is, in the daily changing of the cosmos, in the turning of earth from sun to moon and back again, and when "the river will rise." The sacred is located, then, to recall Nancy's notions of transimmanental imagery, in motion and movement, in passings in the natural world. Hers is a riverine passing through the singular plural world, one that etches still more passageways, conduits to new modes by which resisters may engage one another in networks of further actions. They will need both to flow and meander through such passageways in search of alternative ways to create world, to transimmanently engage the powers of sovereignty and the transcendental God that still grounds the brutal work of *immonde* and *glomus.*

Significant, too, is that the voice associated with God is nameless. Ortiz does not attach, at this crucial juncture of her narrative, any of the traditional titles that might be derived from the symbolic order which mediates the sovereign ethos (Father, Ruler, Almighty, and so on). Instead, she leaves God nameless. There is a hint of naming, but only in the suggestion: "and God is the name of the nameless voice." Interestingly, though, this nameless voice is one that is called to by humans and which the world hears. But both the calling and the hearing of the nameless voice that is "God" are never done by a single individual. "No one calls alone" to this nameless voice named "God." Once again, this accents the intrinsically collective and communal character of the vision

---

80. Ibid.

and imagery developed from the underside of imposed social suffering, here torture. The world "will hear" the nameless voice after it is cried out to *collectively*, amid the shared struggle for being and life, which grows through the practices of justice and peace that constitute being and life. Not surprisingly, given the naturalist faith, and given that she had sunk deep into the singular plural world (even, as she once dreamed, to the ground floor of its ocean), it is the watery movement of nature, of a river rising, that occasions the world's hearing of the voice that the grieving call out to together, even from the dead. This is the matrix of meanings in a singular plural world in which "God" for her becomes meaningful. God is thus inserted, in a life-giving way, into a neocolonial necromancy.

Still—and I must stress this one more time—there are vestiges of the transcendent ethos in this. Those weighing-in transimmanentally do not jettison every aspect of transcendence, particularly the hope of overcoming, or rising, in some sense. However grotesque those vestiges may seem, those ruins persist. Their ashes remain. They cannot simply be swept aside. Here the "rising of the river" carries a transcendent reference. There is a "rising," after all—but it is of the river and still very much within and for the earth and those who inhabit its spaces and times. That rising river, together with the light, is what is said to be "greater than" the sufferers' grieving, and "more than" their death and dying. As the references to the play of light and rising of rivers connotes, this greater, this more, is found in the twisting and refracting singular plurality of a vital, always surprising, natural world.

Finally, amid and through all this, there is the spectral presence, not just as seething but also as subverting. It should be recalled that the commentary on "God" of this passage occurs in Ortiz's narrative just after she recounts her burning to ash the artist sketches of her torturers. The spectral, the portentous, is conveyed not only by that act of burning as context for her reflections on God, but also by the very title of the song on which she comments, the title that she returns to as the final phrase of the paragraph on God: "and the river will rise." In this rising there is not only threat, but also spectral confidence, a certain, strange—grotesque, again—hope that even the tortured and always tortured will rise, a fact to which Ortiz and her supportive community have borne remarkable witness through the courage and tears of continual rising to resist, again and again, against the citadels of sovereignty and transcendence that reinforce the torture state and weight of the world. Her own organizing, and directorship of TASCC (Torture Abolition and Survivors Support Coalition), gives practical and institutional expression to that spectral rising.[81]

Reengaging the Transcendentalizing Communities

A final conceptual move in the grotesque transcendentalism returns us to the domain of practice, wherein her spectral imaging is at work to create survival and resistance. Here I point to her courage to dare stepping again into the spheres of ritual meaning operative in transcendentalizing religious communities. The clearest examples of this come at two points.

First, it is noteworthy that when planning her vigil across from the Clinton White House on behalf of the tortured, and in an attempt to get full disclosure of information about her torture, she chose to inaugurate the vigil on a Palm Sunday, when the church commemorates Jesus' entrance into Jerusalem. In spite of her reservations about the transcendentalizing Christian faith she embraced before, and a lingering sense that she still could not make the obeisance to a sovereign god that says, "Yes, God, I commit my life totally to you," she was willing to proceed with the vigil on Palm Sunday, enabling her to frame her thoughts about the Guatemalan situation "in a faith context."[82] There is in this the incongruity of the grotesque, this implanting of one's transimmanental faith within the ritual calendar of the transcendentalizing religion. This may be all the more so given that the Christians celebrating with her, during the time of the vigil, unlike her, may very well have been venerating the cross as a divine salvific symbol. But her own practice of survival and resistance involved a daring to risk that incongruity. Here it is evident that the transimmanental mode of weighing-in against sovereign power at times demands risking the incongruity, a perceived inconsistency—a working within the ethos of transcendence, in spite of an aim to rupture the destructive ways of that transcendental ethos.

The second, and perhaps most poetic, example of spectral imaging at work within a context of grotesque transcendentalism comes in her discussion of that decision to celebrate Mass with her family and friends.

---

81. For the TASCC Web site, see http://www.tassc.org/index.php?sn=164, accessed September 21, 2010.

82. Ortiz, *The Blindfold's Eyes,* 344.

It was, as she tells it in *The Blindfold's Eyes*, a Mass that she observed after a ritual of "purification and celebration" performed at the end of yet another press conference. This Mass, we might say, was yet another somatic performance, at which she ritually incinerated in the flames of burning sage the artist sketches that had been made of her torturers. This was not because she was now proclaiming her "healing" from torture. Nor was this a return to a commitment to forgiveness, which would encourage her to forgive her torturers. More to the point, it signaled her capacity to wonder if there was something other than the "wholly evil" even in her torturers. Simultaneously, the ashes of their sketched images reminded that she was freed from the fear and hatred inside her, which was one of the ways that the torturers had maintained their places within her. "The weight had lifted from me, as the faces of my torturers had vanished to ash."[83] She not only celebrated Mass, but also she said the Lord's Prayer with her family and friends in that gathered community.

* * *

Where does this "grotesque transcendence" leave us for an understanding of transimmanence and its spectral practice? What sort of encounter with the world's weight do we confront? Victor Anderson's words in his book *Creative Exchange*, which treats of the concept of the grotesque for theological reflection, offers some important reminders.[84] It is typical of the grotesque to recover and leave unresolved prior and basic sensibilities such as attraction/repulsion and pleasure/pain differentials. The need to overturn, or to triumph over, onerous and repressive exercises of sovereign power can suggest that liberating practices should be lacking in any qualities reminiscent of oppressive power's constitution and ways of operating. In her spectral practice, however, especially regarding this grotesque transcendence, Ortiz's trajectory of survival does not include a stripping away of all such vestiges of the transcendent. The lesson here for radical practice may be that forging actions as spectral for the undoing of oppressive power need not mean a purge of all those elements (or persons) associated with that which is being resisted. On the contrary—and

---

83. Ibid., 390.

84. Victor Anderson, *Creative Exchange: A Constructive Theology of African American Religious Experience* (Minneapolis: Fortress Press, 2008), 10–13.

Anderson emphasizes this, too—radical practice may live and work with confusion and ambiguity precisely about this retention. To be sure, there will be reflection about how to wield the retention, just as for Ortiz there was reflection on how to reengage elements of the transcendent. But *that* there is retention, and even ambiguity and confusion about the retention, is what invites acceptance. Often this means resisting "cognitive synthesis," especially the kind of ordering reflection of Theology that traffics in doctrinal structures and systems. Anderson, like Ortiz, features discourse full of symbols and artful images, but he resists offering a great synthesis. This leaves radical practice and reflection open to engage the onerous concentration of the world's weight by deploying a wider array of creative energies and pathways, of journeying that might release the teeming vitality of a singular plural world. In this there may be the need to highlight "the absurd and the sincere, the comical and tragic, the estranged and familiar, the satirical and playful, and normalcy and abnormality."[85] Is not this the lesson in playfulness Ortiz received in her encounter with the dolphin splashing in the sea, or the lesson in horror and mourning she received when a Maya woman pressed her son Victor's bone-piece into her palm?

---

85. Ibid., 11.

Epilogue

THE THEOLOGICAL
AND THE POLITICAL

I see growing on the ripples of the water
The revivifying specter
Of a barbarous freedom drunk on its tears.[1]—Victor Serge

In time flesh will wear out chains
In time the mind will make chains snap.[2]—Victor Serge

One way to summarize this book's presentation of "the theological" is to see
it as my attempt to formalize a thinking that is carried in the visionary
poetry rendered here by Victor Serge amid his political struggle. The risk
will be that his poetry is rendered sterile by more formal concerns of
theory. But if the poet also is a thinker, could there not be a thinking into
the world's being, into its "body of sense," as intimated in this visionary
poetry offered from a life of struggle that included imprisonment under
regimes of both a capitalist France and the Bolsheviks' Soviet Union? His

---

1. Victor Serge, "Stenka Razin," in *Resistance: Poems*, trans. James Brook (San Francisco: CityLights, 1972), 21. Used by permission.
2. Victor Serge, "Be Hard" (fragment), in ibid., 33. Used by permission.

line, "in time flesh will wear out chains," was once included as a closing word of encouragement to me in a letter from Mumia Abu-Jamal,
a prisoner and revolutionary journalist who had been on death row in
Pennsylvania, then for over almost twenty years, now for almost thirty.[3] I
knew what Abu-Jamal meant as he used these words to evoke our shared
struggle and hope—but what would it entail to *think* that elusive meaning? If thought and body "*are* only their touching each other, the touch
of their breaking down, and into, each other," what kind of thinking can
touch the flesh that can wear out chains, what kind of mind will make
them snap? The theological, I suggest in this epilogue, is the name for
this kind of thinking, this kind of mind and flesh. This thinking involves
identifying several formalizations of the theological. Let me identify five
of these as a summary of this book.

First, there is the formalization that situates the theological as a *transdisciplinary discourse, in a space of knowledge production that is intercultural and countercolonial.* Perhaps for those in the guild academy
who organize themselves primarily by "disciplines," this may be the more
difficult point to grasp. Not only is the discursive practice of the theological not identifiable with the discourses of guild Theology, it is neither
to be found in any one other "discipline" or "area study," nor in any
one academic "Center" or "Institute" of the academy, especially of the
Western academy. Instead, it is a discursive practice, a use of language
and thought embodying spectral practice, which can take place at any of
those academic sites and at other public sites of reflection, too. In order to
deal with systems of global capital, neocoloniality, imperial dominance,
and the suffering they create, this transdisciplinary discursive practice will
usually also have to be intercultural, countercolonial, and counterimpe-
rial, if it is to deal with the transimmanental dimension of human being
steeped in the agonistic political.

This points to a second formalization of thinking that is the theological. *It has as its subject matter, and recurrent concern, the dimension of
transimmanence,* as I have explored with the aid of Nancy's and others'
thought. For those still prone to identify "the theological" with Theology,

---

3. Among Mumia Abu-Jamal's hundreds of published essays and several books, see
his earliest book, *Live from Death Row* (New York: Addison-Wesley, 1995). For analysis of
his case and struggle, see Amnesty International, *The Case of Mumia Abu-Jamal: A Life in
the Balance* (New York: Seven Stories, 2000), and on exculpatory evidence for him, see
Justice on Trial: The Case of Mumia Abu-damal. A documentary film (New York: Big Noise
Films, 2010).

relinquishing the transcendent and learning the transimmanental focus are necessary disciplines—better, they constitute a freeing meditation. The notion of transimmanence presents a changed terrain of subject-matter, beyond transcendence and immanence, where the reference to the transcendent is let go and so also is any obeisance to the primacy of doctrinal cognition that orders thought and practice to the transcendent, either as "wholly other" and outside world, or as "incarnate" within it. This yields not something less, but actually something more—something more than enough. It is to have opened up *in the world* the teeming singular plurality of the world's bodies, instead of the straightened and disciplined chain of world and human being ordered to the transcendent in a politics of verticality. In transimmanence, the scholar of the theological explores the intricacy, opaqueness, and grotesqueness—occasionally the strange luminosity—of the world's own being, its body of sense.

A third formalization is the *social ontology of the agonistic political,* as the field in which transimmanence lies, or, if that be too wooden an expression, as the milieu of which transimmanence is a dimension. The dimension of transimmanence emerges, this work has argued, in the milieu of a weighted world, and the theological has this transimmanence of "the political" as its milieu. Human being is steeped in this weighted world, what the book's political ontology has presented and explored as "the agonistic political." Some might portray Nancy's notion of transimmanence as only a continual circulating of meaning among singularities, a multiple, changing and sliding through social relations, a kind of teeming vitality of a polyform world of interiors and exteriors. This captures much of Nancy's major concern, it seems to me, but it also misses what is evident in Nancy, too, especially in later writings, namely, that this transimmanence is always in tension. Its world is labile, always capable of shifting weights of bodies and the weighing between them. The weighing between, most notably, can shift from world weighing as "extension" to world weighing as "concentrated." It is the concentrated weight that brings a sense of crisis in Nancy's writings, as world extended is under threat, in "brutal collision" with homogenizing globe, with concentrated capital (and, I have always added, with coloniality and neocoloniality of power, especially as worked by imperial state powers).

This shifting of the world's weight is the agonistic milieu of transimmanence. The practical social ontology of Schatzki and Bourdieu enables my formalization of the agonistic political to be brought closer to the lived world of human being and practice. They enable our theorizing the agonistic as inscribed in all interaction, in formation of the human, from infant and child to adult, as male and female, as sexually, racially, and religiously constituted, through a somatized sociality in which bodies and their dispositions are shaped by a struggle for recognition and accumulation of symbolic capital. These practice theorists enable us to spot the many ways the agonistic is at work in human life. They equip us to see the gradations in that agonism, between the world's weight some experience as extension (less agonistically because spaced with intimacies and distances making for some freedom of bodies), and weight many experience as concentration (most intensely agonistic, because bodies are crammed, piled, arranged, ordered, without the spacings that preserve singular plural being).

A fourth formalization that constitutes the theological as a thinking into the world's bodies, into its flesh, is *analysis of the "prodigious art-force of the image"* (Nancy) or *"symbolic force by way of artful form"* (Bourdieu). This art-force is more respected, and theorized, by Nancy than by Bourdieu. For Bourdieu, the symbolic is largely a function that extends the influence of an alchemy of ascendance, which creates "symbolic violence," by reference to the transcendent, and thus sets up dominations across different social fields, from hearth to workplace, from *homo religiosus* to *homo academicus*. This book began its formalized analysis of images' art-force with Nancy's greater sense of their power, and then developed it further, as critique of Bourdieu, in conversation with a variety of thinkers on the politics of aesthetics (JanMohamed, Butler, Wright, Biehl, Rancière, and others). What the imagistic art-force does is to throw into bold relief a crucial dynamic at work in the agonistic political, that shifting, again, between world as bodies weighing-in extension, in one form, and bodies weighing as concentrated, in its other form. But it does this in a way that simultaneously portends the undoing of its onerous, sovereign power. Whether the art-force is in the power of the skull that meets us from Richard Wright's poem, in the force-full specter of liberation carried by the poems of Guantánamo detainees, or in the spirited self-affirmation of Catarina's "raw poems" from a zone of abandonment—in all these and more, the agony of concentrated weight is registered in their art, as is their defiance of reduction to bare life, to mere meat or to ex-humanness. They persist with their art-force and thus display their language, their desire—their life. The analysis of such art-force could be, and should be, pursued far beyond the few examples I have pondered—from Guantánamo, Wright, and Catarina—taking scholars of the theological into new readings of transimmanental life in a wide array of the artfully defiant symbolic forms, wherever they are found.

Does this all constitute a kind of denial of death? Have I merely transposed past concerns of Theology with outside world and some supernatural realm into the defiant art of the world's immanence, its sufferers' outcries? I think not. There is no denial of death here, in the sense of that dying that is a necessary, and sometimes welcome, dissolving into other beings, a decaying that is a lying-beside other beings and entities of world. What these prodigious art images *do* decry, what they defy, is not this inevitable dying, but death by concentration, by the agonistic weight of the world piled upon peoples in the practices of domination and sovereignty, in a politics of verticality. The legitimacy and finality of that concentrated weight is what is denied. In a helpful image, Nancy limns what death in a singular plural world could/should be. "Our dead," he writes, would have "a winding-cloth to define the spacing of one, and then another, death." Instead, in the concentration of the world's weight, in the "world-wideness of bodies," we have "cadavers in a mass grave that aren't dead . . . they are wounds heaped up, stuck in, flowing into one another, the soil tossed right on top, no winding-cloth . . ."[4] That is concentration, and that is the sinister kind of death denial that results all too often from the politics of verticality and worships at the shrines of the transcendent. The artful images of the victims of these concentrations are only defying that necropolitics, denying the legitimacy of "life" ordered in its concentrated form. The cadaverous cultural politics still surround us. Few in the mainstream arts or media decry, or even mourn, the piling of cadavers by, say, U.S. projects in global sovereignty that foster and allow the number of Iraqi civilian deaths to rise into the thousands, perhaps to over a million. As Bruce Springsteen sang, "We don't measure the blood we've drawn anymore/We just stack the bodies outside the door."[5]

---

4. Jean-Luc Nancy, *Corpus,* trans. Richard A. Rand (New York: Fordham University Press, 2008 [French 2006]), 77.

5. Bruce Springsteen, "The Last to Die," on his compact disc *Magic* (New York: Columbia Records, 2007). The song title is taken from former Vietnam veteran John Kerry (later a U.S. Senator from Massachusetts and Democratic Party presidential candidate) in his testimony before Congress, when he asked, "Who'll be the last to die for a mistake?" Springsteen's song points the question to the U.S. killing in Iraq. For a discerning critique

The fifth formalization of the theological by which this book can be summarized, and the one that reminds again of practices, concerns the theological's *sense of expectation, its cultivation of transformative possibility as carried in spectral practice.* The prodigious image, recall, has a power, yes—in its narrative turnings, its lyric, its melody and rhythm, its arresting tapestry or shape—but it is always something carried, inscribed intersubjectively, in practice. It is the practice that directs and points the image's art-force toward the dissolution of concentrated weight. Practice, because it has what Schatzki terms a "teleo-affective structure," is both strengthened by such prodigious art forms, which engage the affective life powerfully, and also gives *telos* to human activity, points symbols' artful force toward the globe's *immonde*, its onerous concentrated powers of sovereignty. It enables the art form, in and through practice, to be both an anticipation of, and also an acting into, a future of bodies' liberation from concentrated weight, bodies in motion, reshifting to world as extended, weighing through diverse motions in a singular plural world. This means that the theological is both reflection upon and usually interactive with movements of persons, groups, and institutions whose practices are forged to dissolve the world's concentrated weight. These movements may be both internal to the academy as well as at work amid other public spheres.

The expectation at work in spectral practice is worked out in the more specific forms that I identified in this book's final chapter. The movements that give image art its diverse force, its teleo-affectivity with respect to onerous concentrations (of exclusion and domination), usually involve four kinds of spectral practice: somatic performance of wounded bodies, anamnestic solidarity, revivifying naturalism, and a grotesque transcendentalism. I have illustrated each of these through my close reading of Sister Dianna Ortiz's survival and defiance of the weight of torture. Obviously, numerous examples from various other movements for countering imposed social suffering might be cited in order to illustrate these four kinds of spectral practice. Rather than name the variety of actions, in other movements, which may be analogous to the four I have distilled from Ortiz's journey, I prefer to allow readers to draw their own lessons, to make their own connections to other regions of practice, working

---

of the politics of Springsteen's music, see Bran K. Garman, *A Race of Singers: Whitman's Working-Class Hero from Guthrie to Springsteen* (Chapel Hill: University of North Carolina Press, 2000), 195–258.

however they may for the liberation of bodies, wherever the world's weight concentrates in the agonistic political.

Is this liberation of bodies like the freedom Serge envisioned, "barbarous" and "drunk on its tears"? Maybe—*if* the art-force is prodigious enough, and its practices sufficiently spectral. The concentrated world already weighs so brutally; its defenders will surely see newly created worlds as monstrous, Hydra-like threats to their orders—hence as "barbarous." But also, for those bearing the world's most onerous weight—and for those of us who share their rage however indirectly, often all too feebly—there might also be that kind of anticipation which is exhilarating enough that it strikes us, too, as "monstrous," barbarous, in the sense of "being more than we dared hope for." Part of the barbarous quality of this liberation, especially as "drunk on its tears," might be that the freedom of transimmanence which comes through spectral practice emerges when we are most wrung out, hence vulnerable to being surprised by hope, even while we feel ourselves only to be plodding on, bending ourselves toward it in daily practices of our struggles for freedom and liberation.

What, then, of the theological and the political? The theological is a dimension of the agonistic political. It belongs neither to the way of transcendence, nor immanence, but to the transimmanental dimension of the agonistic political. There we meet the artful form born of the agony of concentrated weight, but pointed forward to a life of the world that defies the onerous and oppressive globe that burdens our time. The wounded bodies of the oppressed still perform. The dead are not only remembered, they are seething in their presence/absence, and so the dead circulate in the present, particularly through anamnestic practice. Nature and its peoples, though compressed, piled, and abandoned, experience revivifying connection. Even the transcendent, so long erected to shore up the most deadly of sovereignties, is engaged, pulled in—grotesquely, to be sure—as part of its own undoing, part of the creation, finally, unendingly, of world. This is how "flesh wears out chains." And so the oft-incarcerated body of Victor Serge still sounds:

> *I see growing on the ripples of the water*
> *The revivifying specter*
> *Of a barbarous freedom drunk on its tears.*[6]

---

6. Serge, "Stenka Razin," in *Resistance*, 21.

ACKNOWLEDGMENTS

This book is dedicated to Wonhee Anne Joh, theologian now teaching at Garrett Evangelical Theological Seminary. Since and before our marrying, our shared life together for years now has touched every dimension of my being and life. This book, as well as some previous work, was written within the grace and regimen of our intertwining and enriching life and work. I have lost track of which book or idea was shared with whom in the years of our discussions and debates. I do remember, as just one of many such examples, Anne putting into my hands Judith Butler's book, *Precarious Life*, and later Butler's *Frames of War*, at just the right moments of my research and writing this book. These and many more such acts mark our deeper intellectual exchange and spirit of mutual intellectual challenge that are difficult to render in words. If I gender-bend just a bit, I would hope to be muse to her as much as she has been to me. More significantly, I know that with the coming into one another's and our children's lives, my life is somehow right—still one of adventure, desire and delight—now also grounded or, well, set on course. This book's dedication to her is just one way to express a love and gratitude that cannot adequately be expressed in words.

This book first struggled forward in a three-volume, 800-page manuscript completed in 1998, a long meditation on my political work throughout the 1980s and 1990s in areas of criminal justice, prison activism, anti-death penalty and anti-racism struggle, and critical resistance to U.S. policies in Latin America and its wars worldwide. Many of the themes of spectral practice, haunting and ghostly "seething presences" were broached in that work, *Ghosts of American Lands: A Spirituality of Revolutionary Populism.* The writings on ghosts, and on the land as a veritable "protagonist of history," as expressed in Laguna Pueblo writer Leslie Marmon Silko's publications, especially her novels, *Ceremony* and *Almanac of the Dead,* and also her essay collection, *Yellow Woman and the Beauty of the Spirit,* all long ago became veritable scripture to me. They turned me in the mid 1990s to more rigorous readings in decolonial and postcolonial theories, which I had begun reading during the assaults by the United States on Iraq in 1991. So, I express my deep gratitude to works like Silko's and others, to the movements and peoples in the demanding worlds of U.S. activism, which provoked that earlier work, creating communities of accountability for me, even as I try to meet the canons of scholarship and teaching in theological and higher education.

To Fortress Press, I owe a debt of gratitude, for staying with this book through its many drafts, from an overly long manuscript begun in 2007, into its present form. I especially thank Michael West, Susan Johnson, Joshua Messner, Olga Lobasenko, Marissa Wold, Neil Elliott, David Lott, Sheila Anderson, and Kristin Goble. Readers for Fortress Press—Professors Mary-Jane Rubenstein of Wesleyan University and Corey D. B. Walker of Brown University—read the manuscript in its entirety with a criticism that was supportive and deeply humbling, and so I redrafted my work in light of many of their comments. To be sure, the remaining limitations of my approach and writing are still entirely my responsibility. But that I had their critical eyes for a time, I am deeply grateful. Corey Walker also enabled my airing many of this book's core ideas in an earlier essay that I wrote on Abdul JanMohamed, Richard Wright, and Giorgio Agamben, in which I analyzed the "state of exception" currently applied to death-row prisoner Mumia Abu-Jamal in a special issue edited by Walker titled "Theology and Democratic Futures," for the journal *Political Theology.*

I am also grateful for further careful reading and constructive criticism that was offered by Professor Laurel Schneider of Chicago Theological Seminary and, again, Corey D. B. Walker at an American Academy Religion session on the book in a pre-publication panel in October 2010. I could not incorporate all of their very helpful critiques into the book by that time, but I remain deeply appreciative and instructed by the time they gave to this text.

Thanks, also, to many others who read portions or the entirety of this book at some point of its drafting. Wonhee Anne Joh constantly considered portions of this with me and lived with my tensely posed self across the years of its writing, amid her own career and writing, publishing, parenting, and teaching pressures.

The first reading with fruitful and detailed comments on the entire manuscript was undertaken by James W. Jones of Rutgers University. I remain indebted to his critical eye and grateful for our almost 20 years of continuous friendship.

A reading of the whole, with numerous comments, also generously came from Professor of Ethics, Nimi Wariboko, of Andover Newton Theological School. Others, Sigurd Baark, Elías Ortega-Aponte, Derek Woodard-Lehman, Nate Van Yperen—all of these doctoral candidates at Princeton Theological Seminary—offered critical discussion and spirited conversation of several of the theoretical moves in this text. Princeton neighbor, Robert MacLennan offered judicious and provocative commentary on some of the earliest drafts of this book. Also, an opportunity in early 2010 to present these ideas in a seminar on Political Theology at the University of Chicago Divinity School, which I was invited to do by its instructor, Professor Kathryn Tanner, was instrumental in the process of my seeing a way toward some of this book's most important moves.

Administrators at my institution, Princeton Theological Seminary, particularly Dean Darrell Guder and President Iain R. Torrance, have been supportive throughout, not only by creating support committees for faculty research and sabbaticals, but also by graciously giving me a few weeks extra leave from some committee duties at a crucial time, all in order to prepare the final form of this book.

I cannot conclude without also expressing my appreciation for those many with whom I feel myself yoked in a journey of "spectral practice," as articulated in this book—a "haunting" of all those powers that concentrate for so many a life of exclusion, marginalization and oppression—an intolerable indignity to us all. Without naming all of those who seem on that journey with me, I am happy to name some of those whose thought and practice shape my being and reflection, even though I do not presuppose that they see the world and the future as I do. They will know, each in a different way, why our journey might be "spectral," why it is necessary, and what is at stake. These include, again, Wonhee Anne Joh; my daughters Laura and Nadia Kline-Taylor, Joshua and Alex Joh-Jung, and, again, Jim Jones. I include also Mumia Abu-Jamal, Johanna Fernandez, Tameka Cage, Cornel West, Vijay Prashad, Jamal Joseph, Pam Africa, and Suzanne W. Ross, as well as the many colleagues at my own institution who press for structural change and with whom I have team-taught over the years.

Mark Lewis Taylor
Evanston, IL/Princeton, NJ

INDEX